LEADING FROM THE INSIDE OUT

A COACHING MODEL

Virginia E. Bianco-Mathis
Strategic Performance Group and Marymount University

Lisa K. Nabors
Strategic Performance Group

Cynthia H. Roman
Strategic Performance Group and University of Maryland

SAGE Publications
International Educational and Professional Publisher
Thousand Oaks ▪ London ▪ New Delhi

For information:

Sage Publications, Inc.
2455 Teller Road
Thousand Oaks, California 91320
E-mail: order@sagepub.com

Sage Publications Ltd.
6 Bonhill Street
London EC2A 4PU
United Kingdom

Sage Publications India Pvt. Ltd.
M-32 Market
Greater Kailash I
New Delhi 110 048 India

Printed in the United States of America

Library of Congress Cataloging-in-Publication Data

Bianco-Mathis, Virginia.
Leading from the inside out: A coaching model / By Virginia E.
Bianco-Mathis, Lisa K. Nabors, Cynthia H. Roman.
p. cm.
Includes bibliographical references.
ISBN 0-7619-2392-6 (p)
1. Leadership. I. Nabors, Lisa K. II. Roman, Cynthia H. III. Title.
HD57.7 .B513 2002
658.4′092—dc21 2001006639

This book is printed on acid-free paper.

02 03 04 05 10 9 8 7 6 5 4 3 2 1

Acquisitions Editor: Marquita Flemming
Editorial Assistant: MaryAnn Vail
Copy Editor: Elisabeth Magnus
Production Editor: Diane S. Foster
Typesetter: Rebecca Evans
Proofreader: Scott Oney
Cover Designer: Michelle Lee

LEADING FROM THE INSIDE OUT

Contents

Preface

This book is about creating and practicing the most effective approach to leadership we have ever seen—coaching leadership. We have structured the book for leaders and for those who work with leaders to use in a practical, purposeful way. We present a five-step model that leaders can apply for developing themselves, their teams, their organizations, and their communities. Of course, many books have been written on the topic of leadership, and many books have been written about coaching. What makes our book different?

First, we have combined what we believe to be the best elements of compatible leadership and coaching models with our own unique approach to the subject. The result is a holistic model that is competency based and provides leaders with a framework for personal and professional growth. Second, we have reviewed recent literature and research, and we present theories and findings in a way designed to provide a context for the model we propose. Third, we share stories and cases that we have gleaned from our work with clients so that our readers can learn from their experiences. Finally, we have created worksheets, job aids, scorecards, and other tools for you to use in your own development work.

A brief word on limitations. As we worked to present a new model that leaders can apply in developing themselves, their teams, their organizations, and their communities, the volume of material we reviewed and created grew exponentially. Consequently, we had to make difficult choices about what to omit. We do not explore many of the cultural challenges that face leaders operating in a global environment. Though we know our approach has been embraced by other cultures, our perspective has a Western orientation. We do not explore the spiritual dimension of leadership in depth, preferring instead to present a cognitive, behavioral focus.

In many ways, this book represents the culmination of a journey that we have been making throughout the last 20 years. In other ways, this book represents a beginning—a new look and a different focus on the skills, knowledge, and ability it takes to be an effective leader. In writing this book, we made a choice to be purposeful in sharing our learning and in creating and sharing meaning with you, our readers. We believe that coaching leadership is a powerful discipline—simple to explain, difficult to initiate, challenging to practice, and rewarding to experience. We wish you that reward, and we hope you find this book to be an invaluable tool in its pursuit.

Acknowledgments

We would like to acknowledge our clients and colleagues for everything they have taught us. The lessons learned and the experiences shared have been memorable.

We are grateful to our students who keep our thinking sharp and with each semester continue to challenge us in new ways.

Words can hardly express our gratitude and love for our families—we are truly blessed to have their unconditional support for all we attempt personally and professionally.

We acknowledge the tremendous efforts by Allison Pinckney, our word processor and graphic artist. With great skill and some magic she makes it all look right.

We are thankful for the tireless work by Marquita Flemming, our editor, and her staff at Sage. It is truly a pleasure working with such professionals.

Finally, we acknowledge each other. As business partners, we know each other better than we do our siblings, and we don't even fight about whose turn it is to do the dishes. It is an honor to work with such talented women. Every day is filled with adventure, achievement, and fun. We intend to keep it all going—we know how lucky we are.

—Virginia E. Bianco-Mathis
Lisa K. Nabors
Cynthia H. Roman

part 1

Introduction

Rooted in conversation, coaching is evolving as a natural form of leadership.

— Laurence F. Lyons,
"Coaching at the Heart of Strategy"

A Way of Being

The leaders we discuss in this book lead from their hearts: They know and believe in themselves, and they bring that knowing to their vision of leadership in their organizations. Hence, the title of this book, *Leading From the Inside Out: A Coaching Model.*

Over the years, we have coached many types of leaders—CEOs, vice presidents, executive directors, project managers, line managers, and highly trained specialists. We have worked in many different types of organizations, from high-technology companies to not-for-profit associations, from government agencies to manufacturing industries. In every case, we found the most powerful leaders to be those who embrace coaching as a way of being. We have designated these leaders as "coaching leaders"—those who align beliefs with action, communicate honestly, focus on the future, and relate to others in an open and authentic manner.

In this book, we explore the competencies, philosophies, and specific behaviors of coaching leadership. We share a blueprint that you can follow as you travel your own leadership path. By the end of this chapter, we unfold the four levels of the coaching leadership model—self, team, organization, and

Table 1.1 A Summary of Comparative Mind-Sets

Traditional Ways of Leading	*Coaching Ways of Leading*
■ Pushes/drives	■ Lifts/supports
■ Tells/directs/lectures	■ Asks/requests/listens
■ Talks at people	■ Engages in dialogue with people
■ Controls through decisions	■ Facilitates by empowering
■ Knows the answer	■ Seeks the answer
■ Uses fear to achieve compliance	■ Stimulates creativity, using purpose to inspire commitment
■ Points to errors	■ Celebrates learning
■ Problem solver/decision maker	■ Collaborator/facilitator
■ Delegates responsibility	■ Models accountability
■ Creates structure and procedures	■ Creates vision and flexibility
■ Does things right	■ Does the right things
■ Knowledge is power	■ Vulnerability is power
■ Focuses on the bottom line	■ Focuses on process that creates the bottom-line results

SOURCE: Crane (1999).

community. But first, let's review some underlying concepts concerning coaching and leadership.

The Coaching Leader

Let's look at the trends in today's organizations that call for a new way of leading. The disintegration of hierarchies, the preponderance of teams and virtual teams, and technological breakthroughs have increased the need for successful interpersonal relationships and "leader relationships." Leaders can no longer hide behind policies, structure, or concrete boundaries. Things happen "in the white space," not in the chain of command. High performance can best be facilitated through a leadership style that is based more on coaching principles than on power and control. Whereas traditional leaders have exerted direction, advice, and coercion, coaching leaders rely on their ability to influence, teach, and question. Table 1.1 shows a comparison between the two mind-sets. As you can see, traditional leaders lead their followers, whereas coaching leaders lead through their followers.

Most of the business gurus will tell you that leadership is different from management. They will also tell you that leadership is preferable in today's business environment. Why? Because leadership requires followers. And followers today expect their leaders to be role models of character. Our view of coaching leadership is that leadership starts with the self. The most successful leaders are those individuals who know and are comfortable with who they are. Their personal and professional lives are aligned with congruent values and principles. They are comfortable in their own skin, and they practice what they preach. Coaching provides you the vehicle to determine who you are and how you will be as a leader.

What position in an organization do you have to hold in order to be a coaching leader? Coaching leadership is less about position than about influence. Coaching leaders have influence over individuals, teams, and/or organizations. You may be a coaching leader if you are accountable for supporting your employees to attain greater quality and better performance. Or you may be a coaching leader as the owner of a small start-up company who is setting goals and developing strategies for success. Following is a list of people we believe can be both leaders and coaches:

- CEOs and executive directors of large and small organizations
- Senior executives in the public and private sectors
- Midlevel managers
- Supervisors
- Team leaders
- Department heads
- Project managers
- Entrepreneurs

So are you a leader? If you are, your next step is to determine if you should be a coaching leader. If one or more of the following conditions apply to your leadership situation, then read on.

- Commitment from other people is needed to carry out your decisions.
- Individuals receiving your feedback must change their behavior for the organization to be more effective.
- Open and honest communication is needed to achieve your organization's goals.
- Translating your vision and values into performance is required.
- The goal is improved business performance and increased competitive advantage.
- Employees see you as important to their goal achievement.
- People want to develop their knowledge, skills, and competencies to achieve goals.

What Is Coaching?

The practice of coaching has become very popular in the last 10 years. Coaches practice independently or in organizations, or they apply coaching as part of other jobs. Below are some recent definitions of coaching:

> Coaches are committed to change, so they can stay aligned to challenging and believable futures that are in constant flux. They are committed to external performance when that can be attained and to internal renewal and resilience when that is necessary. (Hudson, 1999, p. 16)

> Coaching helps every executive build an individual path to achieve personal or organizational aspirations. When consolidated, all these paths transform today's managers into tomorrow's leaders. (Goldsmith, Lyons, & Freas, 2000, p. 1)

> [Coaching is] challenging and supporting people in achieving higher levels of performance while allowing them to bring out the best in themselves and those around them. (Hargrove, 1995, p. 15)

> Coaching delivers results in large measure because of the supportive relationship between the coach and the coachee, and the means and style of communication used. (Whitmore, 1996, p. 7)

> This relationship is an alliance between two equals for the purpose of meeting the client's needs. (Whitworth, Kimsey-House, & Sandahl, 1998, p. 3)

> [Coaching is] a system of feedback as well as techniques such as motivation, effective questioning, and a conscious matching of management style to each coachee's readiness to undertake a particular task. (Landsberg, 1997, p. xiii)

Our view of coaching leadership combines a number of the above elements. Coaching leadership is a way of being based on the commitment to align beliefs with actions. Coaching leaders communicate powerfully, help others to create desired outcomes, and hold relationships based on honesty, acceptance, and accountability.

Earlier, we discussed how coaching leadership differs from traditional approaches to leadership. It is also critical to understand how coaching compares to related practices. In Table 1.2, we compare the leader as coach to the therapist, the trainer, and the mentor. Significant points you should note are the orientation to time (past, present, and future), the emphasis on questions versus advice, and the individual's accountability for learning and outcomes.

Why Coaching Leadership Today?

Leadership has always been about followers. What's different in the 21st century is the changing nature of the professional workforce. Not only are workers' needs different than they were 25 years ago, but demographic changes make recruitment and retention of skilled employees a critical issue. As a leader in the 21st century, you must be aware of and accept followers for who and what they are. Trying to change your employees to reflect the attitudes of a bygone era is a losing proposition.

Two major characteristics of workers today make coaching the ideal way of leading: the desire for choices and the immediate need for information. Workers today want flexibility—in their actions, thoughts, lifestyles, methods, and approaches. For them, unlike their grandparents' generation, job security is no longer the overriding concern. Workers today want more than a paycheck. They want a lifestyle that meets both their personal and professional needs. As a coaching leader, you must provide options and choices to the mem-

Table 1.2 The Coaching Leader Versus Other Practitioners

The Leader as Coach	*The Therapist*
Differences	
Focuses on goals and development	Focuses on problems
Future focused	Tries to understand the past
Focuses on people's strengths	Focuses on people's pathologies
Action oriented	Insight oriented
Similarities	
Both require excellent communication skills and a desire to help	

The Leader as Coach	*The Trainer*
Differences	
Individualized, tailored, customized to the individual, data based	Designed on the basis of generic skills expectations for the organization, group, or position
Requires individual progress	May or may not involve individual progress
Ongoing time frame	Short time frame
Uses powerful questions to promote learning	Uses required information to promote learning
Similarities	
Both involve learning and development	

The Leader as Coach	*The Mentor*
Differences	
Asks powerful questions	Gives powerful advice
Balances individual and organizational goals	Emphasizes organizational goals
Can occur between peers	Usually occurs between a senior and junior employee
Focuses on learning	Focuses on career development
Similarities	
Both need a trusting relationship	

bers of your organization. Employees today expect to make decisions on a variety of alternatives and to take actions leading to a variety of outcomes. Mentoring, though still an important supervisory role, usually supports the "organizational party line." Coaching is about recognizing that everyone is acting with intention and making choices that are consistent with what he or she finds important, meaningful, and satisfying. Being a coaching leader means giving employees the power and opportunity to exercise choices that will make their lives meaningful and contribute to organizational success.

What generation are you a member of? Are you a baby boomer? A "Generation Xer"? Or something else? Employees today want quick recognition, instant feedback, just-in-time information, and immediate success. Having grown up with television, cell phones, computers, and the Internet, today's workers will not wait for what they need or want. They won't wait to take a training seminar that may or may not meet their needs, and they won't wait for a promotion that may or may not happen. Coaching is immediate. Fast-paced workers want tailored development approaches and knowledge that are uniquely meaningful to their situation. Rising executives don't want to sit in a class getting the same information as everyone else—they want to know their own strengths and weaknesses and ways to grow and improve now. Coaching is focused. Think about the degree to which this description fits you. If it doesn't, you must accept the fact that the description probably does fit the majority of your employees. Coaching leaders respond effectively to these employees.

The business environment today also requires new leadership strategies. Despite the fluctuations in the economy, it is far more difficult today to find skilled employees than it used to be. Recruitment and retention pressures are especially great for organizations dependent on emerging information technologies, where the shortage of skilled workers is critical. Coaching is the perfect tool to find and keep good employees. No longer viewed as punishment for poor performance, coaching is seen as a benefit for those employees that the organization is grooming for leadership. Coaching helps employees set and achieve goals for development, and employees who are supported by their organizations in meeting their own goals are more likely to stay.

Businesses need employees who think, feel, and act effectively. Getting and keeping employees is great—as long as they are professional and get the job done. How many times have you dealt with an employee who has potential but just can't get along with clients? Or who can't meet deadlines? Or who has bad habits? In the past, leaders sent employees to training when they had a "problem." Or they engaged the employee in a few "heart-to-heart" chats. More often than not, the problem still existed after these interventions. Coaching is an ongoing way of communicating that targets specific skills, knowledge, attitudes, and behaviors that need to change. Coaching provides honest feedback to help employees be more effective.

The Roots of Coaching Leadership

Like many other theories of management, our model of leadership development is grounded in our allegiance to the principles and practices of the organizational and behavioral sciences. Specifically, the theorists who have researched human needs, leader personality, attitudes and assumptions, and the nature of organizational/work environments influence our thinking. Leadership is about exerting influence on other people's motivation to behave and perform in certain ways.

Abraham Maslow's (1970) hierarchy of human needs (Figure 1.1) suggests that people satisfy their needs in sequence. They progress step by step from the lowest level in the hierarchy to the highest. As they progress, a deprived need

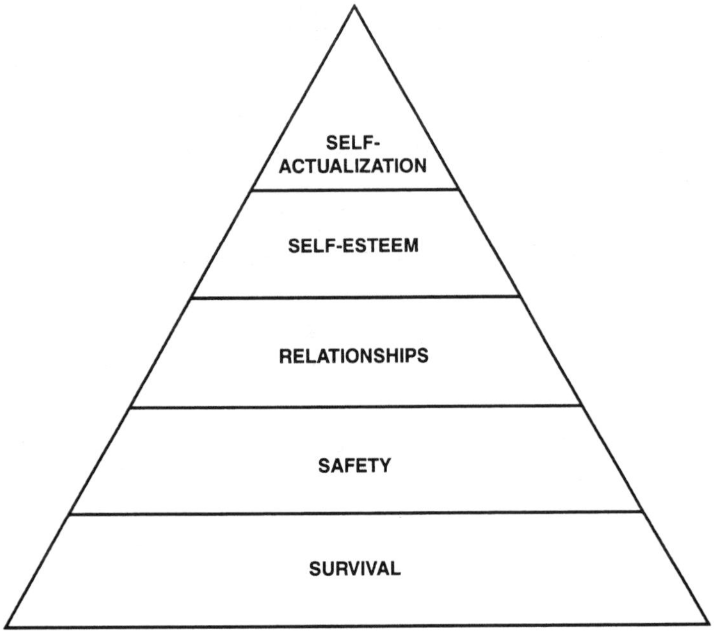

Figure 1.1. Maslow's Hierarchy of Needs

dominates attention and determines behavior until it is satisfied. Then the next higher-level need is activated, and progression up the hierarchy continues. At the level of self-actualization, the deficit and progression principles cease to function. The more the need for self-actualization is satisfied, the stronger it grows (Maslow, 1970). This theory is important for leaders to understand because needs influence a person's work attitudes and behaviors. By helping people to meet their needs, the coaching leader can positively affect their satisfaction and growth.

David McClelland (1961) identified three needs that are central to human motivation. The need for achievement is the desire to do something better or more efficiently, to solve problems, or to master complex tasks. The need for power is the desire to control other people, to influence their behaviors, or to be responsible for them. The need for affiliation is the desire to establish friendly relationships with other people. By recognizing the strength of each need in themselves and in others, leaders can create more responsive work environments.

Douglas McGregor's classic book *The Human Side of Enterprise* (1960) asserted that managers should give more attention to the social and self-actualizing needs of people at work. McGregor encouraged managers to shift their view of human nature from a "Theory X" perspective to a "Theory Y" perspective (see Table 1.3). McGregor pointed out that managers holding either Theory X or Theory Y assumptions can produce follower behaviors that confirm the manager's original expectations. For example, if a manager believes that employees need direction, he or she may provide direction so often and in such detail that employees come to rely on that direction for all their work.

In addition to the assumptions a leader has about people in general, research has addressed the relationship between leadership style and the partic-

Table 1.3 McGregor's Theory X Versus Theory Y: Managerial Perceptions of Employees

Theory X	*Theory Y*
Avoid work	Will work toward goals
Avoid responsibility	Will assume responsibility
Need direction	Can self-direct
Cannot make decisions	Can make decisions
Not achievement oriented	Want to achieve
Not dependable	Are dependable
Motivated by money	Motivated by interest or challenge
Not concerned with organization's needs	Are concerned with their organization's needs
Must be controlled	Want to be supported
Cannot change	Want to develop

SOURCE: Adapted from Douglas McGregor, *The Human Side of Enterprise*, New York, McGraw-Hill, 1960. Used with permission of McGraw-Hill.

ular situation requiring leadership. Fred Fiedler's (1965) contingency model of leadership is based on the premise that good leadership depends on a match between leadership style and situational demands. Leaders tend to be either task motivated or relationship motivated. Fiedler argued that leadership style is part of one's personality; therefore, it is relatively enduring and difficult to change. The key to leadership success is putting the various styles to work in situations for which they are good "fits." Leaders can maximize their own and others' success by (a) understanding the leadership demands of various situations and (b) understanding their own and others' leadership styles.

So far we have discussed how the literature has contributed to our understanding of human needs, managers' assumptions, and the fit between leadership style and situation. Another element that is critical to the role of the coaching leader is the organization itself. The early work of Chris Argyris showed his concern with the nature of organizations. His book *Personality and Organization* (1957) pointed out that traditional, hierarchical organizations may conflict with the needs and capabilities of mature adults. Like McGregor, Argyris believed that managers who treat people positively and as responsible adults will achieve productivity. He suggested that managers expand job responsibilities, allow more task variety, and adjust their behavior to include more participation and better relations. Argyris's later work *Theory in Practice: Increasing Professional Effectiveness* (Argyris & Schon, 1974) built on these beliefs about alignment by suggesting that leaders themselves need to address the misalignment between their actions and what they really believe. Argyris suggested that organizations will not truly change unless leaders commit to learning where the discrepancies exist and what the implications are for the organizational environment.

The emerging literature in organization development has contributed to our understanding of leadership coaching with its emphasis on systems thinking and the organizational change process. Kurt Lewin, a pioneer in organization development (discussed in Marrow, Bowers, & Seashore, 1967), developed the processes of action research and survey feedback to plan organizational change. Lewin's writing and research have guided our coaching steps to include the application of data feedback to the development of goals and change strategies. Although Lewin focused primarily on groups and organizations, we have extended his approach to those individuals practicing coaching leadership.

In addition, our model of leadership is indebted to continuing research in psychotherapy that supports the importance of relationship factors in positive psychological development (Campbell, 2000). Carl Rogers (1951) described three conditions necessary for client change: genuineness, empathetic understanding, and positive regard. Roger Carkhuff (1969) added three more conditions: respect, concreteness, and self-disclosure. More recent solution-focused techniques (Juhnke, 1996; O'Hanlon & Weiner-Davis, 1989) have had significant impact on coaching practice in organizational settings. Coaching methods such as challenging, championing, and requesting (Whitworth et al., 1998) are adaptations of supportive interventions by counselors in therapeutic relationships.

Finally, we concur with current management gurus such as Stephen Covey (1991), Charles Manz (1992), Daniel Goleman (1998a), and Peter Drucker (1999) who promote the practice of self-examination by leaders. Goleman (1998a) asserted that the most effective leaders are alike in one way: They all have a high degree of what he called "emotional intelligence." He stated that with coaching, people can develop the five components of their emotional intelligence: self-awareness, self-regulation, motivation, empathy, and social skills. Drucker (1999) advocated that leaders use vigilant self-management to determine when and where they can be most effective during their careers. He stated,

> History's great achievers—a Napoleon, a da Vinci, a Mozart—have always managed themselves. That, in large measure, is what makes them great achievers. But they are rare exceptions, so unusual both in their talents and their accomplishments as to be considered outside the boundaries of ordinary human existence. Now, most of us, even those of us with modest endowments, will have to learn to manage ourselves. We will have to learn to develop ourselves. We will have to place ourselves where we can make the greatest contribution. And we will have to stay mentally alert and engaged during a 50-year working life; which means knowing how and when to change the work we do. (pp. 65-66)

A Leadership Coaching Model

Over the years, and thanks to the shared learning we have experienced with our clients, we have come to believe that coaching leadership involves four levels:

1. Self: the leader within
2. Team: the leader's relationship with others

3. Organization: the leader and the organization
4. Community: the leader and the community

Although each of these levels can be and often is regarded separately, the coaching leader is committed to development in all four areas at the same time. Leading from the inside out requires the coaching leader to examine and articulate deeply held beliefs about leadership, to coach others who are followers, to develop systems and processes to create a coaching organization, and to reach out to the community with the spirit of coaching. The model is like a living organism in that each element is affected by the other elements. Your work on yourself will affect how you set goals for organizational change, which will concurrently affect how you communicate with your employees. This in turn will help you decide how to reach out to your specific community. And there are infinite numbers of other input-output relationships among the elements of the model.

This book is organized into five parts, enabling the reader to focus on each element separately:

1. Introduction
2. The Leader Within
3. The Leader and the Team
4. From Traditional to Coaching Organization
5. Beyond Organizational Walls

Within each level of our leadership coaching model is a series of five steps:

1. Establishing the coaching relationship
2. Collecting and analyzing data
3. Processing feedback and planning actions
4. Taking action
5. Evaluating your progress

As in the action research model familiar to practitioners of management and organization development, these steps focus on planned change as a cyclical process in which data about the individual, group, or organization provide information to guide subsequent action. As in the coaching model itself, these steps don't necessarily occur in a linear fashion. And the boundaries separating the steps are more fluid than lockstep. Feedback loops can form from any step in the process. The entire process forms a cycle that repeats itself as an individual, team, or organization sets new goals for development and change (see Figure 1.2). For example, one leader we know changed his personal action

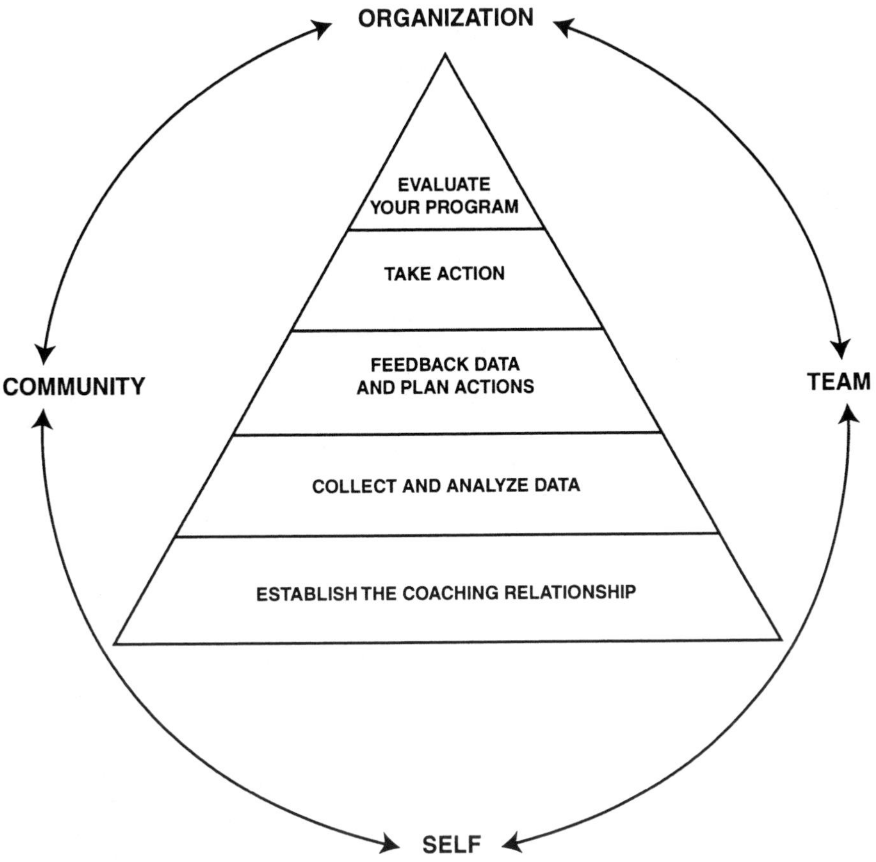

Figure 1.2. Leading From the Inside Out: A Coaching Model

plan entirely after the executive team decided to reorganize their company using project management teams.

Our coaching model provides leaders with a blueprint to follow at different levels of the organization. In addition, coaching leaders must demonstrate specific competencies at each step in the process. The competencies for success as a coaching leader differ from those of a traditional leader. As a result of our work and research in organizational systems as well as our coaching relationships, we have developed a set of competencies for each step within each level in our coaching model (see Table 1.4). These competencies encompass the core behaviors and skills needed to develop effectiveness as a coaching leader. We discuss each competency in depth and give many examples as we address each level of the model.

In keeping with our belief in the integration of beliefs with actions, we have developed four principles to guide you in your practice of being a coaching leader. These principles, shown in Exhibit 1.1, are embedded in each level of our coaching model and guide the steps of coaching.

In summary, our coaching model represents the coaching leader as part of a complex system that, at its best, is constantly growing, changing, and adapt-

Table 1.4 The Coaching Model: Competencies for the Five Steps of the Coaching Process at Levels of Self, Team, Organization, and Community

Steps of the Coaching Process

Level (Part of Book)	*Establishing the Relationship*	*Collecting and Analyzing Data*	*Processing Feedback and Planning Actions*	*Taking Action*	*Evaluating Your Progress*
Self (Part 2)	Reflection Learning Honesty Determination	Honesty Inquiry Advocacy Resiliency Self-management	Clarification Reframing Goal setting Accountability Transition management	Dialogue Reflection Problem solving Decision making Risk taking	Openness Courage Commitment to learning
Team (Part 3)	Vision Integrity Courage Openness Passion	Inquiry Reframing Listening Sorting Patience	Truth telling Empathy Ability to generate and evaluate alternatives Conviction	Interdependence Willingness to risk Execution Reinforcement	Measurement Learning mind-set Follow-through Recognition Future focus
Organization (Part 4)	Commitment Vision Sense of urgency Collaboration Self-knowledge Teaching	Participation Establishment of trust Courage Persistence Education	Focus on the vision Provision of a challenge Ability to act as a change agent	Alignment with the vision Follow-through Facilitation of continuous learning Acknowledgment of others' contributions	Decision making Passion Rewarding of others' contributions
Community (Part 5)	Investigation Vision Brainstorming Education	Research Involvement Focus	Negotiation Drive Training	Systems thinking Program management Establishment of relationships Fostering of a vision Acknowledgment of accomplishments	Assessment Participation Exploration

ing. Coaching leaders influence the entire system by taking accountability for aligning their values and beliefs with their actions at all levels of the organization. As each part of the system changes, feedback loops enable the entire organization to become a community of coaching practice.

Exhibit 1.1 **The Coaching Model's Four Principles**

1. *Future focused:* The goal of coaching is to achieve the organization and leader's goals, not to dwell on or label past actions or behaviors.
2. *Data based:* Leadership coaching should be based on feedback data: self-assessment and feedback from organizational members. Basing leadership development on untested assumptions and potentially inaccurate conclusions can result in the leader's wasting time and effort.
3. *Action oriented:* Coaching is always more about what the leader does than what he or she thinks or feels. We believe that sustained change in actions is best achieved by examining deeply held values and beliefs. Coaching conversations will go deeply into the mental models that drive the coaching leader's behaviors and often confront the incongruence between espoused values and actual values. But ultimately the coaching leader encourages change in action.
4. *Results driven:* Results are what matter in organizations. Likewise, the coaching leader works toward established goals, measured and evaluated by the standards defined by the leader and the organization.

How to Read This Book

We hope you will read this book with anticipation for the process of learning and patience with yourself. Becoming a coaching leader is an exciting and intense journey of discovery about yourself and your world. The patience comes into play as you try to "be" with the ideas and behaviors we discuss. This is not easy stuff!

We wrote this book for you, a leader in your organization. Why? For three reasons: (a) You can make change happen, (b) you need to learn how to be a coaching leader, and (c) we want you to be fulfilled as well as successful. Let's talk about each of these three reasons.

We consistently find that leaders have more leverage for helping people and organizations succeed than individuals who do not play leadership roles. Many failed change efforts, whether they involve individual change or organizational change, are due to lack of leadership involvement. If you, as an organizational leader, don't hold yourself accountable for the future of your people and your organization, then you have no business calling yourself a leader.

Second, it is sad but true that many leaders don't have the skills to be good coaches. Most leaders today grew up with a management approach that was defined by hierarchy, control, and direction. Today's workforce and today's organizational environment demand a different leadership approach. Leaders, no matter how charismatic and experienced, often are ignorant of coaching styles of leadership. When confronted with today's diverse workforce and unpredictable business scenarios, leaders often revert to what they are comfortable with—sometimes with disastrous consequences. This book will give you the steps and strategies you need to master to be a coaching leader.

Finally, we wrote this book out of our concern for you. It's lonely at the top. Many of the leaders we've worked with experience isolation, stress, and frustration. They rarely have open, honest communication with anyone in their organizations, and they often operate on inaccurate assumptions, untested inferences, and misguided conclusions. If you adopt a coaching way of being as a leader, you will have a framework for understanding yourself, dealing with multiple constituencies, and managing change effectively.

We suggest that you read the entire book first to get the big picture of what being a coaching leader means to you. Then go back and reread each part. Each part of the book addresses a different level of the coaching model: self, team, organization, and community. As you read, think about examples out of your own experience. Notice how you're reacting to what you read. Take notes on anything that comes to mind. Talk about your insights with others. Finally, complete the planning worksheets. Don't attempt to complete the worksheets until you have read and reflected on the material in that part. Your learning may change over time as you reflect and apply what you learn. After a couple of weeks, go on to the next part. Don't rush the process. This is not a cookbook—it is a road map to your life of coaching leadership. There will be long stretches of straight driving, and there will be detours. Enjoy the sights. Pay attention to the speed limits, and don't worry if others pass you. The learning is in the process, not at the destination. In fact, it's okay if you never reach your destination. You don't want to miss out on the fun along the way!

part 2

The Leader Within

Success in the knowledge economy comes to those who know themselves—their strengths, their values, and how they best perform.

— Peter Drucker,
"Managing Oneself"

Getting Started

Are you willing to be and do what it takes to be a leader? Take a deep breath because it will not be easy. I can hear you saying, "I know that. I have what it takes." Maybe you do. You probably think that you have the necessary experience, knowledge, skills, and commitment. That's fine. Now ask yourself the following questions:

- What is my life's mission? Am I living it?
- What brings me joy? Do I make it happen?
- Do I have a vision of myself as a leader? What is it?
- Do I practice what I say I believe in? How do I know? How deeply am I willing to look?
- Do I live every day as if someone is grading how well I'm living that vision?
- What are my fears? How do these fears inhibit me as a leader?
- How do I reflect on my actions and learn from them?
- How much am I willing to change?

In this section, we will challenge you to consider what you believe about yourself, to define your role as leader, and to confront the reality that you probably don't practice what you preach.

Critical to being a leader from the inside out is your willingness to be coached yourself. Self-development is where leadership starts and ends. You cannot hope to effectively lead others until you do the hard, painful work of examining your own life. The process of coaching others and teams provides ongoing data for you to continue developing the leader within. Coaching the leader within is about surfacing and articulating the learning that occurs in this dynamic relationship. So as you begin this journey of making coaching a way of being, keep in mind that your leadership is a work in progress—a never-ending process of integrating what you learn about yourself with how you lead others and your organization.

Step 1: Establishing the Coaching Relationship

Helen was an executive who had it all. She was highly regarded in her industry for her experience and expertise. She had a great income and lots of status in her professional community. She was on track to become a vice president and fully expected the promotion within the next few years. Then, out of the blue, her company hired someone else for the position of vice president—a man with no experience in Helen's industry. In what was even more of a shock, Helen was summoned to a meeting by the vice president of human resources. She was told that several employees had complained about her and that she needed to improve her people skills. Helen was stunned. She had never seen it coming. How did this happen? How could she be so betrayed by the company she had given her life to? What should she do now?

Coming to grips with the leader within you starts with an examination of who you are: your beliefs, your values, the lens through which you view your place in this world. To Helen's credit, she realized, very painfully, that the assumptions she had about her own effectiveness were incorrect. She knew that it was useless and foolhardy to indulge her self-pity and blame the organization for not recognizing her worth and potential. Helen considered her options and decided to get a coach.

Sometimes it takes a rude awakening like the one Helen experienced to cause an individual to make the decision to get a coach. Sometimes it's because you want to achieve something bigger, something better in your life or in your organization. What is your reason? Following are some good reasons for you to get a coach:

- You want to change the culture of your organization. As the leader, how should you communicate and behave?
- You have received some feedback that your leadership could be improved in some areas. Though you discount the feedback, you decide that now is as good a time as any to look into some development activities.

- You have achieved more than you ever hoped for. But there's no joy in it for you. You don't have the relationship with family or others that you really want.
- You want to make a difference in your world—to your family, your organization, and your community. But you don't know where to begin.
- You never seem to have enough time to get everything done. You've missed too many deadlines, self-imposed or otherwise.
- You don't have anyone you can talk to honestly.
- You'd like to strengthen your relationship with the board.
- Your employees expect you to meet all their needs and don't care about yours.
- You want to build the capacity of your senior team.
- Others (family, employees, colleagues) don't respond to your ideas with great enthusiasm. You don't understand why.
- You are experiencing conflicts with others who are important to you. This seems to be a pattern.
- You want to be CEO or (fill in the blank) within 5 years. How can you make that happen?
- Someone else (boss, colleague, fill in the blank) has suggested that coaching might be helpful to you. Yikes! What does that mean?
- You have made a significant change in your life (marriage, divorce, child, move) that you find difficult to manage along with your job.

If any of the above reasons are familiar to you, then coaching may be a powerful tool to help you. There are many other reasons as well. But know what your reason is. In addition to knowing why you may need a coach, you must be ready to commit to the effort that coaching requires of you.

Tom was a midlevel manager who was ambitious and smart. He had a lot of great ideas to contribute to his company, if someone would only listen. Instead, the levels of bureaucracy and the degree of micromanagement he encountered frustrated him. Tom's frustrations grew into temper tantrums with his employees and disrespect to his superiors. His performance evaluations suffered. When the director of human resources offered the company's executive coaching services to Tom, he thought, Why not? He decided to get a coach. However, when his coach asked him to commit to a process of self-examination that involved the pros and cons of his leadership style, he became very impatient. He didn't really want to change. He just wanted advice on how to "get around" the inefficiencies and incompetence in the organization. He dropped out of coaching after two sessions. His stated reason: He was too busy doing everything because no one else could do it. He didn't have time to meet with his coach. After 3 months, Tom found another job.

One might argue that Tom needed to leave the organization. Perhaps yes, perhaps no. And therein lies the reason why coaching might have been useful to Tom. A good coach could have helped Tom determine his goals and what he needed from himself and others to achieve them. After sufficient coaching, Tom might or might not have decided to leave his organization. But without the self-examination and self-learning that occurs during coaching, Tom might go on to repeat the same attitudes and behaviors in his next position.

To test your commitment to coaching, ask yourself the following questions:

- Am I ready to be everything I want to be?
- Am I willing to consider not doing everything I want to do?
- Am I committed to coaching? Even when the going is slow?
- Am I willing to have an honest relationship with a coach?
- Am I committed to coaching even if the dialogue is painful?
- Am I willing to go deeply into the values and mental models I hold dear?
- Am I willing to make my coaching process a top priority in my life?
- Am I willing to change my attitudes? My behaviors?
- Am I willing to align my beliefs with my actions?
- Am I willing to accept the consequences of what I'm not willing to change?

Some of you may be thinking that you don't need a coach because your spouse or your best friend relates to you as a coach. You are fortunate to have such a positive relationship in your life. Tell that person how much you appreciate him or her! However, consider what a coach might offer you that other relationships may not.

A coach

- Holds your agenda, not his or her own
- Keeps your big picture in mind
- Is your champion
- Listens without judgment
- Is curious about you as a total person
- Holds you accountable for achieving your goals
- Is relentless in making requests for you to take action
- Challenges you to go beyond your comfort zone

Obviously, we believe that you need a coach. If you aspire to be a coaching leader but are not willing to be coached yourself, how can you coach individuals, teams, or your organization? Ironically, if you are resisting the idea of having a coach, you are a prime candidate for being coached.

Finding a Good Coach

Coaching as a profession is growing rapidly. The International Coach Federation (ICF), at <www.coachfederation.org>, is an important voice in the drive to establish credentials and standards for all coaching practitioners. Another organization is the OD Network, which represents organization development consultants, many of whom practice executive coaching.

You should interview prospective coaches. As you do this, ask them what preparation and training they have for their coaching practice. Anyone can hang out a shingle and say he or she is a coach. When you begin to look for a coach who is right for you, know what you are looking for. At a minimum, a good fit between you and a coach should satisfy you in the areas outlined in Table 2.1. You should explore everything from the coach's philosophy and background to his or her fees and policies. Of special note to those of you who will have your coach's services paid by your organization, ask if and how the coach will report to anyone in the organization.

Remember that the process of selecting a coach is important. If your organization is sponsoring your coaching relationship and has contracted with one or more coaches, make sure that you have the opportunity to choose among several coaches or that you at least have veto power.

When you choose a compatible coach, you make a commitment to develop yourself as a leader. At the beginning of your coaching relationship, you and your coach must address two major issues: (a) the nature of your relationship and its boundaries and (b) the goals you want to work on.

Defining the Coaching Relationship

How successful your relationship with your coach is depends on how explicitly you define and discuss the roles and expectations of your relationship. The successful coaching relationship is one in which the coach believes the client to be "creative, resourceful and whole" (Whitworth et al., 1998, p. 3). This means that the coach agrees to create a safe space for you to begin your journey into learning and growth. In turn, you agree to be accountable for your own self-discovery, choices, and actions. As you explore who you are as a leader, it will be tempting to regard your coach as the adviser, the expert, or the solution giver. Discuss this with your coach right from the very beginning. Your coach must be willing to be with you where you are and not lead you to his or her or someone else's goal or outcome. On the other hand, your coach must be willing and skilled to challenge you and ask the hard questions. By regarding you as creative, resourceful, and whole, the coach is holding you to your own choices, decisions, commitments, and actions. The coach supports you to be as much as you choose to be.

Do you agree to be regarded as creative, resourceful, and whole? You will succeed sometimes, fail often, make tremendous leaps of learning, and backslide into the pit of self-defeat. It is the journey of leadership.

Defining Your Goals

Setting the goals for self-development is more than defining what you want to do. It is more about who you want to be—your values, principles, hopes, and

Table 2.1 Interviewing a Prospective Coach

What to Ask About in Your Interview With a Prospective Coach	*What We Recommend as Minimum Requirements*
Focus on personal or organizational coaching	The coach should know the differences and similarities between the two. The coach should be able to help you develop as an individual and as a leader in your organization. Ask: ■ What is his/her definition of coaching? What models does he/she follow? ■ What data would the coach like to have? ■ What does he/she need from you?
Coaching experience	Experience in coaching leaders and professionals in organizational settings. Ask for references and contact them.
Training/education in coaching	This is a personal decision for you. We like academic background in the behavioral sciences and specific training in coaching.
Ethical guidelines	The coach should adhere to the International Coach Federation's ethical guidelines for coaching (on their Web site at <www.coachfederation.org>).
Fees	Coaching is expensive and worth it! Expect to pay $300 and up per month for 2 hours of personal and/or telephone contact.
Expertise	Leadership experience and an understanding of communication and organizational dynamics are necessary to effectively coach other leaders. Ask the coach what he/she believes about the relationship between leadership and coaching. The coach should express a sincere desire to understand, support, and challenge you.
Agreements on ground rules and commitments for the coaching relationship	The coach should have a written contract for you to sign. Be sure it addresses fees, missed appointments, conflicts, and time commitments. Ask the coach: ■ How would he/she like to work with you? ■ What is his/her approach to confidentiality? How will the coach report to the organization?
Results	Ask the coach: How can I expect to be different as a result of this relationship?

dreams. You will need to set goals for yourself and reflect on the following questions:

- How does the coaching process relate to my role as a leader?
- Who do I want to be as a leader?
- What is my life vision?
- What are my values?

- How will my coach help me live my values?
- What hopes do I have about myself?
- What fears do I have?
- What makes me happy?
- How will I engage in a dialogue of development?

As you get caught up in the day-to-day tasks and problems of your life, your relationship with your coach will be a safe place to deal with them. Your coach will challenge, acknowledge, and champion all that you can be. The coach will probably ask you a lot of questions. He or she will also ask you to complete some combination of questionnaires, self-assessments, and exercises. Depending on how coaching is sponsored in your organization, you may also be asked to share performance evaluation data with your coach. The purpose of these "intake" activities is to gather data. We'll address the process of data gathering in a later section. For now, suffice it to say that the most effective coaching is based on data—both self-assessment data and the feedback of others. After you have completed your intake activities, you and your coach will spend several hours summarizing and making meaning out of the data.

Competencies

When you are dealing with self, the first step—establishing the coaching relationship—must be carried out on two levels. First, you must establish the coaching relationship with your newly chosen coach. Second, you must establish a coaching relationship with yourself. Both dimensions require the use of four key competencies: reflection, learning, honesty, and determination.

Reflection

To get started with your coach and get comfortable with the entire coaching process, you must be aware of what you want from coaching. This requires the skill of self-reflection. You will need to challenge yourself. How easy is it for you to talk about yourself? Does an aversion to anything "touchy-feely" make it difficult for you to face your feelings, beliefs, and thoughts? Do you have a sincere desire to change? What do you believe needs to change about yourself? Notice that we're not asking you to state who or what else needs to change because coaching is about you. The issues you might choose to work on could range from your need to control and micromanage, to your hesitancy to make decisions, to your fear to appear inexperienced. It is about the changes you are ready and willing to consider to help you lead from the inside out.

Learning

The decision to hire a coach must come from your commitment to learn about yourself. Even more important than what you learn is how you learn. In the relationship with your coach, you will be in a learning process. The stages of the learning cycle are

1. *Concrete experience.* This stage emphasizes personal involvement with people in everyday situations. You and your coach will bring to the surface the feelings and beliefs you had during these everyday engagements.
2. *Reflective observation.* Your coach will challenge you to rely on your own thoughts and feelings to form opinions and to understand ideas and situations from different points of view.
3. *Abstract conceptualization.* This stage involves critical thinking. You and your coach will engage in a dialogue to consider the logic and ideas you have to help you make meaning out of your experiences.
4. *Active experimentation.* Your coach will help you experiment with influencing or changing situations. Trying on new behaviors leads to a new concrete experience, which starts the cycle all over again (Kolb, 1984).

Honesty

According to many executives, what they value the most about their coaching relationship is honest communication, something they rarely find in other relationships in their professional circles. Honesty is more than telling the truth. It is your commitment to bringing to the surface the deep truth about who you really are.

Janice was a senior attorney in a federal government agency. When her agency offered executive coaching to its senior managers, Janice thought this would be a good way to get some targeted help in dealing with her staff more effectively. The initial telephone interview with the prospective coach was friendly and professional. During the face-to-face interview, Janice discovered that her coach was open and candid about what coaching could and couldn't do for her. Janice knew that one important issue needed to be brought up so that she could see if this relationship was right for her. She took a deep breath and stated, "You will probably want to know something about my personal life. Well, I am a lesbian. I have a partner and we're raising a child together." The coach smiled and said, "Thanks for starting out our relationship with such openness. I am heterosexual; does that pose any concerns for you?" Janice replied, "Being a lesbian affects my entire life, and it's important that I can talk about that with you. The fact that you're heterosexual means that you might not be able to understand what I've been through." The coach said, "That's true. My approach is to celebrate and champion you as the magnificent person you are, in all aspects of who you are. I honor our differences, as well as the similarities we may discover. But you have to decide how important that difference is to you in working with me." Janice felt a wave of relief that this hurdle was over.

Janice chose to reveal her sexual orientation because it was important that her coach know her in a deep, meaningful way. The coach acknowledged the choices available to Janice with the new knowledge they shared. The transformational power of coaching lies beneath the secrets, in the heart of how we see ourselves in relation to ourselves and to others.

Determination

We guess that you know a lot about determination already. Otherwise, you wouldn't be reading this book. However, the kind of determination that we're talking about is not the workaholic, adrenaline-addicted determination that got you to the successful place you're in now. It's the determination to live and work from a place of leadership, a different way of being. Laura Berman Fortgang, author of *Take Yourself to the Top* (1998), described determination as having eight components (p. 41):

1. Get off adrenaline.
2. Give up having problems.
3. Start investing in other people.
4. Clean up your integrity.
5. Take responsibility.
6. Develop your intuition.
7. Tap into your vision.
8. Become the leader you are, NOW.

As you can see, this type of determination frees one from the usual stress and complications of a burdened, unexamined life. You need to take care of yourself and your relationships, move to a higher level of awareness, and take responsibility for becoming the kind of person and leader you need to be.

In summary, the first step to leading from the inside out is to establish a coaching relationship. In having a coach for yourself, it is critical to do the difficult, sometimes painful work of discovering who you really are and how you are ready and willing to change. By assessing your commitment to learning and change, you are demonstrating what you will ultimately require of your followers, organization, and community. Find the right coach for you, and start this wonderful journey.

Step 2: Collecting and Analyzing Data

Becoming a coaching leader differs from other developmental or skill improvement efforts. One major difference lies in the reliance on objective and subjective data to determine goals. Objective data include various quantitative measures of performance, such as sales quotas or deadline achievement. Subjective data involve the feedback of others, such as performance evaluations, customer feedback, or employee and peer feedback. Another form of subjective data is self-assessment data, such as personality and communication style inventories, skills assessments, and interest inventories.

The Importance of Data

Why is it important to base leadership coaching on data? Successful relationships are built on the perceptions people have about themselves and one another. Perceptions, then, are the only reality there is. But it takes a thick skin to listen to how other people perceive you.

An assistant vice president we know resisted feedback from colleagues and employees who perceived her as demeaning and bullying. She rationalized that her behavior was the only way she could get ahead in her Japanese-owned company. When she came to us for coaching, she had been turned down for promotion to vice president. She was told that she needed to be a better leader in her relationships with others. Subsequently, her coaching focused on what leadership meant to her and what the discrepancies were between her views and those held in her company. She began to try on new attitudes and behaviors with her coworkers. It wasn't easy because she viewed her feedback with suspicion. But she developed patience—with herself and others. After a year, small improvements in her relationships with her employees and colleagues helped her to develop a new way of leading. She never did get promoted to vice president, but she did win the respect of those who worked with her. She began to envision new roles for herself, new business goals, and new ways of coping with the sometimes disappointing realities of business decision making. Interestingly, her relationships with her grown children also improved.

Have you solicited feedback from others? If not, why not? To what degree do you trust the perceptions of those around you? Remember that receiving feedback from others does not require your agreement. It requires only your willingness to explore its meaning and implications. And there is another aspect of feedback to take into consideration. One person's feedback may be interesting but may be important only to how you relate to that person.

A pattern of unexpected feedback from different sources can be an important signal that you need to examine the attitudes, beliefs, and assumptions you hold that may be limiting your effectiveness. One CEO we know discounted feedback he received from employees and coworkers until he heard the very same words from his spouse and teenage children. Only then did he commit himself to change. Feedback for successful leadership may come from both your personal and professional relationships.

Table 2.2 Sources and Methods of Feedback

Sources of Feedback	*Methods of Data Collection*
Yourself	Surveys and self-assessments Interviews by your coach
Your boss	Performance evaluation Organization performance documents Interviews by your coach
Your employees	Meetings, conversations Surveys, interviews by your coach
Peers and coworkers	Meetings, conversations Surveys, interviews by your coach
Family members	Day-to-day feedback Surveys, interviews by your coach

What Data Do You Need?

Spend some time thinking about the data that you need to develop yourself as a coaching leader. Consider where these data might come from. Table 2.2 outlines several sources of data, including yourself, coworkers, and family. It also lists a variety of methods of data collection, ranging from informal conversations to more formal surveys.

Gathering data will help to verify, contradict, expand, or reinforce your own self-knowledge. Your coach may also choose to gather data using research-based instruments. Exhibit 2.1 explores self-assessment and research-based inventories that are often used in leadership coaching.

Competencies

As a coaching leader, you will need certain competencies to determine the data you need, to draw meaning from the data, and to ascertain themes from all the information you collect. These competencies are honesty, inquiry, advocacy, resiliency, and self-management.

Honesty

Why is being honest with yourself so hard? Today's business leaders wrestle with incongruence in their own thinking. What inconsistent messages do you hear in your head?

- I must control my life to win, even though the game rules change every day.
- I must remain rational, even though I feel great stress and pain.
- I must have all the answers, even though I don't know what I'm doing.
- I must be successful, even though it doesn't make me happy.

Exhibit 2.1 **Examples of Assessment Instruments**

Self-Assessment

- Personality assessments

  Examples: Myers-Briggs Type Indicator (MBTI; Myers, 1998), Fundamental Interpersonal Relations Orientation—Behavior (FIRO-B; Schutz, 1996), or Birkman Inventory (1996)
- Values clarification exercises

  Examples: exercises found in *Co-Active Coaching* (Whitworth et al., 1998), *Simply Live It Up* (Belf & Ward, 1997), or *Life Launch* (Hudson & McLean, 1995)
- Self-management exercises

  Examples: CleanSweep, found in *The Portable Coach* (Leonard, 1998) or in *Take Time for Your Life* (Richardson, 1998)
- Professional management competencies

  Example: *The Career Architect* (Lombardo & Eichinger, 1992)
- Leadership style assessments

  Examples: *The Visionary Leader* (Sashkin, 1996), the Emotional Intelligence Inventory (Goleman, 2000), or the Leadership Practices Inventory (Kouzes & Posner, 1993)
- Style and skills in such areas as management, supervision, communication, and conflict management

  Examples: the Thomas-Kilmann Conflict Mode Instrument (Thomas & Kilmann, 1974) or the LaMonica Empathy Profile (La Monica Rigolosi, 1980)
- Customized 360-degree surveys that include self-assessment of competencies in a number of areas

Feedback From Others

- Leadership style assessments

  Examples: *The Visionary Leader* (Sashkin, 1999), the Emotional Intelligence Inventory (Goleman, 2000), or the Leadership Practices Inventory (Kouzes & Posner, 1993)
- Organizational climate surveys

  Examples: *Targeted Culture Modeling* (Hay Group, 1995) or the Denison Organizational Culture Survey (Denison, 1995)
- Style and skills in such areas as management, supervision, communication, and conflict management and others
- Customized 360-degree surveys that cover competencies in a number of areas

Are there other inconsistent messages you cope with? Being honest with yourself requires noticing when burdensome "musts" and "shoulds" crop up in your thinking. Don't try to fight these self-destructive messages. Just notice them. Try substituting authenticity when you feel stuck by the inconsistencies.

There are several ways in which honesty with yourself will be tested during data collection and analysis at the level of self. One is your choice of self-assessment tools. Make sure that whatever tool you choose is comprehensive, well researched, reliable, and valid. Another test of your honesty is how you answer questions, whether on an inventory or during questioning from your coach. Answer questions truthfully, not how you think the questions should be answered. Third, be honest with yourself in choosing others to provide feedback. Don't choose only those who think you walk on water. Your coach can guide you on whom to choose and who will give you the most meaningful data for self-development.

Inquiry

According to Peter Koestenbaum, philosopher and adviser to global economy leaders, self-inquiry "doesn't take away from decisiveness, from being a person of action. In fact, it generates the inner toughness that you need to be an effective leader" (quoted in LaBarre, *Fast Company,* 2000, p. 226). Meg Wheatley, author of *Leadership and the New Science* (1999), recently commented on the value of meditative practices for leaders—being aware, listening, letting go, not taking things as they appear (McLeod, 2001). These practices contribute toward the discipline of personal mastery. Self-inquiry is devotion to critical thinking. It is a developmental process that requires you to challenge and perhaps change your thoughts: how you think and reason, what inferences you make, what assumptions you make, what conclusions you draw, and ultimately what actions you take.

Effective inquiry requires an attitude of curiosity about self and a desire to dig deeper into one's "mental models." Self-inquiry is a powerful tool to learn more about what drives our actions. Once we ask ourselves those questions, we can begin the process of making deliberate choices to change. Recently, Senge explained how leaders need to go beyond just wanting to change:

> So it's not simply a matter of good intentions. As it would be in any discipline-based religion or artistic field, it's a matter of hard work and knowing how to do it. Do you have the tools? Do you have the methods? Do you have the teachers or mentors? All the things that help a person along any developmental path. (quoted in McLeod, 2001, p. 30)

Here are some powerful inquiries you need to apply directly in the data-gathering process at the level of self:

- What are my intentions in this situation? What is preventing me from being successful in achieving my intentions?
- How did I reach this conclusion? What other conclusions are possible?
- What inferences am I making about the other person, organization, and so forth?
- What assumptions am I making in my thinking? What other assumptions are possible?
- What beliefs do I hold (about leadership, etc.) that cause me to think this way?
- What are the consequences of thinking this way? What are the benefits?
- What are some other ways of thinking about this?

Keeping these questions in mind during data collection will give you practice in the kinds of conversations you will have with your coach and the coaching conversations you will have with others in your organization.

Advocacy

Stephen was a vice president of a large federal government contractor. He worked his way up from junior engineer to running a billion-dollar military contract. Stephen learned from his experience working with generals and admirals to always be ready with "the answer." His prowess with complex data analysis had won him an excellent reputation with his clients and peers, and he was an excellent negotiator for his company's business development. Like many other technology-based companies, Stephen's company was having difficulty retaining young, talented engineers and computer scientists. Recently, employee focus group data indicated that Stephen and other senior managers were perceived as arrogant, uncaring, and impatient. Stephen was frustrated that his communication style, which he had always thought of as a strength, was not working with his employees. Fortunately, Stephen had an executive coach who questioned Stephen's assumptions about effective interpersonal communication.

Like most leaders, Stephen had been well trained and rewarded for successfully advocating his point of view. He was articulate, politically astute, and relentless. But then these very attributes started causing him problems. How about you? Do you value your ability to influence and persuade others? Self-advocacy is less about your skills of powerful persuasion and more about stating your views with reasoning, with the intention of learning more about yourself and others.

Researchers have explored the uses of inquiry and advocacy in dialogue (Bohm, 1990; Senge, 1990). More recently, a distinction has been made between skillful discussion and dialogue (Isaacs, 1999). Despite these distinctions, we use the word *dialogue* to describe the skillful use of both inquiry and advocacy to learn and solve problems in organizational conversations. The next time you feel compelled to state your position on something, try framing your views in a manner something like the following:

- "I am taking this action because of my belief that ____."
- "I believe ____ because of the following reasons: (1) . . . (2) . . . (3)."
- "I came to this conclusion because I assumed that ____."
- "I make this assumption because of the following facts: ____."
- "I am inferring that you think/believe ____."

Obviously, self-advocacy is never enough in a productive dialogue. You must test your views with statements, such as

- "Do you see it differently?"
- "Do you come to a different conclusion?"
- "What other assumptions can we make?"
- "Is my inference correct?"

We will talk more about the skills of dialogue with others in Parts 3 and 4 of this book. For purposes of data collection and analysis at the level of self, inquiry and advocacy are the actual skills you need to use in assessing what you typically do as a leader and what your reasoning is for doing it.

Resiliency

In today's organizations, many leaders feel the stress of change and tend to cause stress for others. How do you handle stress? Can you bounce back? The coaching leader practices the attitudes and behaviors of resiliency and coaches others to be resilient.

Darryl Connor (1995), president of ODR International, wrote that resiliency is required of leaders who aspire to lead companies at "the speed of change" (p. 1). A resilient leader is

1. *Positive:* views life as challenging but opportunity filled
2. *Focused:* has a clear vision of what is to be achieved
3. *Flexible:* is pliable when responding to uncertainty
4. *Organized:* applies structures to help manage ambiguity
5. *Proactive:* engages change instead of evading it

Self-Management

Self-management is also an important competency of the coaching leader. Self-management is the discipline of eliminating the mental, physical, and emotional clutter of your life and replacing it with thoughts, beliefs, structures, and processes that free you to be a leader. Do any of the following examples of clutter and/or self-management apply to you?

Examples of Clutter	*Self-Management Techniques*
Messy desk	Cleaning off desk every 3 days
Helping with all requests	Saying "no" once a day
No energy	Exercising three times per week
Not meeting deadlines	Scheduling time for what's important
Others?	Others?

In examining how competent you are at self-management, getting feedback from others during the data-gathering and analysis stage can be enlightening. Do you practice what you preach? Feedback from others will tell you the degree to which you are seen as a role model in your organization. The following case highlights this point.

Susan was chomping at the bit when her company offered her coaching to develop her leadership potential. Thirty-five and single, she was a successful department director and was seen as a rising star in her company. At her first meeting with her coach, she said her goal was to become vice president within a year. At her coach's suggestion, Susan met with her boss to determine specific competency areas that she should develop. With typical zeal and determination, Susan quickly developed an action plan that included training, mentoring, and new projects that she volunteered to take on. Susan asked her coach to help her by giving her feedback on her progress and identifying areas for continuing improvement. The coach agreed and also asked Susan to complete an exercise called the Wheel of Life (Whitworth et al., 1998) and to write a life mission statement. Susan was puzzled as to how these activities would contribute to her development, but she reluctantly agreed to the request. As she related to her coach later, it was the first time she had considered the degree to which her life's work was in alignment with what was truly important to her. She began to see how her ambition could serve her in ways that would enhance her leadership potential—not only within her company but also to fulfill her dreams for a successful life. As a result, Susan expanded her action plan to include efforts in conservation, opportunities to meet new people, and more physical exercise.

Susan is an example of many leaders or aspiring leaders who have not integrated leadership into their way of being. This scenario shows how Susan developed into a role model of an integrated life. What kind of life do you want to lead? According to Peter Koestenbaum, "Nothing is more practical than for people to deepen themselves. The more you understand the human condition, the more effective you are as a businessperson. Human depth makes business sense" (quoted in LaBarre, *Fast Company*, 2000, p. 224). Becoming a coaching leader is first about becoming a successful human being. Getting feedback helps you define what that will look like for you.

In summary, your commitment to be a coaching leader requires you to integrate who you are with what you do. Data from self-assessment and feedback from others will also reveal any gaps between how you see yourself and how others see you. This analysis is critical to identify your strengths, weaknesses, inaccurate assumptions, and erroneous inferences. It provides the foundation for action planning, which we will address in the next section.

Step 3: Processing Feedback and Planning Actions

Think about your last performance appraisal. Did you enjoy the experience? Most people don't enjoy hearing what they perceive as criticism from others. Often they perceive that criticism as unfair or unjustified. Yet assessing others is an important part of organizational life today—assessing peers, employees, even bosses. In this section, we're asking you to suspend any negative assumptions you have about feedback long enough to consider how feedback from others, and yourself, can help you set goals for your development as a coaching leader. We will present five steps that will help you to accept feedback and transform it into goals for positive change. Then we will discuss five major competencies you need during this phase.

Hearing the Feedback

In the last section, we discussed the various sources and types of feedback you will need to explore who you are as a leader and how you need to change and develop. Your coach will present feedback to you in the form of a summary of the major strengths and weaknesses perceived in your leadership behavior. It is especially helpful to hear how your self-assessments compare with feedback from others. In our experience, some leaders are very tough on themselves and are surprised to learn that others see them more positively than they see themselves. Other leaders tend to have blind spots around the impact of certain behaviors and rate themselves higher than others do. In the latter scenario, it is easy to tune out the feedback with dismissals such as

- "My boss just doesn't understand how hard it is to manage around here."
- "They haven't seen enough of my behavior to judge me on that."
- "He never says anything positive about anyone."
- "My employees are trying to blame me for their poor performance."

Although it is understandable that we humans try to escape the pain of hearing something negative about ourselves, becoming a coaching leader is a shift in thinking about yourself. You no longer need to be perfect, the best, or the winner. Coaching leadership is not a game to win or lose. Coaching leadership is a learning stance in life. How can you learn and grow if you have nothing to learn? Table 2.3 outlines some questions you can ask yourself to "hear" the data effectively.

Peter Drucker (1999) advocated the development of strengths over the effort to improve problem performance. He stated, "It takes far more energy to improve from incompetence to mediocrity than to improve from first-rate performance to excellence" (p. 67). Drucker went on to describe a process of feedback analysis in which an individual records key decisions or actions and writes

Table 2.3 Comparing the Gaps Between Self-Assessment and Feedback From Others

Self-Assessment	*Feedback From Others*	*Comparison*
What are my top three strengths?	What are my top three strengths?	What are the differences in how I perceive myself and how others perceive me? How large are the gaps in perception? What ideas do I have for the reasons for the gap? How could I verify those ideas?
What are my top three weaknesses?	What are my top three weaknesses?	What are the differences in how I perceive myself and how others perceive me? How large are the gaps in perception? What ideas do I have for the reasons for the gap? How could I verify those ideas?
What do I notice about my reactions to these data? ■ Surprise? ■ Ambivalence? ■ Pleasure? ■ Other?	What do I notice about my reactions to these data? ■ Defensiveness? ■ Resistance? ■ Pleasure? ■ Other?	What are the differences in my reactions to how I perceive myself and how others perceive me? What are my feelings all about? How does that affect me as a leader? How can I be more open?

down what he or she expects will happen. A year later, the individual compares the actual results with his or her expectations. This method will show you, in a relatively short period of time, where your strengths lie. According to Drucker, most people think they know what they are good at. They are usually wrong.

Accepting the Feedback

According to Joe Folkman (2000, p. 300), we are unwilling to change what we do not believe needs to be changed. But how do you decide what needs to be changed? The first place to start is with the gaps between how you perceive yourself and how others perceive you in your top three strengths and weaknesses. Because these areas reflect something more than isolated responses, you must accept these perceptions as meaningful. Notice that I did not say that you must agree that these discrepancies are accurate. You must, however, be willing to consider the answers to the following questions:

	Benefits	Consequences
To Me	Of changing my behavior? Of not changing my behavior?	Of changing my behavior? Of not changing my behavior?
To Others	Of changing my behavior? Of not changing my behavior?	Of changing my behavior? Of not changing my behavior?

Figure 2.1. Approaching Your Feedback

- To what degree am I willing to accept the perceptions of others as valid?
- To what degree am I willing to change my behavior in these areas?
- What do these behaviors look like?
- What is the impact of these behaviors on others? On their productivity? On their commitment to the organization?

Figure 2.1 further depicts how you should approach the feedback.

Setting Goals for Development

There are several criteria for determining which areas to work on. First, what are the organization's expectations for your performance as a leader? If one of your top three weaknesses is related to a competency expected in your position or a position that you aspire to, then you can safely assume that this development area will have high leverage for you.

A second consideration for goal setting is the degree to which you want to change. How clearly is the behavior tied to the values you have identified as important to you? One way to determine your passion to change is to assign a number to where you are now and where you'd like to be (Whitmore, 1996, p. 113). Below is an example of one leader's top three weaknesses:

Top 3 Weaknesses in My Feedback Data	*As I See Myself on a Scale of 1 to 10*	*As I'd Like to See Myself on a Scale of 1 to 10*
Meeting management	3	7
Giving performance feedback	2	9
Including others in decision making	4	6

In meeting with his coach, the leader in this example determined that he is much more committed to improving the quality of his feedback to his direct reports than he is to managing meetings better or including others in his decision making. This doesn't mean that he will not improve his other weaknesses. It just means that his most immediate passion is around performance feedback.

Folkman (2000, p. 301) also recommended first choosing the few critical issues that can easily be changed. Finding a "quick win" can both provide momentum for the leader and demonstrate that the leader is serious about change. In the case described above, the leader decided that improving his approach to leading his staff meetings was easiest to change. Ultimately, with the help of his coach, he decided to work on both meeting management and performance feedback at the same time.

Creating an Action Plan

Now that you've identified your major goals, it's time to create an action plan. The first step is to translate each goal into objectives. Whitmore (1996, pp. 55-56) stressed that good objectives need to be not only SMART, but also PURE and CLEAR:

- SMART: Specific, Measurable, Agreed, Realistic, Time-phased
- PURE: Positively stated, Understood, Relevant, Ethical
- CLEAR: Challenging, Legal, Environmentally sound, Appropriate, Recorded

Whitmore also offered a set of powerful questions to guide the what, when, why, who, and how of leadership development action planning:

- What are you going to do?
- When are you gong to do it?
- Will this action meet your goal?
- What obstacles might you meet along the way?
- Who needs to know?
- What support do you need?
- How and when are you going to get that support?
- What other considerations do you have? (pp. 81-83)

Whitmore recommended that you rate on a 1-to-10 scale the degree of certainty you have that you will carry out the actions agreed. A self-rating of less than 8 indicates that you are unlikely to take the action. If you have rated yourself at less than 8, how can you reduce the size of the task or lengthen the time scale so as to enable you to raise the rating to 8 or above?

Exhibit 2.2 is an example of one objective from a leader's action plan.

Communicating Your Action Plan

Communicating your action to others is an important part of this step. Sometimes leaders are reluctant to communicate their action plans to others:

Exhibit 2.2 **Sample Action Plan**

Goal: Improve meeting management.

Objective: What are you going to do? Distribute meeting agenda to team members 3 days in advance of meeting.

When are you going to do it? Meeting of January 4.

Will this action meet your goal? Not by itself.

What obstacles might you meet along the way? Unexpected tasks delay creation of agenda.

Who needs to know? Team members, secretary.

What support do you need? How and when are you going to get that support? Input from team members no later than 3 days before meeting; get agreement last week before Christmas.

Other considerations: Agenda format, who is responsible, time allocated.

"It's embarrassing. It's a sign of weakness. And what if I don't meet my objectives? I can lose face with those who know of my failure." Bringing up these concerns, perhaps with your coach, is crucial to understanding what mental models guide your decision making and your actions. Exhibit 2.3 is an example of a leader who explored his reasoning process for not wanting to share his action plan with his team. Note that the questions for reflection enable the leader to question the validity of his reasoning process and move toward commitment to change.

Competencies

You need five competencies to accept feedback as valid, learn from others' perceptions, and plan actions for change: clarification, reframing, goal setting, accountability, and transition management.

Clarification

Effective problem solving requires valid information. You must clarify your understanding of others' perceptions by the use of skillful questions. Examples include the following:

- What does having a preference for introversion mean? What are some specific examples of how I demonstrate this preference?
- What does "poor listening" mean? What behaviors are perceived as poor listening? What behaviors are perceived as good listening?
- What is the impact of poor listening on my peers? My employees? On me?

Exhibit 2.3 **Coaching a Leader to Communicate His or Her Action Plan**

Current Reasoning

- People expect their leaders to be strong and successful.
- People expect their leaders to win and not make mistakes.
- Objectives for improvement indicate current vulnerability or weakness.
- People have difficulty changing.

Current Behavior

- Hide or cover up any area of weakness.
- Act as if you have all the right answers.
- Avoid new or "risky" behaviors or actions.
- Blame others or "the system" if a mistake occurs.

Results

- The leader does not change his or her behavior or beliefs.
- The leader does not learn.
- The leader shows poor performance as a leader.
- Followers are frustrated and disillusioned.

Questions for Reflection

- What is it about setting objectives for development that indicates lack of strength?
- How could sharing objectives indicate strength?
- What does winning mean to you?
- Can making mistakes ever lead to a win? What would that look like?
- How easy is it for you to change?
- What is your level of confidence that you can change?
- What would enable you to raise your level of confidence?

New Reasoning

- People admire leaders who show their humanness.
- People expect their leaders to be honest.
- Learning from mistakes can be seen as a strength.
- Winning is overcoming mistakes and obstacles.
- Change is a matter of choice.
- I have the confidence to be vulnerable.

New Behavior

- Share data and action plan with followers.
- Request help from others as needed.
- Take risks with new behaviors.
- Explicitly discuss mistakes and lessons learned.

Results

- The leader shows new actions and behaviors.
- The leader learns and develops as a leader.
- The leader shows improved performance as a leader.
- Followers are more committed and loyal to the leader and the organization.

Reframing

Reframing involves looking at a situation from another perspective. For example, you may receive the feedback that your employees ranked your communication skills second to your decision-making skills. You might react by thinking, "I'm not as good with people as I thought I was." Try reframing your perspective to "Decision making is a critical leadership competency, and my communication skills were ranked in my top three strengths also. I'm very pleased."

Goal Setting

Goal setting represents your first step in planning positive change. Making the choice to change requires a learning stance when listening to feedback and a willingness to consider alternative behaviors. Thus, you need to explore the mind-sets that may cause you to resist change before setting specific goals. You need to set goals that are consistent with your values even when these are not consistent with your strengths (Drucker, 1999, p. 69). In the case of one religious leader we know, feedback from his peers suggested that he needed to be more visible with external constituents. Although the leader had long recognized the need for this kind of visibility, his introverted nature made it difficult for him. He and his coach explored ways to decrease his discomfort and build confidence. Once you clarify a goal for development, your next task is to identify specific objectives, which can then lead to changes in your behavior.

Accountability

When you clarify your action plan, you become accountable for change. You should address the following questions: (a) What will I do? (b) How will I do it? and (c) How will others know? A creative regional manager we coached translated her objectives into a jar full of coins! She created several objectives having to do with supervisory behavior. She identified a list of behaviors she wanted to change with her team members. She asked for her employees to give her praise when she demonstrated a new behavior. When she had the opportunity to behave differently but didn't, her employees would also tell her, and they would put a marble in a designated jar. The manager had to replace each marble with $1.00. At the end of the week, the money was collected and used for "happy hour snacks." The manager was conditioned to change quickly.

Your action plan should be a specific, documented blueprint for your leadership development and must be monitored and followed with diligence. Nothing will destroy your integrity more quickly than to betray a promise to change. Each objective in your action plan should include how you will measure successful change in behavior.

Transition Management

The self is not a thing but an unfolding process. Bridges (1991) addressed three phases of internal transition that we experience during change: endings, the neutral zone, and new beginnings. He advised anyone deciding to change to acknowledge the grieving process of defining clearly what is over and what isn't. For you to commit to change and growth, what will you have to let go? It might be certainty, security, or control. Making the decision to change is hard.

In summary, the step of processing feedback and planning actions involves five smaller steps: (a) hearing the feedback, (b) accepting the feedback, (c) setting goals for development or improvement, (d) creating your action plan, and (e) communicating your action plan. These steps require specific competencies and behaviors. They will enable you to begin the most important part of becoming a coaching leader—taking action.

Step 4: Taking Action

Jennifer was an ambitious young staff accountant who had team leadership responsibilities. The new vice president of finance, Tom, recognized her potential and supported her growth and development. When Jennifer submitted her application for an open director position, Tom was pleased but worried that Jennifer didn't have the knowledge, political savvy, and management experience to be effective at that level. He arranged for a coach to work with Jennifer on her skills, style, and behavior.

The coach quickly realized that Jennifer had little understanding of what being a director in her company really entailed. The coach asked Jennifer to interview several directors throughout the company to get their perspective on performance expectations at that level. Jennifer's initial enthusiasm waned when she discovered that long hours, negotiating skills, and a thick skin were management necessities. Her coach asked her to identify her values and goals in life and to honestly compare them to the realities of management life in her company. Jennifer spent several sessions talking with her coach about how important her desires for achievement and recognition were compared with her desire to spend as much time as possible with her young children. These conversations with her coach were enlightening. The coach asked Jennifer many questions regarding her beliefs, values, intentions, and actions. She posed situations that Jennifer might face and challenged her reactions and responses. Jennifer gradually accepted the fact that she wanted the challenge of management and that she would be bored and unfulfilled if she chose to delay her ambitions until her children were older. Jennifer relished the opportunity to "tangle with the big boys." She and her coach planned strategies to prepare her for management responsibilities and to meet her family obligations. Though Jennifer did not look forward to the inevitable judgments of some of her friends and family regarding her decision, she was satisfied that she was being true to herself, and, more important, she was excited about her future. For his part, Tom was pleased that he could recommend Jennifer for the director position with confidence that she would be willing and prepared to handle the tough new responsibilities.

This case illustrates how the step of taking action happens during a process of ongoing conversation, reflection, and practice between the coach and client. If the relationship between you and your coach is successful, you will have a safe place in which to report on your progress. Imagine that! A safe place to talk openly and honestly about your successes, failures, fears, hopes, and aspirations. If you, like many of the leaders we have known, have no one to talk to about your innermost thoughts and feelings, the coaching relationship will be a relief. In addition to honest dialogue, your coach will give you homework assignments designed to further your problem solving and decision making. By having this kind of relationship in your life, you will in turn be emboldened to coach others in your organization.

Taking action to develop yourself as a coaching leader involves the following elements:

1. Holding regular meetings with your coach
2. Determining what actions you will take to learn and develop between meetings and how they relate to your objectives
3. Making a commitment to carry out those actions
4. Keeping notes on your actions, your reactions, and the outcomes
5. Sharing your progress with your coach
6. Sharing your progress with your boss, employees, and peers
7. Reinforcing and celebrating your successes
8. Learning from your mistakes

As you take action, everything you have done so far to examine and explore who you are as a leader will be put to the test.

Holding Regular Meetings

By this time, you have agreed to a schedule of meetings with your coach. In general, it's best to meet with your coach at least once every 2 weeks for an hour. Some people prefer half-hour appointments on a weekly basis, especially if the appointment is by telephone. However, it's critical that you set up a schedule that takes priority in your life. Postponing or missing appointments frequently not only disrupts the momentum of learning and development but signals that you are not taking your own development as a leader very seriously. Yes, it requires commitment and tenacity. Yes, you will have to say "no" to some other emerging requirement. But we bet that you will be rewarded by increased self-confidence, self-motivation, pride, and excitement about who you are becoming. Other people will notice the change in you. In subsequent chapters, you will learn how to coach others. How can you expect others to commit to their development if you don't demonstrate the same commitment?

Three months of meetings with your coach are the bare minimum for achieving meaningful progress in your development. We recommend 6 months to a year of meeting twice a month. At the end of 3 months, talk with your coach about how well the process is working for you. At that point, you can mutually determine if you want to continue the relationship as it is currently defined, redefine your relationship, set new goals, or end the coaching relationship. Good coaches are not interested in a permanent relationship. On the contrary, they want you to succeed as a leader without them.

Table 2.4 Coaching Agendas

Type	*Description*	*Notes*
Action	Information, knowledge, skills that enable leader to take action Opportunities to practice and get feedback	■ Interpersonal communication ■ Meeting facilitation ■ Project management ■ Writing ■ Delegation ■ Budgeting
Reasoning	Discovering assumptions or faulty reasoning that leads to faulty behaviors	Under what circumstances will behaviors contradict stated beliefs? What assumptions would lead to these behaviors?
Fulfillment	Desire to create a balanced life in which personal values, goals, and beliefs are aligned with both personal and professional behaviors	■ Spending enough time with family ■ Maintaining a desired lifestyle ■ Achieving a lifelong ambition without giving up an income ■ Making career change ■ Wanting a more satisfying personal relationship

Determining Actions Between Meetings

What kinds of actions will help you grow, develop, and be more effective as a leader? Witherspoon (2000, p. 166) asserted that coaching involves one or more of the following areas: skills, performance, future development, or a personal agenda. In our work with leaders from all walks of life, we have found their "agendas" to be typically in the following areas: action, reasoning, and fulfillment. Table 2.4 explains these three agendas.

Below is a case that demonstrates the balancing of these action areas.

Helen hired a coach when she realized that growth and advancement in her company were limited. She had been in a line management position for many years and had a great deal of experience. However, she was bored and was looking for a challenge. Her coach helped her to identify what kind of life she wanted to lead and what career goals she had. Helen became intrigued with the idea of consulting, and she wanted to see different parts of the country. During coaching, Helen was challenged to examine her inferences about consulting. She interviewed several consultants and was surprised to learn of the many demands they faced from clients. Armed with her new insights, Helen was more determined than ever to pursue her goal of becoming a consultant. She practiced with her coach how she would respond in job interviews with consulting firms. The positive feedback she received during actual interviews further reinforced Helen's goals. Helen eventually accepted a position with a global management-consulting firm that not only allowed her to travel but also provided many new training and development opportunities.

Helen spent time in all three agenda areas. She gained information, knowledge, and skills to prepare her for a new career. She explored and tested her assumptions about what a life of consulting would be like for her. Finally, she was able to realize a goal that fulfilled her hopes and dreams.

As you think about the actions you will take to develop yourself as a leader, remember that this is the time to stretch. You can try out new skills, correct some faulty assumptions, plan for that next job or role, and deal with that haunting problem that keeps you up at night. Using these three areas as a planning tool, we challenge you to develop one good objective in each area and take effective action.

Making a Commitment

What does it take for you to make a commitment? Someone to nag you? Post-it notes on your computer? Reinforcement when you do well? Threats of dire consequences if you don't take action? Making a commitment and carrying it out is crucial for effective leadership. Later in this discussion, we will talk about the value of sharing your progress with your boss, employees, and peers. Making your commitment visible and tangible by sharing your plans with others is an excellent way to keep you committed to taking action.

Keeping Notes

The last thing busy managers need is the task of keeping notes. Yet keeping notes on your self-development will help you for several reasons. First, it will force you to think about your actions in a deliberate way that focuses on learning more than achievement. Second, it will guide you to new courses of action if one approach didn't work well. Third, it will record your progress and give you a chance to celebrate. The worksheet in Exhibit 2.4 is one we give our coaching clients to complete prior to each coaching session.

There are many ways to take notes. If this form doesn't appeal to you, what would be a way for you to document your progress that would be meaningful to you? One artistic CEO we know took notes free-form in a sketchbook. Another busy executive dictated his progress into a tape recorder. Whatever works!

Sharing Your Progress

Robert Hargrove (1995, p. 214) stated that collaborative conversations, such as those with a coach, elicit powerful commitments from people and must be explicit. Sharing your progress on actions with your coach is a powerful way

Exhibit 2.4 **Presession Worksheet**

1. What went well for you this week? What was it about this situation that was positive? What did it feel like? How did it support your values? How can you build on that?
2. What didn't go well for you this week? What choices did you make? What did you learn from this experience? What was the perspective you had on this situation? What are some other perspectives?
3. Where are you in achieving your objectives? What can you do to move forward? How will this support your values?
4. What will you do to move forward? When will you do it? How will you let your coach know?

to get feedback without fear of embarrassment or failure. It is also a safe relationship in which to shift direction and set new objectives. Creating and committing to new objectives is to be expected as you peel back the layers of understanding about your rich and complex self.

Although many organizations require their executives to report on their coaching progress to their bosses, many leaders hesitate to share their progress with their employees and peers. Why is this? Yes, it would be embarrassing if you failed to keep your commitment. But that's the point. Avoiding embarrassment is a strong motivator for keeping a commitment.

Other leaders don't tell their employees how they plan to change because if they make a mistake or fail in some way, then they won't have to admit failure. It's a way of saving face. Hargrove (1995) noted the enormous price people pay when they hide their mistakes. Because they are so invested in protecting themselves from threat and pain, they are unable to be authentic, learn, or grow (p. 234). The result is that they develop "skilled incompetence"—a set of automatic behaviors of avoidance that are carried out with great skill (Argyris, 1986, p. 75). Over time, these behaviors become so entrenched that leaders cannot even recognize them as defensive behaviors. They become truly skillful at covering up the cover-up.

Reinforcing and Celebrating

It's important to acknowledge your "wins" in taking action.

One executive we know, Susan, had difficulty recognizing when she was successful. She would meet with her coach every 2 weeks and bemoan her lack of progress. Pointed inquiry from her coach made it clear that Susan actually was taking significant action toward her goals. Why was Susan unable or unwilling to acknowledge her successes? After some difficult discussions, Susan realized how holding herself small was keeping her from being the powerful leader she knew she could be. Her coach encouraged Susan to practice being open and explicit about her achievements. An interesting point about this conversation is that this coaching relationship steered clear of therapy or counseling. Whereas a therapist might have asked Susan to explore what had happened in the past to prevent her from acknowledging her successes, the coach focused instead on the gap between the reality of her actions and her beliefs about her competence. Susan was challenged to take a stand—a stand that she was indeed a powerful, effective leader. This action-oriented, data-based approach kept Susan focused on moving forward and building on her successful actions.

Coaching leaders share their successes in the effort to expand positive change to their organizations. A powerful testimonial to this effect is the *Harvard Business Review* article "Retention Through Redemption" (2001), by Navy Commander D. Michael Abrashoff. Below is an excerpt:

> Retaining people sometimes requires redeeming them—changing their lives. But first, I had to redeem myself. I had to become an entirely different type of leader. A different type of person, really. Only then was I able to redeem my sailors, one at a time. Together we learned a different way to think and act. All in all, it was an enormous undertaking. I ran the risk of never getting promoted again. But I realized that the only way to achieve my goals—combat readiness, retention, and trust—was to make my people grow. It worked. The Benfold has set all-time records for performance and retention, and the waiting list of officers and enlisted personnel who want to transfer to the Benfold is pages long. It's a long wait because very few aboard the Benfold want to leave. (p. 4)

Learning From Your Mistakes

Acknowledging and learning from your mistakes is just as important as celebrating your successes. When was the last time you made a mistake? Yesterday? What did you learn from it? Whom did you tell? Who will be affected by what you learned from your mistake? What actions will you take that reflect what you learned? How will that make you a better leader? A better person?

Henry is the controller of a midsize property management company. Henry's coach asked him to talk about choices he had made, describing both successes and mistakes. Henry easily described his successes. However, he struggled to identify any mistakes. When his coach noted the difficulty Henry seemed to be having, Henry said, "I try not to focus on mistakes. I don't think that's productive."

The coach replied, "We make choices based on a number of factors—the data we have available to us at the time, our experience, and our assumptions are examples of those factors. Often in hindsight we recognize that we could have made a better choice. In this framework, how can looking at poor choices or mistakes be productive?"

Henry smiled and began to talk about a choice he had made with his one "problem employee," Jane. Jane resisted change, and Henry had tacitly reinforced her resistance by not giving her new assignments that required teamwork. He said that it had been "the path of least resistance" but that now in retrospect he realized it was a mistake.

The coach asked Henry to talk about the consequences of his approach and the likely consequences of alternative approaches. By the end of the session, Henry committed to using a different approach with Jane. He said he would give Jane two new assignments with expected outcomes and deadlines. One day later, Henry's coach received an e-mail message from Henry saying how pleasantly surprised he had been by Jane's readiness to accept the assignments.

In this case, Henry learned to reframe mistakes as choices made in time, not failures in his leadership. By openly discussing his mistakes, he was able to explore ways to expand his thinking and take different actions. It was significant learning.

Competencies

Because "taking action" is a process of learning, not an outcome, the competencies you need as a coaching leader involve how to learn more effectively. These competencies include dialogue, reflection, problem solving, decision making, and risk taking.

Dialogue

In the previous section, we talked about the need to engage in dialogue by (a) testing the accuracy of assumptions and conclusions that lead us to think and behave the way we do and (b) exploring new assumptions, inferences, conclusions, and beliefs. This is necessary to accept feedback and establish goals for change. In ongoing coaching sessions, you will reflect on what you did to progress toward your goals, what your reasoning and intentions were, and what the impacts, positive and negative, were. You will discuss what you learned about yourself and what you learned about leadership. Dialogue skills balance advocacy for your reasoning process with inquiry into new thinking. Taking action requires getting into the habit of engaging in learning conversations. Table 2.5 outlines some ideas for engaging in a learning dialogue.

Reflection

The process of engaging in a dialogue with your coach about your reasoning and your actions is one of reflecting on who you are. At a deep level, you hold certain "theories in use" that may be in conflict with what you espouse (Argyris & Schon, 1974). In our earlier example, Henry said he believed in teamwork. However, he did not address his problem employee, who resisted new assignments that involved teamwork. We might describe Henry's theory in use as follows:

Condition	*Action*	*Consequence*
An employee resists accepting a new assignment that involves teamwork, even though you promote teamwork in your department.	Back off from insisting on the assignment, explaining that it is the path of least resistance, and justify your nonaction by stating that the employee does her current job well.	The employee is reinforced for not demonstrating teamwork, and other employees doubt the integrity of your words. Teamwork is eroded in your department.

Table 2.5 Engaging in a Learning Dialogue

Inquiry Into Previous Reasoning and Actions	*Inquiry Into Possible New Reasoning and Actions*
I took this action because I believed that ____________________.	What other actions might I have taken? What actions can I take now? What impact do I want to have?
I came to this conclusion because I assumed that ____________________.	What other conclusions might I come to?
I made the following assumptions because I inferred that ____________________.	What other assumptions might I make?
I observed ____________ and inferred that it meant ____________________.	How might I test these inferences? What other inferences might I have made from those observations?

After Henry's theory in use was identified, Henry's coach encouraged him to discuss the beliefs that had led him to take this action. An honest dialogue resulted in Henry's realization that he avoided "confrontation" because he was fearful that he would be disliked. Henry's coach asked him to try on a new belief: Leaders need to be respected and admired, not necessarily liked. The new belief resulted in new actions, which resulted in desired consequences:

Same Condition	*New Action*	*New Consequence*
An employee resists accepting a new assignment that involves teamwork, even though you promote teamwork in your department.	Ask the employee what her reasoning is, and listen with openness to any new information. Advocate for your reasoning, including the consequences of her resistance for her, you, the other employees, and productivity. Ask the employee for her views. Listen with openness. Ask the employee to make her choice regarding the assignment.	The employee accepts the new assignment. She is not comfortable working in a new way but she grows more skillful over time. She and other employees perceive you as practicing what you preach. Teamwork is promoted in your department.

Problem Solving

Managers have typically been well trained to solve problems in the corporate world. What's different about problem solving for a coaching leader? There are two primary differences. First, you need to be more concerned with how you see and interpret your actions than with what the solution is. By reflecting on your reasoning and actions, you realize that you have choices—for example, more than one solution. Your choice of solutions reflects your values, beliefs, and theories in use. Second, you don't let the rules of the game limit your thinking. For you and for those who follow you, you must look for opportunities to think outside the box and take risks. Navy Commander Abrashoff, discussed earlier, risked his career to empower his ship's sailors to solve problems. He was rewarded with technical innovations now used throughout the Navy and higher rate of retention of sailors beyond their initial tours of duty.

Decision Making

In a coaching relationship, you bring your responsibility and commitment to the task of developing yourself. To be committed to the task, you must reflect on your reasoning and actions and make choices regarding what you are committed to and how you will be responsible for taking action. Decision making is the process of determining what choices to make and how to carry them out.

Risk Taking

Perhaps the hardest part of taking action is the willingness to take risks. As you decide what actions to take, bring to the surface whatever inferences you are making about the risks involved. Then ask yourself the following questions:

- What's the worst that could happen if I take this action?
- How likely is that? What is so bad about that?
- What other outcomes could happen from my action?
- How could taking this action benefit me? Others?
- How likely are these benefits?

Coaching leaders inquire into their own reasoning regarding the risks they will incur from taking action.

A vice president we know, Mary, was having difficulty with her marketing director. Over time, difficult conversations had turned into stony silence between the two of them. Upon reflection, Mary decided that she needed to address the silence. She talked with her coach about the reasons for her hesitation—the fear that her overtures would be rejected. The coach asked Mary, "How is that worse than the silence you endure now? Even if your marketing director rejects you, what benefit do you get from speaking to her?" Mary decided to take the risk and speak to the employee.

During dialogue with her coach, Mary developed a "script" for her meeting. And if you're wondering how the meeting went, it didn't go as planned. The marketing director insisted that there was no problem, that Mary was making a mountain out of a molehill. Mary was so surprised she somehow stuttered a reply and ended the meeting. At her next meeting with her coach, Mary reflected on what went wrong and what her next steps would be.

Nobody ever said taking action was easy. But the more you practice, the more you learn. The more you learn, the more your leadership will become your way of being.

Step 5: Evaluating Your Progress

Many individuals we coach describe their leadership journeys as a "calling." Can you imagine doing your job as if it were a "calling"? Throughout this part of our book, we have talked about exploring your self. In this section, we'll explore how you can evaluate your actions and your growth. Did you answer the call? Does your leadership, your life, matter?

When you identified your goals and objectives, you also determined how you would know if and when you succeeded in meeting them. Right? As a coaching leader, you evaluate your self-development on two levels: (a) measuring the effectiveness of each action you took and (b) overall measuring of your successful self-development. During regular meetings with your coach, you will review your progress on each of your actions. Periodically, you will evaluate your entire action plan. Exhibit 2.5 displays a worksheet for evaluating your action plan.

Remember the self-assessment grid we presented in the section on processing feedback and planning actions? You can use the same grid to assess your own success in each area by adding a column to the right. Table 2.6 demonstrates our extended example. Here the individual believes that he has achieved success in his highest-priority action item, giving performance feedback. In addition, he has determined that he has made progress in the other two areas but still has a distance to go in his development.

Beyond the evaluation of actions, objectives, and goals, we believe that coaching leaders constantly evaluate their actions against their life purpose. At the beginning of this section, we posed some questions for you. It is appropriate to pose them again when you're ready to do some intense self-evaluation of your progress as a coaching leader:

1. What is my life's mission? Am I living it?
2. What brings me joy? Do I make it happen?
3. Do I have a vision of myself as a leader? What is it?

Exhibit 2.5 **Action Plan Analysis**

1. Were my actions completed? On time?
2. What percentage of completion was achieved?
3. If an action was not completed, do I still intend to accomplish it?
4. If the action was not completed, what prevented its accomplishment?
5. What did I do differently from what I had planned and why?
6. What benefits did the completed activity produce?
7. If I were to do it again, how would I do it differently?
8. What do I plan to do now?
9. If an action was completed, what is my degree of satisfaction with the outcome?
10. Who will benefit the most from this action?
11. Specifically, what was improved as a result of the activity?
12. What money was saved or what value was added to the organization as a result of the action?
13. What did I, my team, and/or my organization learn?
14. What did I discover about what needs to be done next?

4. How well are my beliefs and values aligned with my actions? How do I know? How deep am I willing to look?
5. Do I live every day as if someone is grading how well I'm living that vision?
6. What are my fears? How do these fears inhibit me as a leader?
7. How do I reflect on my actions and learn from them?
8. How much am I willing to change?

Elisabeth Kübler-Ross, author of *On Death and Dying* (1969), found that when people look back upon their lives, they ask three questions that determine their sense of meaningfulness:

1. Did I give and receive love?
2. Did I become all I can be?
3. Did I leave the planet a little better?

Can you answer "yes" to all three questions?

Competencies

The competencies you need to evaluate your self-development are openness, courage, and commitment to learning.

Table 2.6 Self-Assessment for Evaluation

Top Three Weaknesses in My Feedback Data	*As I See Myself on a Scale of 1 to 10 in January*	*As I'd Like to See Myself on a Scale of 1 to 10 by September*	*As I See Myself on a Scale of 1 to 10 in September*
Meeting management	3	7	5
Giving performance feedback	2	9	9
Including others in decision making	4	6	5

Openness

How successful were you in achieving that objective you set for yourself? Be honest! We have asked you to embrace feedback. Now we're asking you to be open to failure, or at least mistakes. Demonstrating openness about one's failure or lack of progress can be very painful. Robert Quinn, in his book *Deep Change* (1996), described his own journey of deep change:

> I became fascinated by my own defense mechanisms, all the ways I could deny the fact that I was sometimes lazy or lacked courage. I became intrigued with the link between embracing disconfirming feedback, seeing and hearing unpleasant things about myself, and the process of growth. It wasn't long before I realized that if I was not continually growing, I was slowly dying. Perhaps in confronting the choice of slow death or deep change, I have come to understand that life is a constant process of deaths and rebirths. In understanding this, I am more free to grow and become more responsive to the individuals around me. (pp. 24-25)

Courage

To grow and achieve real change, you must have the courage to discuss how your intended actions differed from your actual actions and why. As we discussed for Step 2, collecting and analyzing data, inquiry into gaps between intended actions and actual behaviors is important in self-assessment and getting feedback from others. That line of inquiry is also important in evaluating your progress. As you evaluate your growth as a coaching leader, keep track of actual conversations and situations that did not go as well as you intended.

Commitment to Learning

Coaching leaders have committed to a learning way of life. The steps of self-development do not stop with evaluation. In fact, evaluation leads to revised or new goals for development, as can be seen in the following case.

Annette was vaguely unhappy. She had always dreamed of being an executive, and now she was one. After a year of working toward this promotion, she had been rewarded with the title of vice president of marketing and a nice salary increase. Yet something was not right. Annette looked back to the values she had identified a year earlier with her coach and gained some insight. Her values included achievement, but she had also listed fairness, giving to the community, and learning. When she looked at the way she spent her time in her company, she realized that she was not "living" all of her values. Annette developed a new action plan that would include leadership in her local chamber of commerce and graduate classes in management. She also resolved to start a mentoring program in her company. Annette had achieved one major goal, but she still was "heeding her call."

Annette's learning had evolved. She had reason to celebrate, but she was already starting a new journey in her development as a coaching leader.

Leading from the inside out always involves returning to the self—yourself. That in itself is reason to celebrate. But wait, there's more. It's time to build on your new self-understanding. You are ready to build a coaching relationship with your team!

WORKSHEET 2.1: The Leader Within

Step 1: Establishing the Coaching Relationship

DEFINING THE DESIRED OUTCOMES

1. **What I want from coaching is:**

   ____

   ____

2. **My commitment to hiring a coach is:**

   ____

   ____

3. **The right coach for me is:**

   ____

   ____

Tips and Examples

- ❑ Understand the differences between coaching, counseling, training, and mentoring.
- ❑ Determine how coaching is related to leadership.
- ❑ Know the difference between doing leadership tasks and making leadership a continual way of being.
- ❑ Explore what is important to you.
- ❑ Create a vision for your future.
- ❑ Ask the right questions of a prospective coach.
- ❑ Choose your own coach, or at least have veto power.

QUESTIONS TO CONSIDER

1. **What do I want coaching to do for me?**
2. **What does leadership mean to me?**
3. **Do I have a sincere desire to change?**
4. **What do I want from a coach?**
5. **What is my vision for my life?**

Tips and Examples

- ❑ Coaching can be about growth, development, meaning, or improvement. But it is never about the status quo.
- ❑ Set goals and make agreements early in the coaching relationship.

(continued)

WORKSHEET 2.1: The Leader Within *(continued)*

RESOURCES AND TOOLS

1. **My resources for finding a good coach are:**

   ____

   ____

2. **I expect my relationship with my coach to have the following characteristics:**

   ____

   ____

Tips and Examples

- ❑ Training schools and professional organizations are good resources.
- ❑ Coaching and leadership experience count in a coach.
- ❑ You get what you pay for.
- ❑ Find out what the coach expects from you.
- ❑ Make sure the coach you hire has a written contract.
- ❑ The coach should expect you to be creative, resourceful, and whole.
- ❑ The coach should let you set the agenda and create the goals.
- ❑ The coach should be willing to address your whole life.

COMPETENCIES

On a scale of 1 to 5 (1 = nonexistent; 5 = outstanding), rate yourself on the following competencies for this step:

1. **Reflection** **1 2 3 4 5**

   Two specific ways I will demonstrate this competency in this step:

   a. ____

   b. ____

2. **Learning** **1 2 3 4 5**

   Two specific ways I will demonstrate this competency in this step:

   a. ____

   b. ____

3. **Honesty** **1 2 3 4 5**

   Two specific ways I will demonstrate this competency in this step:

   a. ____

   b. ____

(continued)

WORKSHEET 2.1: The Leader Within (*continued*)

4. Determination **1 2 3 4 5**

Two specific ways I will demonstrate this competency in this step:

a. ______________________________

b. ______________________________

Tips and Examples

- ❑ Be clear about your values.
- ❑ Be committed to yourself.
- ❑ Take the initial step of hiring a coach for you.
- ❑ Be honest with your coach.
- ❑ Be open to new ways of thinking and behaving.

WORKSHEET 2.2: The Leader Within

Step 2: Collecting and Analyzing Data

DEFINING THE DESIRED OUTCOMES

1. **What I want to know about my own beliefs about myself is:**

   ____

   ____

2. **What I want to know about me from others is:**

   ____

   ____

3. **I want feedback from the following individuals/groups:**

   ____

   ____

Tips and Examples

- ❑ Examine what about yourself may be limiting your effectiveness as a leader.
- ❑ Ask your coach about personality assessments, values clarification, self-management exercises, competency and skills assessments, and leadership style assessments.
- ❑ Ask your coach about ways to get feedback from others: leadership style assessments, climate surveys, 360-degree surveys.
- ❑ Remember that interview data from others are confidential.
- ❑ Likewise, only you and your coach have access to your data.

QUESTIONS TO CONSIDER

1. **What do I need to understand about myself to develop as a coaching leader?**
2. **How open am I to the perceptions of others?**
3. **Whose feedback is important to my development?**
4. **To what degree do I integrate leadership into my whole life?**

Tips and Examples

- ❑ Dig deep into your needs, your values, your strengths, and your weaknesses.
- ❑ Consider getting feedback from employees, peers, customers, boss, friends, family.
- ❑ Consider your blind spots in perceptions.
- ❑ Your personal life and your professional life must both be considered in your leadership development.

(continued)

WORKSHEET 2.2: The Leader Within *(continued)*

RESOURCES AND TOOLS

1. **Self-assessments I will complete are:**

   ____

   ____

2. **Organizational data I can use include:**

   ____

   ____

3. **The methods I can use to collect data are:**

   ____

   ____

4. **I expect my coach to help me collect data by:**

   ____

   ____

Tips and Examples

- ❑ Examples of self-assessments are the Myers-Briggs Type Indicator (MBTI; Myers, 1998), the DISC Personal Profile System (Carlson Learning Co., 1994), the Fundamental Interpersonal Relations Orientation—Behavior (FIRO-B; Schutz, 1996), the Clean Sweep Program (Clean Sweep, 1995), the Wheel of Life (Whitworth et al., 1998), and the Leadership Practices Inventory (Kouzes & Posner, 1993b).
- ❑ Consider customized 360-degree surveys and personal interviews for feedback from others.
- ❑ Tie your data collection to organizational expectations.
- ❑ Your coach should be skilled in interviewing and resourceful in data collection methods.
- ❑ Collect data early in the coaching process.

COMPETENCIES

On a scale of 1 to 5 (1 = nonexistent; 5 = outstanding), rate yourself on each competency for this step:

1. **Honesty** 1 2 3 4 5

   Two specific ways I will demonstrate this competency in this step:

   a. ______________________________

   b. ______________________________

2. **Inquiry** 1 2 3 4 5

   Two specific ways I will demonstrate this competency in this step:

   a. ______________________________

   b. ______________________________

(continued)

WORKSHEET 2.2: The Leader Within *(continued)*

3. Advocacy **1 2 3 4 5**

Two specific ways I will demonstrate this competency in this step:

a. ______________________________

b. ______________________________

4. Resiliency **1 2 3 4 5**

Two specific ways I will demonstrate this competency in this step:

a. ______________________________

b. ______________________________

5. Self-Management **1 2 3 4 5**

Two specific ways I will demonstrate this competency in this step:

a. ______________________________

b. ______________________________

Tips and Examples

- ❑ Be honest with yourself.
- ❑ Be authentic with others.
- ❑ Challenge your habits of thought.
- ❑ Question your own reasoning.
- ❑ State your views with reasoning more than persuasiveness.
- ❑ Practice handling stress with resiliency.
- ❑ Eliminate clutter from your life.

WORKSHEET 2.3: The Leader Within

Step 3: Processing Feedback and Planning Actions

DEFINING THE DESIRED OUTCOMES

1. **I will acknowledge feedback from others by:**

   ____

   ____

2. **My readiness to accept feedback will be demonstrated by:**

   ____

   ____

3. **I will communicate my action plan in the following ways:**

   ____

   ____

4. **I will structure my action plan in the following ways:**

   ____

   ____

Tips and Examples

- ❑ Capitalize on your strengths first.
- ❑ Perceptions are the only reality there is for leadership.
- ❑ You must accept others' perceptions; you need not agree with them.
- ❑ Gaps between your perceptions and others' perceptions—these are opportunities for change.
- ❑ Determine what change you are most passionate about.
- ❑ Set "stretch" goals—go way beyond the status quo in your vision as a leader.
- ❑ Make your objectives measurable.
- ❑ Document your action plan.

QUESTIONS TO CONSIDER

1. **How can I capitalize on my strengths?**
2. **How open am I to feedback from others?**
3. **What am I willing to change? What is my reasoning?**
4. **What are the consequences of doing nothing?**
5. **What would be a "quick win" for me?**
6. **How can I make my goals a real stretch?**
7. **Who needs to know about my action plan?**
8. **How will I communicate my progress?**

(continued)

WORKSHEET 2.3: The Leader Within *(continued)*

Tips and Examples

- ❑ Keep reminding yourself that you are creative, resourceful, and whole.
- ❑ Let go of the past and plan for the future.
- ❑ Notice your own reactions—what "hooks" you? Reframe when needed.
- ❑ Determine what behaviors create perceptions.
- ❑ Doing nothing is far worse than failing.
- ❑ Challenge yourself to greatness and create stretch goals.
- ❑ Set goals that are consistent with your values.
- ❑ Consider sharing your development goals with your boss, employees, and other stakeholders.

RESOURCES AND TOOLS

1. I will document my action plan by:

____

____

Tips and Examples

- ❑ Create an action plan template.
- ❑ Brainstorm with your coach.
- ❑ Look for models and benchmarks.
- ❑ Plans can change—give yourself permission.

COMPETENCIES

On a scale of 1 to 5 (1 = nonexistent; 5 = outstanding), rate yourself on each competency for this step:

1. Clarification **1 2 3 4 5**

Two specific ways I will demonstrate this competency in this step:

a. ____

b. ____

2. Reframing **1 2 3 4 5**

Two specific ways I will demonstrate this competency in this step:

a. ____

b. ____

(continued)

WORKSHEET 2.3: The Leader Within (*continued*)

3. Goal Setting **1 2 3 4 5**

Two specific ways I will demonstrate this competency in this step:

a. ______________________________

b. ______________________________

4. Accountability **1 2 3 4 5**

Two specific ways I will demonstrate this competency in this step:

a. ______________________________

b. ______________________________

5. Transition Management **1 2 3 4 5**

Two specific ways I will demonstrate this competency in this step:

a. ______________________________

b. ______________________________

Tips and Examples

- ❑ Use skillful questions to clarify and understand feedback.
- ❑ Reframe by taking different perspectives.
- ❑ Be committed to learning.
- ❑ Be accountable for your own change and growth.
- ❑ Keep your promises.
- ❑ Acknowledge that change is like grieving—be patient with yourself.

WORKSHEET 2.4: The Leader Within

Step 4: Taking Action

DEFINING THE DESIRED OUTCOMES

1. **I will hold myself accountable for action by doing the following:**

   ____

   ____

2. **I will share my progress with my boss, employees, peers, etc., by:**

   ____

   ____

3. **I will celebrate my successes by:**

   ____

   ____

4. **I will demonstrate commitment to learning from my mistakes by:**

   ____

   ____

Tips and Examples

- ❑ Leadership development is a process of change—not a single action.
- ❑ Coaching areas for you to consider: skills, performance, development, or personal/professional issues.
- ❑ Make your commitment to action visible and tangible.
- ❑ You are allowed to shift direction and set new objectives.
- ❑ Saving face is the opposite of authenticity.
- ❑ Shift from saving face to learning.
- ❑ Focus on the present and the future, not the past.
- ❑ Have fun with learning about yourself.

QUESTIONS TO CONSIDER

1. **What am I learning about myself?**
2. **What is working well?**
3. **What isn't working so well?**
4. **What is preventing me from stretching?**
5. **What will compel me to carry out my actions?**

(continued)

WORKSHEET 2.4: The Leader Within *(continued)*

Tips and Examples

- ❑ Confronting one's beliefs and values is the stuff of change.
- ❑ Celebrate your successes.
- ❑ Mistakes are a sign of learning and growth, and that's what leadership is all about.
- ❑ What compels you to action is worth trying.
- ❑ Try on being a leader. Your coach will be your champion.

RESOURCES AND TOOLS

1. The tools I will use to document my progress and actions are:

____

____

Tips and Examples

- ❑ Be accountable for doing your homework and setting an agenda for each coaching session.

COMPETENCIES

On a scale of 1 to 5 (1 = nonexistent; 5 = outstanding), rate yourself on each competency for this step:

1. Dialogue 1 2 3 4 5

Two specific ways I will demonstrate this competency in this step:

a. ____

b. ____

2. Reflection 1 2 3 4 5

Two specific ways I will demonstrate this competency in this step:

a. ____

b. ____

3. Problem Solving 1 2 3 4 5

Two specific ways I will demonstrate this competency in this step:

a. ____

b. ____

4. Decision Making 1 2 3 4 5

Two specific ways I will demonstrate this competency in this step:

a. ____

b. ____

(continued)

WORKSHEET 2.4: The Leader Within (*continued*)

5. Risk Taking **1 2 3 4 5**

Two specific ways I will demonstrate this competency in this step:

a. ____________________

b. ____________________

Tips and Examples

- ❑ Dialogue with your coach will focus on learning, behaviors, and impact.
- ❑ Try on new beliefs and see how your actions will change.
- ❑ Let your choice of actions, decisions, and solutions be guided by your values, beliefs, and mind-sets.
- ❑ When you're stuck, ask yourself, "What's the worst that could happen?"
- ❑ Use critical thinking.
- ❑ Learn by trying it out.

WORKSHEET 2.5: The Leader Within

Step 5: Evaluating Your Self-Development as a Leader

DEFINING THE DESIRED OUTCOMES

1. **I will evaluate how I achieve my goals and objectives by:**

____

____

2. **The new actions will contribute to my life purpose and leadership vision by:**

____

____

Tips and Examples

- ❑ Measure the effectiveness of each action you took.
- ❑ Periodically, measure your overall self-development.

QUESTIONS TO CONSIDER

1. **What is my analysis of my action plan?**
2. **How do my actions support my life purpose?**
3. **How am I a better leader because of my actions?**

Tips and Examples

- ❑ Measure your progress on your action plan regularly and often.
- ❑ Measure the impacts of your actions on you, others, and the organization.
- ❑ Fulfillment is more important than accomplishment.

RESOURCES AND TOOLS

1. **The tools I will use to measure my success are:**

____

____

2. **I will document conversations and events by:**

____

____

(continued)

WORKSHEET 2.5: The Leader Within (*continued*)

Tips and Examples

- ❑ Examples of measurement tools are self-assessment on scales of 1 to 5, feedback from others, surveys, interviews, performance indicators such as timeliness, quality, or quantity.
- ❑ Document action conversations and events that demonstrate success or failure.

COMPETENCIES

On a scale of 1 to 5 (1 = nonexistent; 5 = outstanding), rate yourself on each competency for this step:

1. Openness 1 2 3 4 5

Two specific ways I will demonstrate this competency in this step:

a. ______________________________

b. ______________________________

2. Courage 1 2 3 4 5

Two specific ways I will demonstrate this competency in this step:

a. ______________________________

b. ______________________________

3. Commitment to Learning 1 2 3 4 5

Two specific ways I will demonstrate this competency in this step:

a. ______________________________

b. ______________________________

Tips and Examples

- ❑ Embrace failure, or at least mistakes.
- ❑ Choose between slow death or deep change.
- ❑ Discuss how your intended actions differ from your actual behaviors and why.
- ❑ Uncover your theory in use.
- ❑ Be committed to learning as a way of life.
- ❑ Evaluation leads to revised or new goals for your development.

part 3

The Leader and the Team

The ability to accomplish your goals depends ultimately on investing in your relationships until you have built a powerful partnership that can move mountains.

— Robert Hargrove,
Masterful Coaching Fieldbook

What Is Your Relationship With Your Team?

In the last chapter, you began to examine the process of coaching leadership and how you might apply the five steps to your own development. In this chapter, you will expand on the work you've started and consider how you will apply coaching leadership with your team. Your own development will continue, of course, and the work with your team will run concurrently. The interactions you have with your team and individual team members will serve as practice opportunities for you as you work to take the mechanics of coaching leadership and to make them an integral part of who you are. What you "do" as a coaching leader will ultimately give way to who you "are" as a coaching leader. How would you describe the relationship with your team today? The statements below represent answers we have gotten from many leaders over the years. Perhaps some of them will sound familiar.

- Team discussions are "polite." No problems or issues are brought up and solved.
- Team meetings are used more for project updates than for problem solving and creative thinking.
- Team members take their lead from me.
- Team conversations are a series of statements equating to point and counterpoint.
- The team does not disagree constructively.
- The team does not talk about "feelings."
- Team members are reluctant to admit when they don't know.
- Team members take few, if any, risks.
- Team members do not actively solicit input.
- Team members do not learn from each other.
- Team members do not reveal their thinking or test assumptions.
- Team members rarely, if ever, acknowledge points made by colleagues.
- Team members present their positions and dig in.

Whether your team is barely performing, functioning adequately, or doing first-rate work, coaching leadership can increase their effectiveness and strengthen your organization. Every individual and team interaction you now have with your direct reports will provide an opportunity for you to demonstrate the principles of coaching leadership. As a coaching leader, you observe your team in action. You are in a unique position—you can share information with the team that they otherwise might not have, and, you can solicit information from the team that you otherwise might not get. You will be learning the principles of coaching leadership together. If you do it right, your team will learn how to develop themselves, each other, and their teams. Maybe you'll end up like this:

Pamela smiled in amazement as she surveyed her peers on the program directors team. "There is an energy about us," she thought, "that I never thought I'd see. Eighteen months ago, no one saw it. No one but our new team leader, Jason. He joined us from another firm, and from the beginning he saw things we didn't. He even spoke in a different language—not Spanish or Chinese but a language of questions and silences. Interactions with Jason were energizing and draining at the same time. It was like you had to use more of your brain when you were interacting with him. And the more you put out, the more you seemed to get back.

"We used to only care about our own client groups. It was rare for anyone to help anyone else. We just kept our secrets to ourselves. I guess we thought that made us more powerful or secure. But then we started having monthly meetings with an agenda and minutes and Jason facilitating. We also started participating in leadership development. In the beginning, we had no idea what that was. We assumed it was some kind of training. We never imagined that we'd be learning the most about ourselves and how we interacted with each other and the people who reported to us. We also learned a lot about our bosses on the executive team. They were struggling with their own issues.

"There were several milestones. Jason had us work together to come up with ground rules about our meetings and the way we were going to treat each other. Then we received 360-degree feedback on ourselves. That was an eye-opener. Some people had hockey scores and some people had basketball scores. The feedback was confidential, but by the middle of the first day we were sharing our scores and asking each other for help. The real turning point was when we defined our values and the vision for our team. We had just completed one of those outdoor ropes courses, and we were feeling pretty invincible. We had supported each other through a series of challenges on the ground and 40 feet in the air. Sharing a budget format or talking through our challenges with problem employees seemed pretty easy in comparison.

"Talking with each other, period, got easier and easier. We stopped jumping in on the end of each other's sentences. When someone else was speaking, we stopped thinking about our own responses and started listening and asking questions. Jason seemed to have an endless supply of questions, so we learned from him and then from each other. His questions didn't really sound like us, though. He could ask, 'What led you to think that?' or say, 'Help me understand how you came up with that.' Our questions tended to be a bit more on the direct side. 'Why do you think that?' or 'How did you come up with that answer?' And we didn't always get the tone right. Jason would tease us and say our 'intent' was showing. Anyway, over time we got better in spite of ourselves. It wasn't a question of being 'nicer' with each other. And not all of us became 'best friends.' We learned that no one member of the team was as smart as the entire team when we were really working together. We got ourselves to a point where we were able to learn from each other. We created a budget format that enabled us all to complete our forecasting in half the time with greater accuracy. We worked through contingency plans that kept us competitive as technology changed. And we developed a system with tools for any manager opening a new office that resulted in 100% on-time openings once we brought it online. We even made progress with recruiting and retention. When we went to a panel interview system for management positions, many of us wondered where we would find the time and why we should participate in hiring a manager for another client group. Well, we made the time, we all became more skilled at interviewing, and we started hiring better managers. Investing the time at the front end of the process saved us from cleaning up after poor management at the back end. Turnover at the staff level decreased, customer satisfaction went up, and we began to hit and exceed our numbers quarter after quarter. Jason acknowledged our successes in team meetings and one-on-one. We created a 'Monthly Scoreboard' publication to track our progress. We also played a special role in our national conference, presenting the story of our team's transformation.

"We started out with the purpose of creating a better workplace for our employees and ourselves. We 'aligned' ourselves with a vision of how it could be. Once we did all the work of creating that workplace, we wanted to keep it intact. So when industry cutbacks were hitting the company hard, the threats from the outside gave us focus. It made sense to work together against a common enemy, and we believed that we were stronger together than individually. Luckily, by the time we had to deal with the external threat, we had learned enough about ourselves and each other to do it effectively. The company changed, and so did we. And we're still here. Better than ever."

Jason applied the principles of coaching leadership with this team, and they accomplished substantial results. Team members

- Became aligned around clarified values and goals
- Increased the frequency and quality of their communication
- Learned how to learn from each other and put that learning to work for the organization's benefit
- Focused on expanding their effectiveness as individuals and as a team
- Developed systems and processes that contributed tangibly to the bottom line

In 1 year, these program directors moved from a collection of independent individuals to an effective team with a learning mind-set. By practicing coaching leadership, they transformed themselves and their organization. Like other teams in companies that have moved from "good to great," Jason's team didn't experience one "miracle moment." Instead, they followed a process and continued to make incremental progress, "building tangible evidence that their plans made sense and would deliver results" (Collins, 2001, p. 94).

A Brief Overview of Teams

It is important to appreciate the characteristics of teams so that you will understand the changes you are likely to experience as you begin to practice coaching leadership. In *The Fifth Discipline Fieldbook*, Peter Senge (1994) observed, "History has brought us to a moment where teams are recognized as a critical component of every enterprise—the predominant unit for decision making and getting things done" (p. 354). Katzenbach and Smith (1993) agreed, explaining, "Teams are surpassing individuals as the primary performance unit in organizations of the future" (p. 13). Though it is true that great numbers of teams can be found in every type of organization, most of them aren't as effective as they might be. Why not?

Most teams today, whether traditional, cross-functional, self-directed, or virtual, are made up of bright individuals. What happens to those individuals when they are thrown together to accomplish a specified task?

After decades of studying teams and team development, management theorists and business leaders have suggested many explanations. Although there are countless answers, some of them recur with enough frequency to create a Top 10 list. For the question "Why don't teams work as effectively as they could at decision making and getting things done?" We have found the top 10 answers are: (1) The team can't get past issues of the larger organizational context that affect its functioning (Denison, Hart, & Kahn, 1996); (2) the team can't work through its collaboration and cooperation issues (Argyris & Schon, 1978; Schein, 1994); (3) the team hasn't resolved its direction and orientation issues (Wetlaufer, 1994); (4) the team hasn't worked through its basic assumptions and purpose issues (Bion, 1961); (5) the team hasn't resolved issues regarding its dependency on leadership (Bennis & Shepard, 1956); (6) the team hasn't resolved its defensive routine issues (Argyris, 1994); (7) the team isn't really a team, it is a working group or pseudoteam (Katzenbach & Smith, 1993); (8) the team hasn't resolved its core values issues (Pasmore & Mlot, 1994); (9) the team hasn't resolved its inclusion and power issues (Tuckman, 1965); and (10) the team hasn't resolved its commitment and responsibility issues (Katzenbach & Smith, 1993). With all of these "issues" to work through, you may wonder, short of therapy, how you can get your team to perform at a high level, to develop a learning mind-set, and to work effectively together for the good of the organization. The key lies in the relationship between you and your team. Frances Hesselbein (1996) asserted that one of the three greatest challenges facing CEOs today is relationships (p. 121). Richard Beckhard (1996) agreed, explaining that effective leaders recognize there is a relationship with their followers and purposefully manage its dynamics (p. 125). Some recent literature, though, argues against the importance of relationships. In distinguishing "hot groups" from teams, Lipman-Blumen and Leavitt (1999) asserted that

> it is not mutual loyalty and trust that generate effective performance. Neither is it friendship, nor understanding of one another's idiosyncrasies. Hot groups work the other way around. It is their task, not one another, that hot groups love, along with the process of working on that task together. (p. 50)

We have found that the primary focus for effective team development has to include both task and relationship dimensions. It isn't an either/or proposition.

Knowing how to create and develop effective teams is a critical leadership skill. As Neuhauser, Bender, and Stromberg described in their book *Culture.com* (2000), most of "the actual day-to-day work [in organizations] is being done by an ever-changing configuration of teams" (p. 137), whether interacting face to face, teleconferencing across continents, or communicating in virtual reality. Being a coaching leader positions you to leverage your relationship with your team and their relationships with their own departments and groups. The process requires a fundamental shift in your interactions and an application of new skills. It enables you to tap into an energy source that remains untapped by most teams. As stated in Part 2, we believe the coaching leadership process to be cyclical. However, our model begins with establishing the coaching relationship. When you are working with your team, this happens on three levels: the team leader with the team, the team leader with team members one-on-one, and team members with others (Figure 3.1). Let's start with what you will do to establish the coaching relationship with your team.

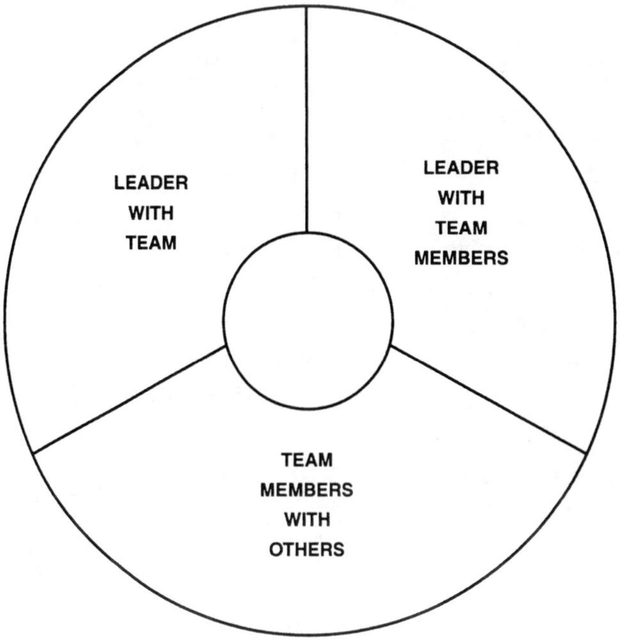

Figure 3.1. Three Dimensions Within Teams

Step 1: Establishing the Coaching Relationship With the Team

Focusing on the Reasons

There are many reasons why you may believe that building a coaching team is right for you and your organization. You may believe that the most effective way to guarantee superior performance is to facilitate it, not to command it. You may believe that your purpose as a leader is to enable your staff to do what you hired them to do and that your job is to eliminate the obstacles in their way. By practicing the behaviors of a coaching leader (see Table 3.1), you will unleash the untapped energy in all the members of your team and leave them with a legacy that results in a sustainable competitive edge for your organization.

Many theorists have compared elements of traditional leadership with coaching leadership (Crane, 2001; Evered & Selman, 1989; Goldsmith, Lyons, & Freas, 2000; Hargrove, 2000; Schwarz, 1994; Staub, 2000). Our purpose in presenting this comparison is to demonstrate the additional depth and breadth of skills required of a coaching leader and to show the impact of those skills on your team. In today's business world, we believe that these skills will enable coaching leaders to create consistently high-performing teams, capable of assessing their strengths and weaknesses, accurately predicting new challenges, rigorously generating and evaluating alternatives, and ultimately choosing courses of action that result in superior products and services delivered to market ahead of the competition. We believe coaching leadership is the most substantial competitive advantage you can bring to your organization. As Hargrove (2000) explained:

Table 3.1 Traditional and Coaching Leaders' Behaviors and Legacies

Traditional Leader Behaviors With Team	*Traditional Leader Legacy With Team*	*Coaching Leader Behaviors With Team*	*Coaching Leader Legacy With Team*
Focus on containing and controlling	Limited development	Focus on expanding and facilitating	Team continues to redefine its role and grow
Initiates action	Team follows direction and waits until told	Holds self and team accountable for initiating actions	Team values keeping promises and performing as agreed
Hides weaknesses	Puts energy into packaging and "spin"	Reveals mistakes and development needs	Team communicates honestly—talks about and learns from mistakes
Minimizes risks at the expense of timely action and creative solutions	Bias toward inaction or using only tried and true methods	Facilitates acting with speed and flexibility; pushes for creative solutions	Bias toward action—team routinely takes calculated risks
Suppresses emotions/ feelings/concerns; presents only good news	Emotions/feelings discounted and considered irrelevant; being rational is highly valued	Considers emotions/ feelings directly related to performance and results	Team acts with awareness of self and others—learns how to develop and maintain relationships
Gives commands	The team doesn't participate, raise questions, or suggest alternatives	Consults with team regarding problems and decisions	Team uses a helping stance—recognizes handoffs and opportunities for support—learns how to work toward solutions interdependently
Criticizes and looks for reasons to place blame	Provokes defensiveness	Gives constructive feedback and positive reinforcement	Team learns to value and practice alternative perspectives and approaches
Avoids conflict or dictates solutions	Discourages critical thinking and surfacing of difficult issues	Uses conflict to stimulate creative discussion and problem solving	Team attacks issues, not each other—everyone's best thinking is expected
Focuses on and rewards technical skills	Team values traditional intelligence	Focuses on and rewards multiple intelligences	Team values differences and pushes members to expand capabilities
Establishes boss/ subordinate relationship with team	People are defined and limited by their positions	Establishes partnership with team	Team members are engaged and accountable
Hoards information/ knowledge	Discourages responsibility and erodes trust	Shares information/ knowledge	Encourages responsibility and builds trust
Tries to dictate or control change	Resistance, fear, and poor performance	Tries to lead and plan for change collaboratively	Team accepts change as a way of life—demonstrates resiliency and ability to adapt

> The bottom line in corporate America revolves around performance. A coach must make sure that every ounce of talent, skill, and teamwork surfaces day after day. If you don't, rest assured that there will be many competent competitors out there eager to take your place. (p. 40)

Whatever your reasons are for choosing coaching leadership, it is important to note that every interaction you have will now contribute in some way to your own learning and that of your team. Every time you communicate information, set expectations, offer advice, receive feedback, resolve conflicts, or celebrate successes, you will be acting as a conduit for the energy that is created by leading from the inside out. As with anything electrical, it is necessary that you and the process be properly grounded. This is achieved by effectively establishing the relationship with your team.

Establishing the relationship with your team and individuals in that team requires that you work through four elements. You will set the context, define the measures, identify the resources, and commit to the process. First, you and your team members will set the context. You should answer questions like

- What is this new relationship going to look like?
- What can we expect from each other?
- What will we be doing differently?

Next, define the measures you will use when you evaluate your progress:

- What metrics are we going to focus on?
- What kind of results are we going after?
- How will we know we've achieved them?

Then identify the resources you are going to need:

- Who is going to help us?
- What level of support are they going to provide?
- Do we have available financial resources?

Finally, you and your team must commit to the process. Restate your reasons for moving in this direction, and describe your plan for handling setbacks. Stake yourself out and articulate the system you will use to maintain everyone's commitment. For example, one team kept a copy of their ground rules posted in their conference room. Everyone had the responsibility to question behavior that seemed to contradict the ground rules. Another team conducted a meeting critique at the end of each meeting. They rated themselves on a list of set criteria, such as "Did we support the ground rules?" If they seemed to have recurring problems in a certain area (e.g., acknowledging others, generating options, building consensus), they got themselves help. Successfully working through these four elements enables you to establish the coaching relationship with your team. Let's look at each one in greater detail.

Setting the Context

When you set the context with your team, you are creating the vision and picture of a team that embraces coaching leadership. You are describing the purpose, what this is going to mean for the team, the challenges ahead of you, the benefits you envision for the team and the organization, and how the process is going to work. Your ability to set the context for a coaching relationship with your team will depend in large part on (a) the credibility you have with the team, (b) the alignment between your personal values and the values you are proposing that the team uphold, (c) the business case you are able to present, and (d) the passion and courage you demonstrate in proposing the changes and in acknowledging the amount of work necessary to successfully incorporate the changes so that they ultimately become "the way it's always been."

Your credibility or track record with the team will help or hurt you as you begin this process. If you have a history of following popular business fads or trends, only to abandon them after an initial flurry of excitement and kickoff events, you will have a hard time convincing the team that you really mean it this time. If you have implemented new guidelines or processes in the past and then have allowed exceptions for your "star" performers, you will have to make a case for how and why things will be different this time around. Consider the case of Dennis.

Dennis is a likable leader. As president of his organization, he takes pride in being accessible and responsive to all employees. He tells everyone that he welcomes feedback and differing points of view. His senior team wonders, though, if that is really the case. On several occasions when they have voiced a dissenting opinion, the senior staff meeting has turned into a "bloodbath." The "bloodletting" seems to be initiated by Jim, one of Dennis's direct reports. Jim acts the role of enforcer, with Dennis's unspoken approval. Once Jim is unleashed, there is no stopping him. No one, including Dennis, makes any move to rein him in. Afterward, Dennis acts as if nothing happened. Now Dennis is saying that he wants to make a shift to coaching leadership and engage in more open "dialogue." Team members are skeptical of his commitment and reluctant to expose themselves to Jim's attacks.

Dennis is going to have to put some clear guidelines or working agreements into place and make certain that everyone, including Jim, follows them. Because Dennis has stumbled in the past, he may want to do something visibly different, like bringing in professional help to facilitate his senior staff meetings. He may also want to practice receiving feedback, from his coach and from his team, and to demonstrate an open response. Speaking to Jim privately about his past behaviors and explaining that they will no longer be tolerated should help. If Jim thought he was helping, he'll now hear the message that his "help" is no longer needed. If he was acting on his own, he'll still have the message that the behavior is no longer wanted. If the behavior comes up again, the facilitator, Dennis, and the team members will have to confront it. If Jim can't or won't regulate the behavior, then he may not belong on this team.

If you have a track record for implementing and sticking to well-thought-out changes, you will enter this beginning step with a leg up on colleagues like Dennis who have to overcome their team members' skepticism. You strengthen your case when you align your personal values with the team values. Demonstrating personal integrity in team interactions enables you to reinforce the stated commitment you've made. Your team will listen to what you say, but they will be most dramatically influenced by what you do. As Teal (1996) explained,

> All managers believe they behave with integrity, but in practice, many have trouble with the concept. Integrity means being responsible, of course, but it also means communicating clearly and consistently, being an honest broker, keeping promises, knowing oneself, and avoiding hidden agendas that hang other people out to dry. (p. 5)

Can you do that?

Ensuring congruence between your personal values and the values you are creating within the team allows you to evaluate behaviors with consistent criteria and predictable responses. Dick Brown, CEO of EDS, observed, "Leaders get the behavior they tolerate" (quoted in Breen, *Fast Company,* 2001, p. 112). You will be raising the bar. Setting the context with your team and the individuals on your team requires that you redefine every element of your interactions—the expectations, the rules, the risks and rewards, the penalties, the working definitions of "winning" and "losing." Here is a job aid and process to help you do this. Begin by asking yourself, "What is my scorecard today as a coaching leader? What do I want it to be in 6 months?" Use Table 3.2 to help you think through these questions.

As you talk with the team about all of these elements, expect to engage in lengthy conversations—one-on-one and as a group. These conversations are likely to be different from those you have held with your team in the past. Chances are you are experienced in presenting rational arguments, complete with appropriate evidence, to support your point of view. No doubt, these arguments outline a substantive business case that leads to the course of action you want the team to follow. Your past conversations were probably characterized by a point-counterpoint approach, much like what you would find in a courtroom or on a playing field, with the "winner" defined as the person scoring the most points.

It is also likely that your past conversations demonstrate what Chris Argyris (1986) called "skilled incompetence." This term describes our ability to respond spontaneously and automatically in such a way that we don't say what we really think, and thereby avoid any upset or conflict. Unfortunately, the unintended consequence of this behavior is that we leave important issues undiscussed and unresolved. Argyris explained that organizations, as well as

Table 3.2 My Scorecard

	Today					In 6 Months				
Working With My Team, I . . .	*Rating (1 = Low, 5 = High)*					*Rating (1 = Low, 5 = High)*				
■ Set clear goals	1	2	3	4	5	1	2	3	4	5
■ Encourage open conversations	1	2	3	4	5	1	2	3	4	5
■ Listen for what is said and what is not said	1	2	3	4	5	1	2	3	4	5
■ Demonstrate effective questioning	1	2	3	4	5	1	2	3	4	5
■ Reveal my thinking	1	2	3	4	5	1	2	3	4	5
■ Look beyond symptoms to find the cause	1	2	3	4	5	1	2	3	4	5
■ Ask for input	1	2	3	4	5	1	2	3	4	5
■ Behave in a credible way	1	2	3	4	5	1	2	3	4	5
■ Respond positively to feedback	1	2	3	4	5	1	2	3	4	5
■ Encourage risk taking	1	2	3	4	5	1	2	3	4	5
■ Hold people accountable	1	2	3	4	5	1	2	3	4	5
■ Recognize contributions	1	2	3	4	5	1	2	3	4	5
■ Model effective team skills	1	2	3	4	5	1	2	3	4	5
■ Demonstrate integrity in my interactions	1	2	3	4	5	1	2	3	4	5

	Today					In 6 Months				
Working Individually With My Direct Reports, I . . .	*Rating (1 = Low, 5 = High)*					*Rating (1 = Low, 5 = High)*				
■ Set clear goals	1	2	3	4	5	1	2	3	4	5
■ Encourage open conversations	1	2	3	4	5	1	2	3	4	5
■ Listen for what is said and not said	1	2	3	4	5	1	2	3	4	5
■ Demonstrate effective questioning	1	2	3	4	5	1	2	3	4	5
■ Reveal my thinking	1	2	3	4	5	1	2	3	4	5
■ Look beyond symptoms to find the cause	1	2	3	4	5	1	2	3	4	5
■ Ask for input	1	2	3	4	5	1	2	3	4	5
■ Behave in a credible way	1	2	3	4	5	1	2	3	4	5
■ Respond positively to feedback	1	2	3	4	5	1	2	3	4	5
■ Encourage risk taking	1	2	3	4	5	1	2	3	4	5
■ Help others link choices to consequences	1	2	3	4	5	1	2	3	4	5
■ Hold people accountable	1	2	3	4	5	1	2	3	4	5
■ Recognize contributions	1	2	3	4	5	1	2	3	4	5
■ Demonstrate integrity in my interactions	1	2	3	4	5	1	2	3	4	5
■ Coach people to succeed	1	2	3	4	5	1	2	3	4	5

individuals, learn to communicate this way and make use of "defensive routines" to guard against "surprise, embarrassment, or threat" (p. 75). Unfortunately, because "defensive routines" prevent honest dialogue about problems and their root causes, they also prevent reflection and learning. The net effect is that the organization and the teams within it stay stuck with old beliefs and behaviors.

Coaching leadership requires that you learn to play a different game with different skills. These skills will allow you to move beyond informing or convincing your team. These skills, referred to under the umbrella of "dialogue," allow you to

- Reveal your thought processes
- Expose your rationale
- Test your assumptions
- Explore "undiscussables"
- Accept new data
- Generate alternative hypotheses
- Select a course of action from well-considered alternatives
- Move forward, confident in the knowledge that everyone who has participated in the conversation has a richer understanding of the content than he or she did before

Effective use of dialogue allows you to make thinking transparent, and it is a critical skill for you as a coaching leader. See Table 3.3 for examples.

Whatever the skill level and experience of you and your team, you can use dialogue to begin to structure and hold more effective conversations. In Figure 3.2, the left side describes traditional team conversations and the right side describes coaching conversations using dialogue skills. Consider where you and the team belong. How does your current position compare with where you'd like to be? What measures will you and the team use to develop your skills and to track your progress?

Defining the Measures

In setting the context, you talk about what you want to achieve. In defining the measures, you discuss and clarify how you will evaluate your progress. What do you expect, specifically, of yourself and others? How often? What can you do if you don't get what you expected? How about the team—what is their recourse if they see you drifting off track? Your agreement may look something like the one shown in Exhibit 3.1.

Substantive discussion of the measures early on in the process will help you later when it comes time to evaluate your progress. Agreement now minimizes or eliminates confusion later. Finally, when you define measures early in the

Table 3.3 Dialogue Elements

What to Do	*What to Say*
State your assumptions.	"Here's what I think, and here's how I got there."
Explain how you got there.	"I assumed that we'd be working with the same vendor." or "I came to this conclusion because I saw an e-mail stating that we were pleased with their pricing and service."
Ask for input.	"Do you have different information than I do?" or "What are you aware of that I may not have known about?"
Encourage different points of view.	"Does anyone see it differently?" or "How else could we look at this?" or "What other options could we consider?"
Explore others' reasoning.	"What leads you to think that?" or "What factors contribute to that conclusion?"
Invite them to present their data.	"Help me understand your thinking on that" or "Can you walk me through that so I can see how you got there?"
Check your understanding.	"Am I correct that you're saying . . ." or "Does this mean that you would like to see . . . ?"
Link their view and yours.	"It seems that we have some overlap. For example . . ." or "We're together on some points, specifically . . ."
Identify a larger context or meaning.	"How will this affect our stated commitment to preferred vendors?" or "Can you describe how this might look to our customers?"
Work to agreement on steps for moving forward.	"What can we build on here to meet our objective?" or "How can we use what we've identified to achieve our goal?" or "What can we do next to move this forward?"

process, they become tools that you and the team use to ensure your success. You are clear about the outputs expected of you, so you can focus on the outcomes you want to achieve.

Each member of your team can probably define what is expected and how performance is judged. But establishing and agreeing on measures is not always easy. First, there's the difference between what is said and what is done. Despite what is written down in performance appraisals or stated in bonus plans, each member of your team can truthfully explain what is actually measured and rewarded.

Second, in addition to the performance you have recognized and rewarded in the past, individuals bring with them what they have experienced in other circumstances. As human beings, we have long memories. One vice president in a large trade association typifies the residual impact past experiences can have. Jan spent 5 years working for a controlling, mean-spirited president who

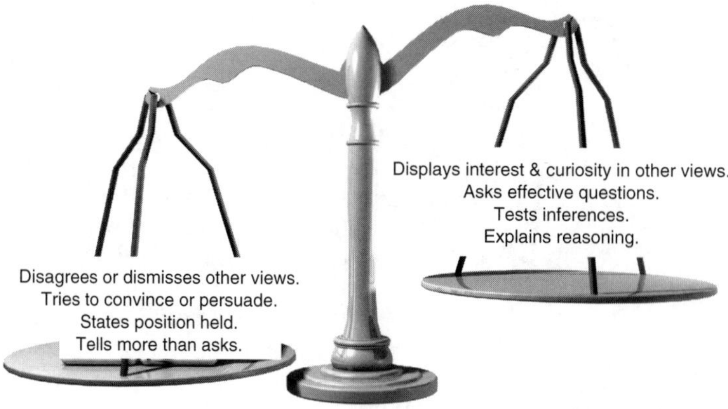

Figure 3.2. The Balancing Act

regularly berated his executive staff. When he left the association, she had the opportunity to work for a skilled, fair-minded, caring CEO. Five years later, when asked why she didn't actively work to support a process change that would have greatly benefited her department, her response was, "You know what we say around here—you can't get in trouble for something you didn't do." Five years with a good leader had not been sufficient to erase the measures set in 5 years with an ineffective leader.

What you pay attention to—and the behavior you reward—overshadows anything you may once have written in the organization's values statement, stated in your annual message, or described in the objectives section of a performance appraisal document.

So how should you define measures? First, you honestly acknowledge any "givens" that you cannot change (e.g., shareholder expectations, market conditions, resource limitations). Second, you lay out the criteria that define "winning" within the vision. Third, you invite the team to participate in determining how you all will achieve that "win" and what role each person will play in making it happen. Fourth, you and the team work through scenarios with different variables and plan for contingencies: "What if we lose that bid?" "How will we ramp up quickly if we get that work?" "What do we have to do to identify, attract, and hire the talent we need within 90 days?" Fifth, you and the team come to agreement on the task and the relationship elements of your interactions: "How are we going to practice coaching with each other?" "What impact will this have on our team? On our departments?" "How will we learn these new skills?" "What constitutes victory for us?" You and your team may consider the path to coaching leadership to be filled with "trial and error." Author Teri-E Belf (in press) suggested considering the path "trial and trial" as a way "to honor all that is learning and growth." It's important for you and the team to get clear on your vision and your measures of success because they will guide your development. They will be your compass. You and your team members can measure your progress during this transition if you all know what to expect from each other.

Exhibit 3.1 **Team Agreements**

Leader Agreements With the Team:

- I will ask for and consider your opinions.
- You won't always get your way. I will let you know when something is nonnegotiable.
- I will ask for your feedback.
- I will give you feedback also.
- I expect you to share feedback with me even when I don't solicit it.
- I will listen to you openly.
- I may ask for time to think feedback over before responding.
- I won't kill the messenger.

Team Member Agreements With Others:

- We will raise issues directly.
- We will acknowledge our own contributions.
- We will ask for help.
- We will practice active mutual support.
- We will practice generous interpretations.
- We will work to joint solutions.
- We will support team decisions once made.

If We Don't Honor Our Team Agreements, We Will . . . :

- Throw our penalty flag onto the table and call for a time-out.
- Raise the question to the team by saying, "How does this support our agreement to . . . ?"

Individual Commitments to the Team:

- Ask more questions (John).
- Give more positive feedback (Laura).
- Acknowledge others' points and build on them (Frank).
- Identify points of agreement (Don).

If You Don't See Me Honoring My Commitment, I'd Like You to Help Me by . . . :

- Confronting me at the time (John).
- Speaking to me privately afterward (Laura).
- Telling me one-on-one about your concerns (Frank).
- Slipping me a note (Don).

Identifying the Resources

Once the context is set and the measures are defined, you can identify the resources you and the team need to be successful. Teams use a variety of resources depending on what fits best with where they are in their development. A partial list of resources includes readings, benchmarking of other companies, finding and working with a mentor, leadership development training, 360-degree feedback, outdoor ropes courses, tackling business problems as a team, working with an outside coach, using an outside facilitator, and conducting and receiving the results of an image study or a climate survey. Regular contact is important during this development stage. If the team is not colocated, videoconferencing, e-mails, conference calls, and knowledge rooms should supplement the resources listed above.

Remember, you are beginning a process of evolving toward being a coaching leader, and the team is evolving toward being a learning team. This is not a finite event. The time and money you will be putting toward this change effort are an investment in your future. As with any kind of investment, it is important to have a plan, investigate your options, and carefully weigh your choices. Jim Collins (2001) pointed out that most change efforts are unsuccessful "because they lack accountability, they fail to achieve credibility, and they have no authenticity" (p. 94). In setting the context and defining the measures, you are making public what you intend to do, how you intend to do it, and how you will measure your progress. You and the team will be accountable for the progress you make. Walking your talk will contribute to or detract from your credibility. And rigorous attention to aligning your values and actions with those of your team will demonstrate your authenticity. When the initial euphoria of this process wears off and everyone realizes how hard this development work is, you will have to remind everyone (and yourself) of the commitment you made and why you made it.

Committing to the Process

The final element in establishing the relationship is committing to the process. It is critical for you and the team to understand what you're getting into and to decide that you're in it for the long run. Between the point when the initial excitement wears off and the point when you begin to see the benefits of this new way of interacting with your team—and your team members with their teams—there is a desert to cross: an interval of questions, difficulties, doubts, and hard choices. Your commitment is like a personal water supply that you'll need to use for yourselves and each other to get through this desert.

Everyone is responsible for moving the team forward as agreed. That said, all eyes will be on you to see how you handle yourself. Schein (1996) observed that "transformations occur through a genuine change in the leader's behavior and through embedding new definitions in the organizational processes and routines" (p. 65). You have created a compelling case for embracing coaching leadership. You've set the context, you've defined the measures of success, and you've identified the resources and the systems you will use to support you and the team as you move forward. All that's left is getting everyone to commit to the process, and that is not easy to do.

Senior team members have historically been rewarded for their own areas of responsibility or for what they produced as individuals. In *The Wisdom of Teams*, Katzenbach and Smith (1993) pointed out that "most job descriptions, compensation schemes, career paths, and performance evaluations focus on individuals" (p. 3). Embracing coaching leadership as a new way of being will be difficult for the team. So until the process takes on a life of its own, you will have to provide the energy necessary to sustain it. You will be out in front, leading the charge toward coaching leadership. What will this look like? For a start, you need a plan that you can follow and a support network that will help you. Chances are, when you were identifying resources, you made sure these were in place. You will have outlined what your team could expect from you and vice versa. Generally, leaders and teams aren't so explicit about their performance, behavior, and agreements with each other. This may make you and the team members feel more exposed than you are used to. In the words of Max DePree, "Belonging requires us to be willing and ready to risk. We need to be vulnerable to each other" (p. 24). This new level of closeness is part of coaching leadership.

As you move forward in the process, you'll see how you can use this exposure as an opportunity for growth and development. Refer to the help and support you identified under resources, and clarify how you're going to use that support to stay on track. Even with those resources in place, there is no guarantee that everyone will want to commit to the process.

You may be wondering, "Where do I start?" Start by "asking" more and "telling" less. Because you may be more accustomed to making definitive statements than asking questions, this will take some work on your part. Review the questions in Table 3.3. Let's see how this might play itself out.

Let's say one of your direct reports, Tim, approaches you with a concern about a peer. "Kevin refuses to get me the numbers I need for the investors' meeting tomorrow," he says, with the expectation that you will do something about Kevin's nonresponsiveness because you have in the past. You could respond in a number of different ways. You might say:

1. "Kevin knows you need those numbers. Tell him I said to get them ready this morning."
2. "Why would Kevin refuse to get the numbers? He knows you need them. Let's get him on the phone."
3. "What do you mean, he refuses to get you the numbers?"

Option 3 has the immediate effect of slowing the action (not the choice you would probably default to in a case like this). Asking, "What do you mean?" causes Tim to focus on his language and his interpretation of the interaction with Kevin. As he explains it to you, you may discover that Kevin didn't refuse to provide the numbers. Rather, he is running them now and isn't prepared to release them before 2:00 p.m., which is when he promised they'd be ready.

You can help Tim look at the facts and his reaction to the facts. You can help Tim look at his contribution to the interaction with Kevin and see if something other than this one incident is coloring his thinking. You can help Tim come up with a plan to follow if he needs the numbers early, or if he doesn't get the numbers as agreed. You have the opportunity to demonstrate a course of action for Tim that is in keeping with the new agreements the team has made. You are modeling the behavior of a coaching leader.

The primary capital required to invest in and grow coaching leadership in your team is personal. You have to demonstrate through words and actions your commitment to this new way of leading. As Bob Nafius, Director of Culture Development at Gateway, Inc., explained, "You have to say the same thing again and again. You just don't go off message—no matter what" (quoted in Neuhauser et al., 2000, p. 153). You also have to make yourself vulnerable to criticism from others regarding your steps and your missteps, and you have to provide that same criticism to your team so that this new leadership begins its movement throughout your organization. However, this "criticism" now happens within the context of coaching and development. Learning becomes a key driver as you and the team develop the skills of using data to inform your actions.

You have to demonstrate the courage to stay the course when you're tested and to make course corrections as necessary. Until coaching leadership takes on a life of its own, you as the leader have to provide the energy to sustain it. And you have to tell the truth. Not everyone can do that. You are creating a vision of what it can be like, and you are sharing that vision with your team. You are inviting them to come along with you, but there is no guarantee that everyone will want to. Consider the following examples.

Rhonda was excited when her standards and assessments team agreed to move from a "leader-led" team structure to a "semiautonomous" team structure. They drafted ground rules for themselves and committed to a 1-year trial for the new structure. At the second team meeting, Sally, a team member, asked Rhonda, the team's director, if she could be excused from further participation in the team. Rhonda almost answered Sally directly, telling her what she thought, but she stopped herself and instead replied, "Sally, I don't think that is my decision to make. We've agreed that the team will handle membership issues. Please pose your request to the team."

Reluctantly, Sally restated her request to the team. She told everyone that she didn't want to join them as they pursued this new structure. She wasn't interested in anything they had to say to her, and she had nothing to share with them about their performance or skills. She went on to say that she didn't trust anyone in the team and that she planned to move off of the team at the earliest possible time. For the first time, Sally was giving voice to sentiments that the team members had sensed but had tiptoed around.

Rhonda's previous approach to handling situations like this would have been to take the discussion offline and try to smooth it out even if it meant making accommodations for Sally that went against what the team had agreed. Rhonda tried to help the team and Sally explore alternatives to the all-or-nothing option she had put on the table. After a difficult conversation, everyone agreed that the team and Sally would be better off if she did not participate further. The conversation made Rhonda and the team very uncomfortable. The next day, however, they all agreed that Sally had been unable to get past recent developments in the team's life and that the team and Sally would be better off without her continued participation. Rhonda and the team passed an important hurdle—Rhonda had to take a step back, and the team had to take a step up. Rhonda did not fall into the trap of reclaiming leadership authority. The team didn't fall into the trap of trying to smooth over or ignore a legitimate conflict of values and vision. Although the conversation was difficult, team members were able to lean on their ground rules and each other and move forward to resolve the problem. And they were able to talk about it honestly; describing their feelings and their reactions to doing what they all believed was the right thing.

Here's another example.

The president of a large residential construction company detailed his commitment to leadership development for himself and his top team. Part of the process required participation in an off-site leadership program and 360-degree feedback. The team agreed to support the process, and each individual scheduled his or her attendance in the program and then feedback. After continually moving herself to the bottom of the schedule, the vice president of finance announced her resignation. In her exit interview, she revealed that she didn't believe in the self-reflection that the process required.

These examples show that everyone may not choose to pursue coaching leadership. By outlining the vision and pursuing it faithfully, you align what you say with what you do. This alignment helps your team realize what is required of them and whether they can demonstrate the behaviors necessary. You are setting the context and getting buy-in. You are defining general parameters and inviting the team to discover the specifics with you. You are describing the possibilities of a team that interacts, develops, and outperforms traditional groups through the use of coaching interactions. You are establishing the coaching relationship with your team.

Competencies

The competencies needed in Step 1, establishing the coaching relationship with the team, are vision, integrity, courage, openness, and passion.

Vision

Vision involves painting a picture of the future, a picture so compelling that those around you want to be a part of it. It is setting a direction and focusing everyone's attention on it. According to Robert Staub (2000), "It gives everyone engaged something to shoot for and a larger context within which to plan and set strategy. It provides everyone with an essential sense of direction and purpose" (p. 7). Establishing the coaching relationship with your team requires you to communicate that sense of direction and purpose.

Integrity

Integrity is a measure of your honesty, principles, values, and character. Integrity allows you to create the trust necessary to drive coaching leadership with your team. You build that trust by demonstrating an unwavering commitment to actions that are aligned with your stated values. You erode that trust by saying one thing and doing the opposite. One vice president in a large professional services firm described it this way:

> My boss is a member of the senior team in our organization. They have all said they value communicating honestly and directly. Although they are supposed to speak to each other about problems and concerns, they don't. We know exactly who my boss can't stand. When she is with us, she talks about colleagues and criticizes their efforts. She is very ungracious toward her peers. With them, she acts like a model team player. We see her do this and yet she expects us to trust her. We just wonder what she says about us when we're not in the room.

Courage

Courage is at the heart of coaching leadership. According to Badaracco and Ellsworth (1989), "Courage is necessary to create a vision, to challenge the status quo, and to take risks" (p. 28). Can you do what is required, rather than what is most comfortable or familiar? Will you be able to make the hard calls? Can you hold yourself and your team accountable? Courage enables you to do the right things in support of your vision, even when that means eliminating a traditional line of business or inviting a long-time employee to leave. Many leaders are afraid that confronting people about problem behaviors will "cause them to be disliked" (p. 21). In fact, the opposite is true.

Openness

Openness requires that you demonstrate an interest in discovering and being responsible for your own impact on others. Soliciting feedback and genuinely listening to others are critical. If you genuinely want to create a partnership with your team, you have to be willing to make yourself vulnerable. Clearly stating what you believe in and how you intend to act makes public your intentions. Clarifying what your team can expect from you and what they can do or say if they don't see it gives them permission to act in support of your stated values. According to Peter Drucker (1999), it is "essential to remedy your bad habits—the things you do or fail to do that inhibit your effectiveness and performance" (p. 66). To help you in correcting those bad habits, part of the team's action will include feedback to you if they perceive you are drifting off course. Whether this takes the form of a kick under the table, a private discussion, or an open statement using inquiry and advocacy all depends on the agreements made.

Openness allows the team to say what they're already thinking. You are giving yourself the opportunity to hear more directly how your actions are being perceived. You and the team will learn to hold the kinds of conversations necessary to help you share and correct the perceptions, if necessary, or to inform and change your actions. This also works for the team members with each other. Once you redefine the agreements about actions, feedback, mistakes, and results, the team will find it easier to act in agreed-upon ways.

Passion

Passion is a visible, contagious sense of energy or enthusiasm that will keep you going as you and the team move from doing to being coaching leaders. It is a relentless drive that supports you. Robert Staub (2000) described passion as a terrific sense of aliveness (p. xxvii). Your passion will ignite sparks in your team members and fuel the flames of transformation in your team and throughout the organization. The passion you display for coaching leadership may be obvious or it may be subtle. But it must be unwavering. You need passion to make coaching leadership work. To paraphrase Ralph Waldo Emerson, "Nothing great was ever achieved without passion."

Step 2: Collecting and Analyzing Data

Why Collect Data?

Information is the lifeblood of leading from the inside out. Generally, executives and senior team members do not have access to current information about themselves and the way they are perceived by others in their organizations. They don't have access to this information for several reasons. First, they don't ask. Most executives are focused on their markets, shareholders, customers, and results they expect to deliver this quarter. They typically don't take the time to reflect on their actions and how those actions may be affecting their employees and their ability to deliver desired results.

Second, even if they do ask, it is rare for executives to get the straight story on how they're doing from their employees' perspective. Employees may wonder:

- Do they really want to know?
- Does the executive team really care about how we view them?
- What will happen to me if I do tell them what's really happening?

Employees are particularly reluctant to speak up if there is a breakdown between the executive's stated intentions and his or her perceived behaviors. In other words, if you are perceived as not "walking your talk," employees don't want to put themselves at risk by pointing out your shortcomings.

Third, if executive or leadership teams take the time to ask and are lucky enough to hear from an employee who provides accurate information, they may not listen to the feedback and may not act on the information. This illustrates an inherent problem in collecting data in the first place. If employees step up to the challenge of revealing how the boss is perceived or how well a team demonstrated a specific initiative, there is frequently an expectation that once the information is shared, it will be acted upon. Not only do employees expect prompt action, but also they often have an idea of what that action should look like. Because it is not always appropriate to publicly share actions taken, employees may be left thinking that no action was taken, or at least not the action they wanted. Also, all actions are taken within the context of the organization. Perhaps the boss did something that was unpopular but necessary. Or perhaps employees have only half the story.

In any of these cases, collecting information may not lead to immediate action or desired action, and this will have to be managed so that employees will continue to believe in the integrity of the process and will continue to share information in the future. So how do you decide what information you're going to collect (on the team and on individual members), from whom you're going to collect it, and what you're going to do with it once you've got it? Three activities will help you move in the right direction: agreeing on focus areas, mining information, and identifying and prioritizing themes.

Agreeing on Focus Areas

Initial discussions with the team will create a common language and shared expectations around focus areas. It is important for everyone to know what counts. Several questions will have to be answered: what is expected, what is going to be measured, how it will be measured, and what the data points will be.

At the heart of the matter are several fundamental questions:

- Why are we doing this?
- What do we want to be?
- How do we want to be perceived?

- What impact do we want to have on the organization?
- What are the values we want to embody?
- What are the behaviors that demonstrate and support those values?
- As we go about our work, day to day, what can people expect to see from us?

Many teams look outside at this point to make an informed decision about the focus areas that are important for them. Reading articles about other companies, conducting benchmarking interviews, hosting guest speakers, and using outside consultants are four ways of gathering information to use in identifying focus areas.

The dialogue you will have with your team is likely to be spirited, rich, and even controversial as you consider (perhaps for the first time) the relationship between the values you say are important and the behaviors you actually demonstrate in support of those values. This is a critical part of the process. Getting agreement on "who you are" as a team and as a senior leader in your organization creates the framework for your data gathering. In identifying what's important, you are defining the standard for yourself and your colleagues. As you move forward from here, you'll begin to collect information that will inform you. You can now discover just how close to the standard you are.

Mining Information

There are many ways for you to mine information. Just as in real mining, some techniques are more effective than others, and it is important to know how to tell the difference between pure gold and fool's gold when you come across it. Table 3.4 details several methods for mining information, along with strengths and drawbacks associated with each one.

You and your team should select an approach that is credible for you and the team, that is rich in detail, that is behaviorally focused (what you did and didn't do), and that supports development. After all, the reason you're mining data in the first place is to compare how you're currently doing with where you said you want to be. The information you collect should help you identify strengths you can build on and identify stumbling blocks so you can eliminate them. Let's look at how two different teams collected and used information for their development.

Team 1: The management team from an international manufacturing company followed the directive from their chairman and participated in a 360-degree feedback process. The vendor hired by the company to conduct the process had to extend the deadline for receiving data twice because participants didn't have a sufficient number of inventories completed and submitted. Each member of the team received his or her own feedback during a personal meeting with an outside consultant. Members also completed a personal development plan that was supposed to be discussed with their direct manager and with the human resources department. A team profile was also created using composite data from the 360-degree inventories. This

Table 3.4 Evaluating Methods of Mining Information

Method	*Strengths*	*Possible Drawbacks*
Climate Study: A sample population is identified and interviewed to provide representative perceptions of the organization.	■ Yields detailed narrative data ■ Questions can be customized ■ Themes and backup comments are provided ■ Initial survey can serve as a benchmark	■ Can be costly ■ Best conducted by outside consultants ■ Yields a lot of information—can be difficult to prioritize ■ May be overwhelming
Image Study: Respondents are selected and interviewed to provide data on executives or executive team.	■ Useful as a development tool ■ Yields detailed narrative data ■ Themes and backup comments are provided	■ Individual may not be ready to hear/act on the data ■ Requires professional facilitation ■ Creates an expectation of action
360-Degree Feedback: Colleagues, subordinates, boss, and customers are invited to complete rating forms on team members. Instrument evaluates behavior/performance in predetermined categories. Some instruments allow raters to indicate how important given behaviors are to them.	■ Easy to administer ■ Off-the-shelf packages available ■ Yields primarily quantitative data ■ Development options are often provided ■ Confidential ■ Can be customized for the team ■ Team profile can be created	■ Hard to verify knowledge of participants ■ Data may be skewed ■ Difficult to probe for meaning ■ Creating and implementing of development plan hard to monitor
Employee Opinion Survey: Written or electronic instrument designed to solicit employee opinions on designated topics	■ Easy to administer ■ Can reach large numbers at multiple locations ■ Initial survey can serve as benchmark	■ Creates expectation of action ■ May not explore real issues ■ Can cause credibility gap if issues aren't addressed ■ Frequently is not linked to overall system for learning and development
Focus Groups: Selected representatives are gathered together to discuss specific topics or questions.	■ Participants can build on each other's ideas ■ Allows a cross section of participation	■ Concern for confidentiality—sometimes participants reveal what others have said ■ Requires a certain time investment ■ Have to guard against the traps of "groupthink" and "feeding frenzy"
One-up Meetings: Structured meetings are held between the leader and the direct reports of his or her team members without the team member present.	■ Creates direct access to senior management ■ Promotes responsible dialogue ■ Provides specific, unfiltered information	■ May create false expectations ■ Can cause knee-jerk reactions ■ Requires skilled facilitation ■ Can strain relationships if information isn't used responsibly for development

(*continued*)

Table 3.4 Continued

Method	*Strengths*	*Possible Drawbacks*
Meeting Critique: A written or verbal process is used to evaluate team meetings.	■ Easy to use ■ Inexpensive ■ Provides timely, specific data ■ Easy to track progress	■ Data may be limited ■ Issues not on form may not be raised
One-on-One Feedback: Team members share individual perceptions about each member privately or in front of the team. Can be conducted in rounds, giving the leader and each member access to each other.	■ Supports direct dialogue ■ Allows team to share perspectives and real examples ■ Contributes to stronger relationships	■ Requires a willingness to raise issues and to hear issues ■ Individual skill level may vary ■ Individuals may not share information openly ■ Skilled facilitation may be required
Team Feedback: Team performance is reviewed and evaluated by the team. Possible topics include team functioning, progress on established measures, and skill in interactions.	■ Creates an accountable culture ■ Develops "team" mind-set ■ Promotes open dialogue	■ Requires professional facilitation ■ Can lead to "feeding frenzy" ■ May result in "groupthink"
Color Coding: Leader and team evaluate next-level reports using agreed-on criteria. Leads to team members evaluating each other.	■ Strong development process ■ Provides multiple perspectives ■ Provides a forum for performance discussions ■ Encourages alignment on values and behaviors ■ Creates a learning lab environment	■ Process is lengthy ■ May create defensiveness initially ■ Requires professional facilitation

composite went to the chairman only. Forty-five percent of the management team left the company during or immediately following the process.

Team 2: The project directors' team agreed to pursue an ongoing leadership development process. They started meeting monthly with a professional facilitator. They participated in a 360-degree process that included individual and group feedback. They experienced an outdoor ropes course and worked together to identify values they wanted to demonstrate. They learned how to coach each other, and they participated in technical training to develop their skills in communicating and resolving conflicts. Finally, they developed a feedback segment in the performance appraisals that they conducted with subordinates so they could find out how they were doing. The team leader was open and shared his own strengths and weaknesses. Mutual coaching provided support and confidence, not punishment or embarrassment. After 1 year, every single performance measure was surpassed.

Mining information effectively requires use of four skills. These skills are direct observation, framing effective questions, seeking contrary evidence, and evaluating intent. You and your team will find these skills helpful not only for data gathering but also for more enriched dialogue.

Using Direct Observation

You will have the opportunity for direct observation in many cases when you and your colleagues are together in staff and other meetings, team development sessions, and training. The following case provides an example.

Marla invited Jack to attend her staff meeting so that he could provide her with some feedback. When Jack attended Marla's staff meeting, he saw her interact with her team in a purposeful, direct, supportive way. She had prepared an agenda with their input and distributed it in advance. Marla began the meeting by asking each manager to provide an update on his or her key projects. They did so, and Jack noticed that they weren't afraid to note problems they were encountering and to solicit ideas from their peers. The other managers shared their thoughts without hesitation, and together they worked through every challenge that was raised. Marla stepped in only once when they got stuck and agreed to pursue a piece of information from a peer when they asked her to do so. Team members were focused on their agenda, and they still managed to joke with each other and laugh about their upcoming Halloween plans. Their energy level was contagious, and when Jack left the meeting 90 minutes later (as scheduled), he felt great. Later, Jack was able to share his observations with Marla—things she did, what she said, her team's reactions, and his perceptions of their interactions. Jack asked Marla if she would agree to do the same for him at his next staff meeting.

Framing Effective Questions

Framing effective questions helps someone reflect on things he or she said or did. A series of effective questions helps someone evaluate how he or she might change, modify, or replicate his or her approach. The following case provides an example.

Ron and Carl scheduled their conflict management training together. When it came time to practice describing what happened in a situation without blaming the other person, Ron seemed to struggle. He used the lead-in phrase from the worksheet provided, but his tone was accusatory, and when his partner replied that he didn't think the deadline was firm, Ron blasted him and told him that that was stupid and so was he. His partner replied in kind and walked away. As the observer, Carl asked Ron the following questions. "What happened in that exercise?" "What, if anything, did you try that seemed to work?" "How did Sean react to your statements?" "Did you get the reaction you wanted?" "What might you have done differently?" "How is this exercise similar to interactions you've had with others?" "Why don't we try this again?"

Seeking Contrary Evidence

Contrary evidence is a concept introduced by Paul Green in the video *More Than a Gut Feeling* (1984, LearnCom Group). Seeking contrary evidence is a variation of mining information. It requires you to take a detour when all the information seems to be leading you to a certain conclusion. Specifically, you look for information that supports the opposite point of view. For example:

Joanne was interviewing Hector's peers to gather information about his facilitating skills. Facilitating was a development area Hector had identified through 360-degree feedback, and he had been working on it for 2 months. Martin and Kim both observed that Hector wasn't doing anything differently. He still seemed very directive. "Bossy" was Kim's word to describe Hector's style. Martin said, "He still tells us what to do." After hearing several of these comments, Joanne could have easily fallen into the trap of framing her questions in such a way that she would continue to build a case for Hector's acting directive and bossy. Instead, she did just the opposite. "Tell me about a time when Hector let the team come to its own conclusion, even if it would have been easier for him to make the call." "Give me an example of a time when he asked the team to share their thoughts and didn't assume he knew what you wanted." "Describe a time when Hector specifically observed behavior that violated your ground rules and asked you what you wanted to do about it." When asked in this manner, Hector's peers were able to mention three incidents where he had been less authoritative. Through contrary evidence, Joanne was able to show both Hector and his peers that slow progress was indeed being made.

Seeking contrary evidence requires that you ask the right questions. The evidence may or may not be there. But if you make up your mind too early in the process, you'll never discover it.

Evaluating Intent

Evaluating the intent of the person giving you feedback helps you weigh the information you're mining. Ask yourself the following questions:

- What does this person stand to gain or lose if you act on what he or she has told you?
- What is his or her relationship with the person you're gathering data on?
- Has he or she told the person what he or she is telling you?
- How is thinking this way to the person's advantage?

Sometimes the desire to help is genuine. At other times, it isn't. Consider the following example.

Sandy happily approached Greg (her senior vice president) with feedback about Ellen (her direct boss). "It's really hard for me to tell you this," she said, "but I think you need to know what our client had to say this week when I visited their corporate office." Sandy went on to describe several critical problems with this large account. She painted a picture of lack of interest and poor skills on Ellen's part and a lot of quick thinking and customer care on her own part. When Greg asked if Sandy had shared this information with Ellen, she became agitated and said, "No, you know how difficult it is to get time with Ellen, and I really thought you should know about the circumstances as soon as possible so that you could intervene." Greg thanked Sandy for bringing the issue to his attention. Then he asked her several questions.

- "How did the client happen to approach you about these problems?"
- "What did you do or say to reassure them?"
- "Help me understand what their expectations are now, after speaking with you."
- "Ellen has always done excellent work with this account. Explain to me how you think these problems may have arisen."
- "Talk me through your concerns about approaching Ellen directly."
- "Help me understand why sharing this information with her presents a challenge for you."

Sandy had difficulty answering Greg's questions. In response to his open-ended questions, she revealed that she had conferred with her counterpart at the client site and then had approached the client. Sandy let Greg know that she believed she could do more challenging work and that she didn't feel appreciated by Ellen.

Greg thanked Sandy for her candor. He affirmed his commitment to coaching and developing all of his employees. He acknowledged Ellen's excellent track record and Sandy's statements regarding the client's concerns. He told Sandy that he would bring the matter up with Ellen and he was confident that she would pursue it. Greg shared his intention to contact the client. He also expressed his concern for the way Sandy had handled the situation. He let her know that open communication was something he valued and that he considered all team members responsible for supporting that type of interaction. He let Sandy know that once he spoke with Ellen, she would probably want to speak to Sandy directly and that she should be prepared for that. In fact, he suggested that Sandy might want to initiate that discussion. Sandy said "fine" and left Greg's office decidedly less happy than when she had walked in.

Greg will have to assemble some more facts before he reaches any conclusions. There may be legitimate customer issues to be resolved. And there is a relationship issue between Ellen and Sandy. In the meantime, he has reinforced Sandy's concern for the customer and redirected her approach with her boss. He will coach Ellen on how to handle the client and Sandy. Whatever steps Sandy and Ellen take next will be taken within a coaching framework.

Identifying and Prioritizing Themes

Once you have collected the data about your team and its members, you will be challenged to sort through it and identify themes. None of us can listen to and effectively act on a lengthy list of observations and perceptions. But sorting information into themes enables us to present it in a manageable format. Instead of working through pages of data, we can select from three or four "buckets" and one at a time examine the contents with interest and curiosity. For example, Alan's image study yielded the following comments from subordinates, colleagues, and his boss:

- Has to be right
- Inflexible, rigid
- Steamroller versus light touch
- Can't back down, even when it is more appropriate
- Can seem obstinate, negative, and resistant
- Can come across as terse, demanding
- When others come around to his way of thinking, he has to say, "I told you so"
- Isn't diplomatic
- Knows his stuff, but the engineers are reluctant to approach him

Review the comments and create one or two "buckets" that effectively group the information for presentation. Use the worksheet in Exhibit 3.2 as an organizational tool. For Alan, perhaps you chose the buckets of "personal interactions" or "team player."

Interviews on a senior team revealed the following comments. Using Exhibit 3.2, what buckets would you create for this data?

- We don't think of them as a team. They are a bunch of individuals.
- There is no sense of team between the directors.
- I think Larry (the president) makes the decisions. Everyone knows who is in charge of the company.
- We're not aware of what the directors do.
- Who knows what they're working on?
- We don't get any feedback from the directors.
- They try and outdo each other.
- Communication from the directors could be improved.
- We tend to split off and go our separate ways.

Exhibit 3.2 **Organizing Data**

What themes are evident in the data?

What messages do you hear repeated?

Generate a list of the adjectives/adverbs used. What kind of picture does this list call to mind?

What is new/different in the data? What is familiar?

What are the data saying about the subject? The people you interviewed?

"So what?" Why do these perceptions matter? What is the cost of no change?

- The directors talk about each other to anyone who will listen.
- There is a lot of politics going on at the directors' level. It gets a little bloody sometimes.
- The directors are always jockeying for position. They all want to look the best in Larry's eyes, even at each other's expense.
- They are very competitive with each other. Their egos drive their behavior.
- Larry doesn't hold them accountable. He walks away from it.

For this team, the buckets of "communication," "image," and "role modeling" might work.

Identifying themes or "buckets" of information not only makes information easier to review and work with but also allows us to compare it with other data points. How do the results from your 360-degree inventory compare with the feedback you've been getting on your performance appraisals? What is the relationship between the comments people made in your image study and the quality of the interactions you've been experiencing with your peers? How does the employees' view of the executive team compare with the desired view you've outlined for yourselves? What conclusions can you draw from the way people view the executive team and the results you are achieving? Once you've identified themes and started to work with the data, you can prioritize your efforts. What changes might have the biggest impact? Where should you put your time and resources? The answers to these questions will form the basis of your work in action planning.

Competencies

The competencies necessary for Step 2, collecting and analyzing data, are inquiry, reframing, listening, sorting, and patience.

Inquiry

Inquiry is the ability to question team members with a genuine desire to understand them. Inquiry requires a spirit of discovery and learning. It requires that you suspend your assumptions and pursue information without prejudging the person who is providing it or his or her intention.

In traditional leadership models, the communication of information generally consists of the leader telling the team what to do or how to do it and the team telling the leader what they've done and how they've done it. If things haven't happened as expected, there is frequently a healthy dose of "Why not?" and "When will the situation be corrected?" In the coaching leadership model, the conversation is characterized by revelation. The leader or team members share information, thought processes, and reasoning so that others in the team can add to, correct, and learn from the process. The concepts of mistakes and blame are replaced by discovery and learning.

Making thinking visible allows team members and the leader to test assumptions, formulate questions, coach one another, and ultimately arrive at a conclusion that each person understands. The quality of the conversation is richer, and the team members have the opportunity to learn more than they would otherwise. Practicing open discussion and dialogue removes the posturing requirement. Team members can pay attention to the content rather than putting energy into packaging what they want to sell and working at looking good. No one is expected to have all of the answers, but everyone is expected to get to the answers. Inquiry helps you do that.

Reframing

Reframing is the skill of helping the team find different meanings in the same information. It requires you to explore interpretations and perspectives and to expand the possibilities when assessing information. Instead of automatically assigning meaning, you and the team can use reframing to remove limitations to your learning. See below how Alex helps his team by reframing feedback.

Alex and his sales team bristled when they read the low scores their customers gave them on "acts with integrity." "I can't believe they said this," "I don't know where this is coming from," and "These numbers can't be right" were typical comments from the team. Alex was upset with the numbers, but he kept his team focused on the data with the intent of discovering what was contributing to this perception. He didn't allow the team to get stuck in the numbers or to overreact to the feedback. "Let's see where this takes us," he said. As the team worked through their numerical scores and narrative feedback, comments revealed that their customers thought they honestly represented their products and availability. What they didn't do, however, was follow up if there were any unanticipated problems with delivery. "So our customers are letting us know they want something from us that they're not getting. They are not saying we're communicating dishonestly—they are saying they're not getting something they need from the communication we do have with them. We can work on that."

Internal company systems didn't inform the sales team when delays in shipping or delivery occurred. The data led to a substantive dialogue concerning the sales team's relationship with their customers and the company's systems that weren't supporting those relationships. Once Alex reframed the data and the team got past their initial emotional reaction, they worked through the issue to a positive end.

Sometimes reframing works in another direction.

Rusty and Melinda were reviewing her image study feedback. He asked her what she thought of the comments from her team:

- Melinda always has an answer.
- Melinda keeps a close eye on us.
- Melinda checks on me regularly—usually before I have a chance to go to her as agreed.
- Melinda usually rewrites my status reports, so I just worry about providing the basics.

Melinda was happy to hear that her team considered her the answer person and that they realized how much energy and attention she focused on them. Rusty asked her if there was another way to interpret the data. "Describe the climate you're creating in the team," he requested. Through dialogue with Rusty, Melinda realized she was micromanaging her team. Although she considered them capable, she wasn't demonstrating that through her actions. In fact, she was giving them the opposite message. Working with Rusty, she was able to create a development plan that allowed her to facilitate more and control less. One year later, three members of her team had been promoted, and Melinda had doubled the size of her team.

Listening

Listening requires a sharpened use of your senses. In collecting and analyzing data, you should pay attention to what is said and not said. What is the tone behind the spoken words? Where is the energy flowing? Where is it being siphoned off? You can't listen effectively when your focus is on yourself. Listening as a coaching leader requires that you put the team first—paying attention to all the signals they are putting out there for you to absorb.

Sorting

Sorting is the skill of taking the data and organizing it in such a way that you and the team can extract meaning from it. Individuals can only absorb so much information at once. Sorting chunks the data—it helps to make information manageable. "Buckets" can be used to sort information according to team objectives, identified measures, climate study themes, or agreed-on team values. Sorting isn't censoring. It is simply a way to package the information that you and the team collect so that you can make use of it.

Patience

Patience is the ability to accurately assess where you and the team are and to allow the time necessary for you to grow through the coaching process. Value incremental progress. In a world where we can achieve instant gratification in many areas (e.g., communication, commerce, research), personal and professional growth is a comparatively slow process. Trying out new behaviors, practicing, making and learning from mistakes, and perfecting behaviors take time. Coaching leadership is a long-term investment with many short-term ups and downs. You and the team will take many small steps before the process begins to pick up momentum. Coaching leadership requires discipline. You have to believe the results are worth it.

Step 3: Processing Feedback and Planning Actions

Putting Information to Work for You and the Team

As Peter Drucker (1999) noted, "The only way to discover your strengths is through feedback analysis" (p. 66). Chances are, you now have more information about you, your team, and each of your team members than you've ever had before. The challenge facing you as a coaching leader is whether you can use this feedback skillfully. Doing so will require more than technical skills. Providing feedback to team members and helping them to plan actions requires interpersonal or social skills, a subset of what Daniel Goleman has described as emotional intelligence. The concept of emotional intelligence, popularized by Goleman, includes the skill sets of self-awareness, self-regulation, motivation, empathy, and social skill. As a coaching leader, you should be able to demonstrate all these skill sets. You will be handling relationships and managing emotions in yourself and others. Can you deliver feedback and help team members work through it and make use of it so that they and the team can grow? You will have to handle your own reactions to and emotions about the data, as well as managing the emotions of your team. Goleman observed in *Working With Emotional Intelligence* (1998b), "We're being judged by a new yardstick: not just by how smart we are, or by our training and expertise, but also by how well we handle ourselves and each other" (p. 3). So can you help others identify what matters most? Are you able to create the conversations necessary to help team members talk through their hopes, fears, and goals? Can you help them see the potential payoff in pursuing a new set of behaviors? And can you detail the consequences of choosing to take no action? As John Seely Brown, chief scientist at Xerox Corporation, explained, "To communicate is not just a matter of pushing information at another person. It's creating an experience, to engage their gut—and that's an emotional skill" (quoted in Goleman, 1998b, p. 202). Do you have that skill? The information you have is comparable to raw energy. Harnessed effectively, it can fuel your team's development. Used carelessly, it can cause irreparable damage. Coaching leadership requires you to handle the data you collect in certain ways. For example, you need to

- Put the feedback in context
- Highlight strengths and positive areas
- Provide support in working through difficult feedback
- Generate and evaluate options
- Answer questions
- Provide focus and balance
- Keep the process moving
- Role-model coaching behaviors

Again, John Seely Brown pointed out, "You have to be able to read the situation, the human currents, and move accordingly. The more we operate in less controlled environments, the more we need to be able to read human energies" (quoted in Goleman, 1998b, p. 202). This is why some teams use outside consultants to support them in data gathering and feedback. Many leaders find it helpful to use a facilitator (internal or external) to actively participate in the process or to keep them focused and on track. As you are developing your own skills, it is helpful to have objective support readily available. It is important to remember why you wanted to collect information in the first place. Real data contribute to an informed decision that leads to actions you will take to improve the effectiveness of yourself, the team members, and the team as a whole. Without such information, you are forced to operate from a position of weakness. With the information, the possibilities are endless.

There are, however, inherent barriers that prevent us from hearing and using information about ourselves. In his book *The Heart of Leadership* (2000), Staub described these barriers as ego, fear, and impatience and discussed them as they apply to individual leadership development. He explained:

> Ego makes us unwilling to learn from others, and even from our own mistakes. Fear can cause us not to give or receive needed feedback—it prevents us from acting. Impatience is the unwillingness to allow events and processes to mature and unfold. (p. 25)

We have found that you will need to consider these barriers from another standpoint and work through them as you practice your coaching leadership skills with your team.

Barriers to Feedback

Ego

Ego is the most common barrier that will present itself as you and the team seek out information. Yet as Drucker (1999) pointed out, it is critical to "discover where your intellectual arrogance is causing disabling ignorance and overcome it" (p. 66). Generally, senior-level people have been promoted throughout their careers because they have demonstrated a combination of technical and interpersonal skills. Ironically, often the same interpersonal behaviors that served them well in a more junior position may now be getting in their way. Jack's attention to detail as a controller shows up as micromanaging and poor delegating when he becomes vice president of finance. Linda's drive for perfection at any cost as a sales representative creates burnout for her staff when she becomes the sales manager. Mark's unwillingness to take "no" for an answer as an operations manager results in his staff's scrambling to get things done and hiding bad news from him when he becomes vice president of operations. So how can you convince team members to listen to a selection of junior staff or colleagues who may or may not have the same level of experience or to outsiders who don't know what they face on a day-to-day basis? The answer is simple. If your team members have reached this level in an organization, their success is likely to depend on the ability to get work done through others. They are no longer the focal point—the people they supervise are. And what the people you supervise think of you and the team, and the ways in which they experience you, are key to the results you want to achieve.

You and the team may have gotten to where you are on the basis of what you've done, but you'll be moving forward on the basis of what "they" do. What they think of you matters. Just because something worked yesterday is no guarantee it will work tomorrow. If you want to ensure your future success, you need to tap into the information network that exists around you. Cultivate that network actively and you will collect the information you need to polish the team's performance to a high shine. Below is one scenario.

When the company survey revealed a lower-than-average score in "giving clear directions" and "managing conflict," the account managers weren't happy. They were a competitive team by nature, and they thought highly of themselves. So it pricked their egos to have such clearly delineated areas for improvement. When the team reviewed the follow-up data 3 months later, they found they had increased their overall score 20%. It was hard to admit that they weren't perfect. Not that they believed they were perfect, it was just hard to admit their flaws publicly to each other and to their employees. But in retrospect, coming up with the behaviors that were important to all of them contributed to a lot more open dialogue and some focused professional development opportunities that they hadn't had before. They were now looking at a significant jump forward. Maybe this feedback wasn't such a bad thing after all.

And here is a contrasting scenario.

The managing director looked across the table at the president in disbelief. "You can't be serious," he said. "Somebody went crying to you about my tone of voice and suddenly we're having this conversation?"

"It wasn't somebody, Steven. And it isn't sudden. You and I meet monthly, and I have been telling you for months that your 'scorched earth' approach to getting what you want out of the other departments is no longer going to be tolerated. Didn't you understand my earlier feedback?"

"I heard you. I just didn't believe you. I always exceed my numbers. I am the best at what I do, always have been. I know how to get things done. I'm not going to let someone who doesn't have any idea what it takes to keep this business going tell me how to do my job."

"I'm sorry to hear that, Steven. You are good at what you do. You could be better. If you aren't willing to make some changes, I'm afraid we won't find out just how good you could be since you won't be here."

As a coaching leader, it's your job to help people set their egos aside so they can hear feedback and use it to grow and develop.

Fear

Fear is a common barrier, trapping many leaders in a cycle of inaction, defending intentions, and interpreting or explaining away others' perceptions. A well-thought-out defense or series of explanations allows a leader to protect the ideal self-image that he or she has created. Staying focused on that image prevents them from seeing themselves as others do. This myopic view gets in the way of exploring others' perceptions. The leader becomes locked in a self-sealing cycle of good intentions fueling behavior that may or may not lead to optimal results.

Fear generally results in the leader or team's focusing on the "followers." If the results aren't achieved, it's "their problem." "They don't understand," or "They didn't execute as agreed." Rarely does the leader's focus allow him or her to turn inward and explore "What can I do differently?" or "How am I contributing to this situation?" Fear of information, however, keeps the leader in the dark and creates confusion for everyone else. Everyone else continues to experience the behavior, and their view of the leader is solidified. They may work around him or her to the best of their ability, or they may withdraw to pursue their own objectives outside the leader's reach. The leader knows what he or she intends, but the executives and staff often experience the leader in ways that don't align with those intentions.

Predictably, the leader's credibility is damaged, and the executive team doesn't develop as purposefully as it might otherwise. Pockets of development may occur, but the team forfeits the power of aligned action. Consider the case of Dennis's team.

As described earlier, Dennis stated his intention to shift to coaching leadership. Early in the process, he described what he was doing and why he felt it was so important for him and the team. What he didn't talk about, initially, was his fear of not being liked, of not being seen as the nice guy, and his belief that he had to hold on to control in the team. He asked for everyone's support and held one-on-one conversations with the team members, getting their thoughts and describing where he thought the process would take them. In his meeting with Jim, Dennis explained that he could no longer support Jim's aggressive behavior with the team. He invited Jim to talk to him about his concerns, but Jim had very little to say. After years of working together, Jim knew Dennis and what was important to him. "You know I've always supported you, Dennis. I've always done whatever needed to be done, and I'll continue to do so."

Dennis's team was skeptical about the shift he described because historically Dennis had been unable to deal directly with conflict situations. The team recognized that being a "nice guy" was important to Dennis. Dennis decided to get outside help for himself and the team. He laid out a plan that included conducting an image study of the senior team. In preparing for the off-site, Dennis revealed his concerns about Jim to the facilitator. In response to skillful questioning, Dennis was able to talk about his desire to be liked and his fear that he wouldn't be liked if he was more direct. He also talked about his need to be in control. He came to recognize that Jim's behavior had served his fears but had proven to be harmful to the team.

The image study revealed that the only person who didn't recognize the dynamic in the team was Dennis. Everyone else knew exactly what was going on. When the team went to the off-site, the image study was shared. Everyone got his or her own feedback and data on the team. There were many comments about the interactions of the team, how people felt about them, and what people wanted from Dennis and from the team. Dennis acknowledged the disservice he had done to Jim and to the team. He committed himself to growing as a leader, and he invited the team to develop with him. He went on to make a request of the team. He asked that they hold each other accountable for their team process, and he made arrangements to get coaching support for himself and the team. He admitted that he saw some challenges ahead for all of them—and he reaffirmed his intention to become a coaching leader. He asked for their help. They agreed.

Over time, Dennis made improvements. He was able to redefine what being a "nice guy" meant. He strengthened the relationship he had with his team. Eventually, Dennis was successful in creating a culture characterized by caring and accountability. The team's behaviors and performance changed dramatically.

Exhibit 3.3 **Questions to Work Through Fear**

- Why am I acting this way?
- How is my behavior working to my benefit?
- What message am I hearing in this feedback?
- How is that a problem for me?
- What am I afraid of?
- Is my intention aligned with their perception?
- What am I doing, specifically, that is causing the disconnect?
- What could I be doing instead?
- How hard will it be to change my beliefs and behavior?
- What results would make that effort worthwhile?
- What advice would I give my best friend if he/she received this feedback?
- What would I choose to do if I wasn't afraid?
- How can I use this information to help myself?

If you are going to help your direct reports overcome their fear of information, you must successfully do so yourself. What do you believe about information? How can you use it to develop yourself and your team? What does it tell you about yourself and about others? If you have selected meaningful dimensions around which to collect feedback, you've already bought in rationally to the idea that the information has a value. So what is the problem? Are you afraid that "their perception" won't match "your intention"? In fact, our intentions rarely match their perceptions. Not hearing the information or explaining it away doesn't make the disconnect any less real. On the contrary, it reinforces what others think of you. Hearing the information, refraining from killing the messenger, and showing a willingness to explore the data demonstrate a resolve that your team will notice. You will be modeling a courageous response for them to follow.

Generally our fear comes from that part of the brain that is conditioned to react with a fight-or-flight response—good for fighting dinosaurs, bad for developing leaders and teams. Acknowledge whatever fear you feel, and use a series of questions to work through it (see Exhibit 3.3). Once you have successfully gotten past your own fear of information, you can help your team members do the same. This is demonstrated in the following case.

The data that came from the vice president's group were clear. The group felt that the executive team didn't communicate with them in a consistent, timely way. They cited several examples of hearing from industry sources about pending deals closing or dropping off the table instead of getting the information through internal channels. This hurt their credibility with peers in other companies when they were so clearly not "in the know." The executive team listened to the feedback as presented by their internal consultant and reacted. The initial comments were along the lines of "They always want more information," "If they had their way, we'd spend all our time in meetings with them," "I don't have to tell them anything," and "I'm not changing everything around to suit them."

After some discussion, the five members of the team circled back to the notion that people always want more information and that the president wasn't going to do anything differently. Their consultant asked them to talk through their fears about sharing information. Eventually it became clear that the president had always played his cards close to his chest. He once had gotten burnt when sharing information. He was afraid of that happening again, so his strategy was to share as little as possible. Interestingly, as information coming from him dried up, information getting to him dried up as well. With some work, new agreements were created that strengthened both executive groups.

Here's another scenario involving fear.

Mark couldn't believe it. The feedback he'd just gotten from his new boss, Carolyn, was awful. Not only did she question his technical skills, but she let him know that he was going to have to change some of his personal habits as well. She suggested that he improve the management of his time, the way he treated the support staff, and his interactions with colleagues. How could this be? His old boss always gave him great feedback. He had an MBA, for God's sake. His mother knew the president of the company. Why would Carolyn do this to him?

Carolyn was aware enough to realize that the feedback she had given Mark was a shock. She knew she was taking a risk because he was a good friend of the president's family, but his work was only fair. She was convinced that it was because no one had been honest with him and he was coasting. She suggested that Mark review the notes she had prepared and that they meet again the next morning so they could create a plan for moving forward. She wanted Mark to have the time to think through the data she was giving him.

When they met the next morning, she asked Mark for his reactions and she let him talk through all of them: his outrage, shock, embarrassment, fear, and anger at never having been told some of the things that she told him. While he vented and worked through all of those emotions, Carolyn listened and reinforced her commitment to him. She answered questions, provided examples, and stayed balanced and focused. "This isn't an indictment of you, Mark," she said, "It is a critique of your work products and some of your work habits. I have every confidence that you can change those products and habits if you choose to. And I will help you if you let me." To his credit, Mark decided to work with Carolyn. He worked through his fear of the information and became a stronger professional.

Impatience

Finally, impatience is the barrier that many individuals stumble against in their pursuit of coaching leadership. Once leaders have bought in to the idea of creating this new way of operating and have identified measures, collected data, shared data, and created action plans, the inclination or desire on their part is to throw a switch. They are so action oriented and results focused that they want to change or correct their own behaviors immediately, and they want the same for the people who report to them.

Here are two pieces of bad news. First, changing behavior takes time. Experts agree that for a behavior to become habitual, you will have to practice that behavior every day for at least 30 days. Because most of you don't have the luxury of trying out and practicing behaviors in a pure lab environment, there is most likely an expectation that your business will continue to run profitably throughout this time.

Second, people have memories like elephants. Even as you are trying behaviors that you have determined to be more effective, more closely aligned with the values you have identified and committed yourself to, people continue to experience you as "the old you." It takes a while for the new behavior to break through into people's conscious thoughts. And when it does, they question your motivation. You will do the same thing with other leaders on the team. You may wonder, "Why is Jill behaving in this new way?" and "How long will it last?" Coaching leadership is not a quick fix. As stated earlier, it isn't for everyone. But if it is for you and your team, you will be strongly tested during this part of the process. You must role-model patience, support, and perspective. You must continually hold out the vision as the ultimate goal.

Presenting the Feedback and Exploring the Implications

Your first test is to present the feedback in such a way that the person hears it. Presenting feedback effectively requires that the information be descriptive rather than evaluative and that the presenter use an objective rather than a judgmental framework. Once the information is on the table, you can begin to explore the implications. What does the feedback mean? How does it fit with what you've heard about the team before? How does it compare with other data points (e.g., performance data, survey results)? What, if anything, should you or the team do about it? How will you decide what actions to take? What if you decide to do nothing? All of these questions are likely to come up as you explore the implications of your feedback.

Whether or not you and the team agree with the feedback, it is important to acknowledge the perceptions that exist. Knowing how others view you allows you to assess the effectiveness of your behavior. Are you achieving the results you want to? If your team behaviors are being perceived in a way other than what you intended, why do you think that is? Do you want to change anything that you and the team are doing so that your results will be more in line with what you intended? Let's refer once again to the examples under "Reframing" of Alex's team and the feedback they received from their customers and of Melinda and the feedback she received from her staff. At first, Alex's team and Melinda extracted only one meaning from the feedback. That meaning and their reaction to it limited the way they could use the information. Luckily, they were able to use reframing to extract additional meaning from the feedback, enabling them to consider alternative actions and their implications. They chose to change some of what they were doing so that their results would more closely match their intentions.

Planning for Change

In planning for change, you and the team will have to consider three things: the results you are currently experiencing, the behavior you are currently displaying, and the beliefs that underlie them both. Frequently, when we get results we are not happy with, we look for external explanations. Sometimes we look for ways to assign blame to someone other than ourselves. Departments blame other departments, team members blame other team members, and so on. As a last resort, we will examine our own behaviors and what we may be contributing to the situation. But getting different results requires more than different behavior.

Typically, we behave in a way we think is right, correct, necessary, or appropriate in a given set of circumstances. Most of our behavior is habit—we automatically behave or respond in certain ways on the basis of our experiences and beliefs. As shown in Figure 3.3, our beliefs are like a root system. They are under the surface, nourishing our behaviors and feeding our results. It is these beliefs—these truths we hold about ourselves and our interactions with others—that drive our behaviors. To change the results we're getting, we have to change our behaviors, and to make a long-lasting change in our behaviors, we have to change our beliefs.

Part of exploring change is evaluating the way you and your team operate and "fit" with other individuals and teams in your organization. This is where the emotional intelligence of your team comes into play, particularly the components of "empathy" and "social skill," which bear directly on your "ability to manage relationships with others" (Goleman, 1998a, p. 101). For your team to be effective, you need to develop and maintain an internal and an external focus. You are learning not only about yourselves and the way you interact with each other but also about the way you interact with others outside the team.

If you change certain behaviors, what reactions are you likely to get from team members? From those outside the team? What changes will be credible? For example, let's say team members believe that executives know best about their performance and behavior and don't need any input from staff. Historically, the team has not solicited any information or feedback. If you suddenly call your staff together and start asking for their feedback, they are likely to wonder what you're up to. Further, they may believe that you are purposefully setting them up for some unknown reason.

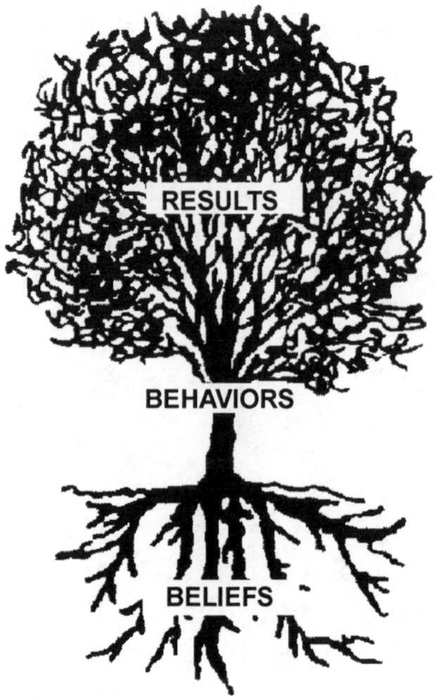

Figure 3.3. Beliefs, Behaviors, and Results

You are likely to experience greater success if you make incremental changes and let your staff know what you are doing and why you are doing it. In the example above, telling your staff that you are committed to soliciting feedback as part of your development plan as a coaching leader demonstrates your openness and willingness to risk. It also role-models for them how to accept feedback if it is offered (providing you don't kill the messenger). Be truthful about what you are doing and why. Recognize the challenges ahead of you. Enlist their help. Team members then develop a vested interest in helping you to succeed, and they learn in the process.

Once you identify the specific changes you'd like to make, you increase your chances of success by creating a written action plan with objectives, specific steps, and time lines. When you are doing this as a team, it is important that everyone be clear about the expectations. An example of part of a team action plan in shown in Exhibit 3.4.

A team might also need to help individual members create personal action plans. The following scenario shows how this might happen.

On the basis of composite feedback, the executive team had to directly confront the fact that the organization viewed Steve, vice president of marketing, as abrasive, sarcastic, unappreciative, and meddling. Steve was surprised. He knew he could be difficult, but he thought that was just part of "being the boss." In dialogue with the team, he agreed to polish up his skills in communicating with staff and in setting performance expectations so that he could manage in a more "hands-off" way. The team assisted Steve in developing an action plan. Steve hired a coach to work with

Exhibit 3.4 **Team Action Planning**

1.0 Objective: Spread the strategic plan throughout the organization.

1.1 Schedule work sessions so each department can identify specific goals.

1.2 Collect and publish each department's goals and objectives.

1.3 Hold one-on-one conversations with employees to create personal objectives and development plans.

2.0 Objective: Utilize advocacy and inquiry in all of our meetings.

2.1 Clarify agreements in staff meetings.

2.2 Draft scripts for major announcements.

2.3 Schedule joint presentations.

2.4 Provide feedback to each other on presentations.

3.0 Objective: Communicate as a united team.

3.1 Suspend judgment and ask questions to uncover team member's reasoning.

3.2 Reflect on individual reactions and record thoughts in journal.

3.3 Complete one "thoughtful conversation" exercise per week.

3.4 Evaluate progress using meeting critique.

---

him and his direct reports. He identified several key actions he planned to take to address the behaviors that were getting in the way. Four months later, he was anxious to see how he was doing.

When his coach first spoke with his staff, they reported "no change." They said, "He's the same way he's always been," and they expressed their doubts in his ability to change his behavior. When the coach probed specifically about behaviors that Steve had committed to eliminate and other behaviors that he had promised to practice, the staff reported that he had stopped what he had promised to stop and had started what he had promised to start. Why the sweeping negative comment, then? Steve's staff didn't like him. They wanted him to be a totally different leader. Even with the changes he was making, they weren't satisfied.

As already discussed, behavior change is difficult. The above situation will require more in-depth team building and coaching. In the end, a decision will have to be made on whether Steve will ever be accepted within this environment. If it is best for Steve to go, this will happen within a framework of support and knowledge, not embarrassment or punishment. Working at data feedback and action planning allows you to make informed decisions and to support the team and team members as they practice the principles of coaching leadership.

Competencies

The competencies required for Step 3, processing feedback and planning actions, are truth telling, empathy, ability to generate and evaluate alternatives, and conviction.

Truth Telling

Truth telling is the ability to share information with your team honestly. No big lies, no little lies, no censoring or spinning—just the information. Sharing information and feedback directly with the people who need to hear it demonstrates your respect for them. Perfecting this skill reflects directly on your credibility.

Describing the way you see someone behave and your reaction or the reactions of others to that behavior is important information you can provide to someone you are coaching. You may have firsthand knowledge and observations gathered in a one-on-one meeting or in a larger group setting. Or you may have gotten secondhand feedback from peers or direct reports. Though it is challenging to provide feedback one-on-one to team members, even more expert skills are needed when giving feedback within a team setting. The most effective teams create and use ground rules or norms that support them in communicating honestly and proactively working through challenges (Druskat & Wolff, 2001, p. 85). In addition to describing the behavior you've experienced, truth telling requires you to help team members explore the implications of the behavior. As a member of the team, you have a responsibility to explore the "So what?" and to ask, "What are our alternatives?" You should consider how your choices affect performance and credibility. In a coaching environment, truth telling invariably leads to informed action. It's important to develop your skills at describing what you or others experienced without evaluating the person's motives. The following case provides an example.

When Diane joined Jeremy for his weekly meeting, she observed that he opened the meeting by complimenting his team on the numbers from last week and led them through some creative problem solving. The energy level was high in the room, and the interchange was open. A short time later, however, Jeremy cut off the discussion when his staff tried to raise questions about the new process for handling customer complaints.

Specifically, he interrupted Jane when she asked if the time frame could be compressed. When Steve started to offer an alternative, Jeremy raised his voice and said, "This has already been agreed to, so let's move on." The next items on the agenda did not generate any discussion, and no ideas were forthcoming on the new order process. After the meeting adjourned, Jeremy asked Diane how she thought he had done in facilitating the meeting.

"Before I answer you, Jeremy, I'm interested in how you think you did."

"Well, I drafted the agenda based on input from everyone and distributed it in advance. We started on time and moved through each of the topics. I may have gotten a little short with Jane when she asked about the timing on the complaint process, but she's been in on that every step of the way, and it felt like she was grandstanding to me. Otherwise, I think it went pretty well."

Diane said, "I know you got the agenda out because you copied me on the distribution. And you did a nice job of recognizing the team's work from last week. I thought you seemed frustrated with Jane. You rolled your eyes and you interrupted her. How do you think the others reacted when you did that?"

"I don't know."

"From where I was sitting, it looked like they shut down. How would you characterize your interaction with Steve?"

"I don't really remember."

"Did you realize that you raised your voice and cut him off in midsentence?"

"No, I didn't."

"Once you interrupted Jane and then cut Steve off, the tone of the meeting flattened out. How would you describe the conversation generated by the last two agenda items?"

"There wasn't any."

"Looking back now, can you identify what happened?"

"I guess I gave everyone the impression I didn't want any."

"Perhaps. Let's talk about what you are going to do now to correct the impression your staff came away with. How will you handle comments in the future when you have a concern about the motivation behind them?"

In this interaction, Diane allowed Jeremy to reflect on what he thought happened. Then she shared her observations. She complimented him on something he did well. They talked through what Jeremy's behavior might have created and how he could correct an impression he didn't mean to create. Sharing observations allowed Diane to create a learning opportunity with Jeremy. She told the truth about what she saw him do and how she saw others react. She let him talk through reasons and alternatives and always brought him back to what happened and what he could do about it. She recognized the work he was doing, reinforced what went well, and redirected his attention in the areas that needed it. Truth telling is what coaching leadership is all about.

Empathy

Empathy, a dimension of emotional intelligence, is best defined as understanding, support, and regard for the team member you are coaching. As Max DePree (1989) observed, "The primary skill of a leader is an ability to understand and liberate the talents of a diverse workforce" (p. 23). Empathy allows you to demonstrate that understanding. In their book *Credibility,* Kouzes and Posner (1993) revealed that it is supportiveness, along with honesty and competence, that determines a leader's "source credibility." And, as mentioned in

Part 1, positive regard is a necessary element for any behavioral change (Campbell, 2000; Rogers, 1951). Your job as a coaching leader is to help people as they undertake the difficult work of changing beliefs and behaviors. Recognize that feedback can be hard to hear. Empathy for other people allows you to understand their feelings, help them to hear the feedback, and support them in taking action. Empathy is not sympathy. Sympathy acknowledges how people are feeling now. Empathy is a link, a bridge of confidence and understanding that helps people move from where they are to where they need to be.

Ability to Generate and Evaluate Alternatives

Generating and evaluating alternatives requires divergent and convergent thinking. First, you survey current circumstances from all sides and create alternative ideas, interpretations, and possibilities. Make sure you have several alternatives to consider. Second, you must evaluate the ideas, interpretations, and possibilities according to agreed-on criteria. Although there are many systems for evaluating information, most of us don't apply those systems with any consistency. It is important to develop this discipline, for it allows you to select a course of action and move forward, confident that you are pursuing the best-balanced choice.

Conviction

Conviction can be defined as belief, certainty, and desire. Conviction is what keeps you and the team on the coaching leadership road. It helps you stay the course when you are tempted to fall back into old habits. Conviction supports you as you move to do the right thing even though doing things right used to be enough.

Step 4: Taking Action

What Happens Now?

Although leading from the inside out requires action in each step, it is here that you and the team are squarely in the spotlight. Up to this point, you have expressed an intention to move in a new direction, and you have gathered the data you need to do so. You have considered the data, and you have created a plan that you believe will carry you toward the goals you have identified. Now it's time for you to put that plan into action. To set yourself and the team up to succeed, consider the following guidelines.

Committing to Actions and Moving Forward as Agreed

Let people know what you're committing to. Describe your plans and your time line. Then do it. As Dick Brown, CEO of EDS, explained,

> It's critical to measure each executive . . . against their commitments. I use the word "commitment" deliberately. It's easier to miss a budget than a commitment, because a budget is just an accumulation of numbers. A commitment is your personal pledge to get the job done. (quoted in Breen, *Fast Company*, 2001, p. 113)

Let the team know that you expect promises to be kept. Create that expectation with each other. It's okay to start small. Give yourself and the team specific, manageable, measurable assignments with dates and time frames. Lay out the upcoming weeks and months, and build in the practice time you need. Schedule your actions in your PC, your Palm Pilot, or your Daytimer. Remember, you are creating new habits for yourself and your team. You are writing a new chapter in your team's history. The story might be similar to this one:

Hal told his executive team that he had heard several messages in his feedback and that one was their concern about the decision-making process. Specifically, he recognized that he didn't always ask for much input before making up his mind. He knew he came into meetings with a course of action already mapped out in his head. He believed there was a benefit to having them more involved in the process, and he made the following agreements:

- Starting with next week's meeting, I will send out an agenda in advance of our meetings indicating when a decision is necessary.
- I expect that you will come prepared to discuss the issue and share your thinking on the topic.
- I will hold my comments until the end of the conversation.
- I don't guarantee that you will always get your way, but I do promise to listen to what you have to say.
- If you see me slipping, you have my permission to remind me of my commitment; interrupt me, or use the talking stick.
- I will collect your feedback about how I'm doing in our standard meeting critique form.

Creating Feedback and Support Mechanisms

Contact the resources you identified in your plan and enlist their support. Once you've shared what you intend to do, ask for their help, and describe specifically what you'd like them to do. Most people will be willing to support you if they know what you need and if it is something they can provide. If you are too general or too vague, however, people will be unclear about what you want, and chances are you won't get the quality of support you need. For example, let's look again at Hal. He described what he was planning to do, and he asked the team for their help. He specifically suggested that they interrupt him or use the talking stick, and he promised to solicit their feedback on the meeting critique form.

As you and the team move forward with your plans, action is taking place in several venues. You have interactions with the whole team. If team members have identified specific behaviors they are working on in this setting, the team can provide feedback and support during and following team meetings. The team might add an evaluation to the end of each meeting, rating the team's overall performance and individual members' specific performance in agreed-on areas (e.g., confronting effectively, asking skillful questions, generating consensus). Or team members might give each other individual feedback one-on-one in either a structured or an unstructured way. Only through constant practice, repetition, and refinement will you and the individuals on your team develop your skills in leading from the inside out.

Rewarding Desired Behavior and Correcting Missteps

As everyone is moving forward with his or her action plans, it is equally important to reinforce the behavior you agreed on when you see it and to correct missteps when you see them. Part of the process is learning from mistakes. The process is strengthened when individuals see you coaching someone with care. The process is weakened, however, if everyone isn't held to the agreed-on standard. If team members continue to make the same mistakes, their commitment to behaving differently is brought into question—and so is yours.

For example, one team agreed to hold regular status meetings with their own departments and to forward a copy of the minutes to their senior team colleagues. During the initial 3-month period, Mark didn't forward any minutes to the team. When they met next, Robert commended the team on their progress in holding meetings with their departments. He then asked Mark why they hadn't received any minutes from his meetings. Mark replied that he had been busy with "real work" and hadn't held any meetings. Robert reminded him of the team's commitment and reaffirmed that keeping their staff informed was part of their "real work." He asked Mark what he might need from the team to make his meetings happen. Mark said he could do it on his own. Robert then suggested that Mark hold his first meeting before the team reconvened and reminded him that he expected to receive a copy of the minutes.

Staying the Course

Changing the quality of interactions between you and the team, between team members, and between the team members and their own direct reports is exciting. It's scary. It's also very hard work. Your resolve and your patience will be tested frequently along the way. For each challenge that you handle well, you are modeling the behavior that you hope your entire team will emulate. For each challenge that you handle poorly, you create an opportunity to evaluate what went wrong, correct it, and demonstrate your resolve and your willingness to learn from your mistakes.

If you are serious about leading from the inside out, every time you practice your new behaviors, you'll experience an adrenaline rush similar to that of any extreme sport participant. The difference is, this rush is self-perpetuating and doesn't require any protective equipment. Every time you put yourself out there, practice what you've been talking about, and do it more and more skillfully, you reinforce the energy running between you and the team. Likewise, every time the team goes out there and performs in a more skillful way, it builds on the energy that is being created by each individual member. Members continue the process with each other and take it out into the rest of the organization.

When you begin, there will be a clear line between your "new behavior practice" time and your "old behavior" time. As you become more skilled at saying what you mean, asking skillful questions, inquiring into others' reasoning, and actively promoting the valued behaviors that you and the team identified earlier, the line will begin to blur. Eventually, you will find yourself leading from the inside out in every interaction.

Competencies

The competencies required for Step 4, taking action, are interdependence, willingness to risk, execution, and reinforcement.

Interdependence

Interdependence requires strong team members who each contribute substantially and recognize that what they do has an impact on their colleagues and ultimately the business. Interdependence is more than understanding product flow or an organization chart. It requires an understanding of the leverage to be gained from working together, a willingness to assume leadership and to relinquish it as appropriate. It is trust in your colleagues and in the strength of the team. It is knowing that everyone is focused on the goal and is doing everything in his or her power to get the team there.

Willingness to Risk

Willingness to risk is the team's commitment to trying out new behaviors and learning from them. This includes disclosing information, asking for feedback, and sharing control. This commitment allows team members to practice skills and to grow in the process. As Rayona Sharpnack explained, "Only two things can come from practice—failure and success—and they both have to come before any real learning can happen" (quoted in Dahle, 2000, p. 276).

That's the mind-set you should create with the team to support the new behaviors you've asked for.

Execution

Execution occurs on two levels for the team. The first level has to do with process—"What did we say?" "What did we do?" and "Did we get better?" The second level has to do with outcomes—"What did we accomplish?" and "How did we change?" Spreading coaching leadership throughout the team requires everyone to be on the field—you've got to show up, practice, and improve. Results count.

Reinforcement

Reinforcement requires letting the team know if you like what you see. If you do, you'll get more of it. You also have to let them know if they drift off purpose so that they can make course corrections. Reinforcement requires paying attention and responding in a timely, informative way to what you see. Compared with a traditional organization, an organization where coaching leadership is practiced has more information in play. You make use of that information when you are reinforcing behaviors with your team.

Step 5: Evaluating Your Progress

How Are We Doing?

Results are at the heart of leading from the inside out. Evaluating your progress and the progress of the team is one of the ways you demonstrate that you are serious. Evaluating the work you and the team have been doing contributes to the credibility of the overall process. After all, the process can hardly be described as results driven if those results are not evaluated.

Measuring and Tracking Progress

It is possible to evaluate your progress in two dimensions at once: the outcomes you and the team achieve and the process you and the team employ. As you consider the elements you are measuring, remember you are looking for movement. This movement may be

- Directly observed by you or others
- Self-reported by team members
- Noted in 360-degree feedback
- Discussed in meetings with department teams
- Evaluated by you and your team

In Step 2, you agreed to collect certain data. In Step 3, you received feedback and created an action plan. Now that you have been working on your action plan for an agreed-on period of time, you can evaluate your progress. You can measure and track your progress incrementally as you move along and at the end of the evaluation period. You can discuss your progress in team meetings, one-on-one meetings with team members, and meetings with people beyond the boundaries of your team.

Linking Actions and Consequences

Holding yourself and others accountable is part of moving forward with this process. Providing feedback in a timely way and clearly explaining the relationship between actions and consequences is critical. The credibility of the entire process hinges on the integrity of the cause and effect to which you have committed. The spectrum of consequences for actions that don't meet agreed-on standards can range from coaching to reprimand to withholding of rewards to punishment or censure of some sort. Errors or missteps are rarely fatal unless they are continually repeated or unless they run totally counter to the values that you and the team have publicly endorsed.

Obviously, the best consequence for results is noting incremental success along the line of continuous improvement—for both the team and the organization as a whole. Actions and consequences need to happen in two dimensions: a change from old behaviors to coaching behaviors and a change from old business results to more successful business results. As we will see in the next part of this book, the purpose of becoming a coaching leader is to improve learning, performance, and results. There is no point in having more effective conversations unless they lead to more successful interactions, work processes, handoffs, and service. When an entire leadership team makes coaching a way of being, the organization gains a competitive advantage that is experienced day to day by employees, vendors, and customers and is reflected in the bottom line.

Recognizing Achievements

It is important to recognize individual and team achievements and to celebrate them along the way. Of course, at the end of the evaluation period, the team and team members can engage in visible celebrations, enjoying the progress they've made and recognizing the effort each person has expended so far. Celebrations can take the form of the following:

- Team off-sites
- Publications detailing successes
- Presentations
- Rewards for individuals and teams

- Parties
- Additional resources

These celebrations can also be used along the way as individuals, and the team, make progress in their efforts to strengthen their leadership. You will recall that Pamela's team, described in the beginning of this section, made use of several of these ideas. They created a "Monthly Scorecard" to track their progress. They talked about progress in team meetings and one-on-one. And they played a special role in their annual conference. In addition to improved team functioning, they experienced successes in many operational areas, including recruiting, retention, budgeting, and office openings. The team talked candidly among themselves and with others about the link between their new behaviors and performance and the business results they achieved.

Competencies

The competencies required for Step 5, evaluating progress, are measurement, a learning mind-set, follow-through, recognition, and a future focus.

Measurement

Measuring requires you to compare your current reality with the desired state you previously defined. Have you and the team achieved your goals? What processes, procedures, and interactions have changed and in what ways? How can you (and others) tell the difference? What are the benefits? The process of measuring informs you about your progress and indicates where you and the team go from here.

Learning Mind-Set

A learning mind-set is the ability to pull information out of your experiences and deepen your understanding of the team and individual members. Curiosity, discovery, and application drive a learning mind-set. A learning mind-set allows you to reflect on your actions, assess the results, and apply that learning to current and future challenges. A learning mind-set places a high value on collecting and sharing information and sees virtually hundreds of opportunities daily that contribute information to an ever-expanding knowledge set.

Follow-Through

Follow-through is moving forward in the way you said you would. It is keeping your promises and being an "honest broker" (Teal, 1996, p. 5). It involves holding yourself and others accountable for the agreements you make and the performance standards you set. Follow-through requires consistency, devotion to the goal, and behaving as agreed.

Recognition

Recognition is noticing what team members and the team as a whole are accomplishing, the progress they're making, and the effort they're expending. It involves rewarding team members for practicing the coaching leader behaviors and developing those skills—for performing as agreed. You can recognize the team in many ways both informally and formally. The important thing is to let them know that you see what they're doing and that it matters.

Future Focus

Future focus requires a relentless pursuit of "What's next?" It involves continuous improvement and ongoing learning. It requires a keen sense of market realities and an eye on the competition. It also means that you and the team always assess your present situation honestly, allowing yourselves to be informed by what is so that you can create what is going to be.

By now, you are well on your way working through the elements of coaching leadership with your team. You are creating a legacy that will last long into the future. In the next chapter, you will begin to explore how you will build on that work as you and your team move this new way of leading throughout your organization.

WORKSHEET 3.1: The Leader and the Team

Step 1: Establishing the Coaching Relationship

DEFINING THE DESIRED OUTCOMES

1. **What I want from my relationship with my team is:**

   ____

   ____

2. **The way I'd like my team members to interact with each other is:**

   ____

   ____

3. **The way I want my team members to interact with their departments or groups is:**

   ____

   ____

4. **The benefits I believe these interactions will have for our team and our organization are:**

   ____

   ____

Tips and Examples

- ❑ Reframe your relationship with the team.
- ❑ Provide the context.
- ❑ Establish a team vision and make it real.
- ❑ Share your reasoning for pursuing coaching leadership.
- ❑ Discuss the risks and rewards of this fundamental change in interactions.
- ❑ Assess your credibility with the team.
- ❑ Create a time line and a plan.
- ❑ Identify the resources you and the team will need.
- ❑ Agree on the new measures for success.
- ❑ Link team performance to business performance.
- ❑ Recognize that everyone may not want to practice coaching leadership.

QUESTIONS TO CONSIDER

1. **In what ways do I want the team to act differently?**
2. **What will our team agreements look like?**
3. **How will we handle it when we get off track?**
4. **What support systems can we create to help?**

(continued)

WORKSHEET 3.1: The Leader and the Team (*continued*)

5. **Which competencies will be most challenging for me? For the team?**
6. **What are some development activities we can use to work on those specific competencies?**
7. **What changes do I expect from myself in interacting with the team?**
8. **How well does this model of leading fit with our organization?**
9. **What will be the easiest changes to make? The most difficult changes?**
10. **What will I consider a successful result?**
11. **What is the final vision I have for the team?**
12. **How am I going to paint the team vision and use it to motivate and incite action?**

Tips and Examples

- ❑ Paint a clear picture of where you want to go.
- ❑ Provide the business case supporting your vision.
- ❑ Deliver the same message again and again.
- ❑ Develop a team charter, including ground rules and communication guidelines.
- ❑ Agree on systems for decision making, problem solving, feedback, and managing conflict.
- ❑ Jointly set goals and milestones.
- ❑ Create visible measurements.
- ❑ Recognize incremental progress.
- ❑ Applaud genuine efforts.
- ❑ Demonstrate the courage required to role-model the new behaviors.
- ❑ Recognize when you or the team fall into old habits.
- ❑ Allow yourselves time to develop new skills.
- ❑ Resist the temptation to "fix" things on your own—let the team work it out.
- ❑ Expect that new agreements will be kept.
- ❑ Call people on inaction.

RESOURCES AND TOOLS

1. **The resources for developing my relationship with the team are:**

   ____

   ____

2. **I expect the relationship with my team to have the following characteristics:**

   ____

   ____

(continued)

WORKSHEET 3.1: The Leader and the Team (*continued*)

Tips and Examples

- ❑ Some possible team resources are outside consultants and facilitators, guest speakers, books and articles, planned training and development activities, one-on-one meetings, team meetings, benchmarking of other organizations, organization climate surveys, and outside coaching leadership training.

COMPETENCIES

On a scale of 1 to 5 (1 = nonexistent; 5 = outstanding), rate yourself on the following competencies for this step:

1. **Vision** 1 2 3 4 5

   Two specific ways I will demonstrate this competency in this step:

   a. ______________________________

   b. ______________________________

2. **Integrity** 1 2 3 4 5

   Two specific ways I will demonstrate this competency in this step:

   a. ______________________________

   b. ______________________________

3. **Courage** 1 2 3 4 5

   Two specific ways I will demonstrate this competency in this step:

   a. ______________________________

   b. ______________________________

4. **Openness** 1 2 3 4 5

   Two specific ways I will demonstrate this competency in this step:

   a. ______________________________

   b. ______________________________

5. **Passion** 1 2 3 4 5

   Two specific ways I will demonstrate this competency in this step:

   a. ______________________________

   b. ______________________________

Tips and Examples

- ❑ Schedule time for the team.
- ❑ Provide resources as agreed.
- ❑ Hold yourself and the team accountable.
- ❑ Acknowledge the challenge ahead.

(continued)

WORKSHEET 3.1: The Leader and the Team (*continued*)

- ❑ Share your own thoughts and feelings.
- ❑ Create a learning space within the team.
- ❑ Fuel the change effort with personal energy and passion.
- ❑ Align your actions with your message.
- ❑ Keep your promises.
- ❑ Seek out feedback and use the data to inform your actions.

WORKSHEET 3.2: The Leader and the Team

Step 2: Collecting and Analyzing Data

DEFINING THE DESIRED OUTCOMES

1. **What I want to know about my effectiveness with my team is:**

   ____

   ____

2. **The information we need about how the team operates and is perceived includes:**

   ____

   ____

3. **The information needed to understand how team members operate with their own departments and others is:**

   ____

   ____

Tips and Examples

- ❑ Solicit feedback.
- ❑ Incorporate regular feedback into your team meetings.
- ❑ Create opportunities to see others in action with their teams.
- ❑ Provide training for the team.
- ❑ Create learning opportunities for the team.
- ❑ Practice the skills of inquiry and reflection.
- ❑ Encourage the team to act as resources for one another.
- ❑ Use outside resources to collect data.
- ❑ Encourage team members to benchmark other organizations.
- ❑ Assign and discuss books, articles, and so forth.
- ❑ Invite guest speakers.
- ❑ Create opportunities to see others in action with their teams.
- ❑ Use business challenges to create real-time team problem-solving opportunities.

QUESTIONS TO CONSIDER

1. **What do I need to know about our team interactions?**
2. **What do I need to know about my interactions with my individual team members?**
3. **What do I need to know about my team members' interactions with others?**
4. **Where can we get this information?**

(continued)

WORKSHEET 3.2: The Leader and the Team (*continued*)

5. **How will we gather the information? What tools will we use?**
6. **How will we share the data we collect?**
7. **How will we use the data we collect?**

Tips and Examples

- ❑ Consider information you collect within a larger context.
- ❑ Look for themes in the data you collect.
- ❑ Identify the recurring messages.
- ❑ Look for the differences (if any) between feedback from employees, peers, and customers.
- ❑ Consider your blind spots in perceptions.
- ❑ Look for disconnects between stated intentions and perceptions.
- ❑ Use data to develop a benchmark.
- ❑ Select the areas where you and the team will focus.

RESOURCES AND TOOLS

1. **Self-assessments we can use to rate ourselves include:**

   ____

   ____

2. **Organizational data we can use include:**

   ____

   ____

3. **The methods we can use to collect data are:**

   ____

   ____

4. **The way we expect to share this data is:**

   ____

   ____

5. **The role we each intend to play within this step is:**

   ____

   ____

6. **Possible categories/themes in which the data can be organized are:**

   ____

   ____

(continued)

WORKSHEET 3.2: The Leader and the Team *(continued)*

Tips and Examples

- ❑ Examples of self-assessments are the Myers-Briggs Type Indicator Team Profile (Myers, 1998), which can be used to generate an MBTI Team Report; the Group Styles Inventory (Cooke & Lafferty, 1993); the Team Development Scale (Dyer, 1987, pp. 69-72); the Team Development Survey (Parker, 1992); and meeting critiques, customized 360-degree surveys, climate studies, and image studies.
- ❑ Tie your data collection to organizational expectations.
- ❑ Be prepared to actively participate in the process.
- ❑ Organize data into meaningful themes—for the team as a whole and for each individual member.
- ❑ Determine how you will share the data.
- ❑ Manage expectations by clarifying the actions you and the team intend to take.

COMPETENCIES

On a scale of 1 to 5 (1 = nonexistent; 5 = outstanding), rate yourself on each competency for this step:

1. **Inquiry** 1 2 3 4 5

   Two specific ways I will demonstrate this competency in this step:

   a. ______________________________

   b. ______________________________

2. **Reframing** 1 2 3 4 5

   Two specific ways I will demonstrate this competency in this step:

   a. ______________________________

   b. ______________________________

3. **Listening** 1 2 3 4 5

   Two specific ways I will demonstrate this competency in this step:

   a. ______________________________

   b. ______________________________

4. **Sorting** 1 2 3 4 5

   Two specific ways I will demonstrate this competency in this step:

   a. ______________________________

   b. ______________________________

5. **Patience** 1 2 3 4 5

   Two specific ways I will demonstrate this competency in this step:

   a. ______________________________

   b. ______________________________

(continued)

WORKSHEET 3.2: The Leader and the Team (*continued*)

Tips and Examples

- ❑ Practice listening for what is said and what is not said.
- ❑ Ask skillful questions.
- ❑ Monitor intent—go after the truth.
- ❑ Consider the source of information—what does the information say about their needs?
- ❑ Extract meaning from the data.
- ❑ Face up to uncomfortable data.
- ❑ Sort data so they can be understood and acted upon.
- ❑ Support the team by keeping the vision out front.
- ❑ Consider the data from more than one perspective.
- ❑ Remind yourself and the team that changing behavior takes time.

WORKSHEET 3.3: The Leader and the Team

Step 3: Processing Feedback and Planning Actions

DEFINING THE DESIRED OUTCOMES

1. We will acknowledge feedback from others by:

____

____

2. Our readiness to accept feedback will be demonstrated by:

____

____

3. We will communicate our action plans in the following ways:

____

____

4. Possible objectives within the action plans might include:

____

____

Tips and Examples

- ❑ Capitalize on your strengths first.
- ❑ Perceptions are the only reality there is for leadership.
- ❑ You must accept others' perceptions; you need not agree with them.
- ❑ Identify the gaps between the team's current performance and desired performance.
- ❑ Consider how you might share your action plans with others.
- ❑ Devote time to working through the data.
- ❑ Agree on how you will acknowledge feedback.
- ❑ Figure out how to get examples or clarification if needed.
- ❑ Generate a planning format that you and the team will follow.

QUESTIONS TO CONSIDER

1. How can we capitalize on our strengths?
2. How open are we to feedback from others?
3. What are we willing to change? What is our reasoning?
4. What are the consequences of doing nothing?
5. What would be a "quick win" for us?
6. Who needs to know about our action plans?
7. How will we track and communicate our progress?

(continued)

WORKSHEET 3.3: The Leader and the Team *(continued)*

Tips and Examples

- ❑ Keep the vision in mind as you plan for the future.
- ❑ Identify resources that you and the team can use to help you.
- ❑ Focus on the actions you can take.
- ❑ Let go of the past; plan for the future!
- ❑ Encourage risk taking.
- ❑ Redefine "mistake."
- ❑ Notice your own reactions—what "hooks" you? Reframe when needed.
- ❑ Determine what behaviors create perceptions.
- ❑ Create a bias for action.
- ❑ Set goals that are consistent with your values.
- ❑ Enlist the support of your colleagues and staff.
- ❑ Consider sharing your development goals with employees and stakeholders.

RESOURCES AND TOOLS

1. **We will document our action plans by:**

   ____

   ____

2. **We will go about the process of action planning by:**

   ____

   ____

Tips and Examples

- ❑ Complete a written action plan.
- ❑ Look for models and benchmarks.
- ❑ Link action plans to business results.
- ❑ Generate alternative actions.
- ❑ Determine what actions you can all agree to.
- ❑ Set "stretch" goals.
- ❑ Make your objectives measurable.
- ❑ Create both team and individual action plans.
- ❑ Plans can change—revise them as necessary.
- ❑ Devote time to reviewing plans and progress at agreed-on intervals.

(continued)

WORKSHEET 3.3: The Leader and the Team (*continued*)

COMPETENCIES

On a scale of 1 to 5 (1 = nonexistent; 5 = outstanding), rate yourself on each competency for this step:

1. **Truth Telling** **1 2 3 4 5**

   Two specific ways I will demonstrate this competency in this step:

   a. ______________________________

   b. ______________________________

2. **Empathy** **1 2 3 4 5**

   Two specific ways I will demonstrate this competency in this step:

   a. ______________________________

   b. ______________________________

3. **Ability to Generate and Evaluate Alternatives** **1 2 3 4 5**

   Two specific ways I will demonstrate this competency in this step:

   a. ______________________________

   b. ______________________________

4. **Conviction** **1 2 3 4 5**

   Two specific ways I will demonstrate this competency in this step:

   a. ______________________________

   b. ______________________________

Tips and Examples

- ❑ Use skillful questions to clarify and understand feedback.
- ❑ Share observations and perceptions honestly.
- ❑ Treat others with positive regard and understanding.
- ❑ Overcome fear, ego, and impatience.
- ❑ Develop ways to track accomplishments.
- ❑ Reframe by taking different perspectives.
- ❑ Help the team consider alternatives and implications.
- ❑ Be committed to learning.
- ❑ Demonstrate a willingness to laugh at yourself.
- ❑ Use humor constructively.
- ❑ Be accountable for your own change and growth.
- ❑ Keep your promises.
- ❑ Acknowledge that change is like grieving—be patient with yourself and others.
- ❑ Role-model coaching behaviors.
- ❑ Keep the vision out in front.

WORKSHEET 3.4: The Leader and the Team

Step 4: Taking Action

DEFINING THE DESIRED OUTCOMES

1. **We will hold ourselves accountable for action by doing the following:**

   ____

   ____

2. **We will share our progress within and outside of the team by:**

   ____

   ____

3. **We will celebrate our successes by:**

   ____

   ____

4. **We will learn from each other's mistakes by:**

   ____

   ____

Tips and Examples

- ❑ Consider the impact of your actions on the team.
- ❑ Consider the impact of your actions with your direct reports.
- ❑ Create the feedback loops you need to ensure your success.
- ❑ Ask for the help you need.
- ❑ Demonstrate your willingness to risk.
- ❑ Encourage each other and recognize progress.
- ❑ Focus on the present and the future, not the past.
- ❑ Consider the team's impact on the rest of the organization.
- ❑ Build in rewards and reinforcement.
- ❑ Create opportunities for the team to share progress.

QUESTIONS TO CONSIDER

1. **How are you helping your team move forward?**
2. **How do you know your team members are moving this work out into their departments?**
3. **Are you demanding the best from everyone?**
4. **How are team members helping each other?**
5. **What is the team learning, and how is the team sharing what has been learned?**

(continued)

WORKSHEET 3.4: The Leader and the Team (*continued*)

6. **What is working well?**
7. **What isn't working so well?**

Tips and Examples

- ❑ Meet with the team and team members regularly.
- ❑ Include an action update discussion.
- ❑ Establish ongoing support mechanisms within the team.
- ❑ Utilize outside coaches and facilitators when needed.
- ❑ Use one-up meetings (structured meetings held between the leader and the direct reports of his or her team members without the team member present) to review incremental progress.
- ❑ Remind team members to keep agreements.
- ❑ Reinforce expectations.
- ❑ Talk through and resolve problem areas.
- ❑ Recognize and resolve any disconnects between team and individual actions.
- ❑ Establish a process for continuous learning and sharing.
- ❑ Leverage the strengths of team members.

RESOURCES AND TOOLS

1. **The tools we will use to document our progress and actions are:**

____

____

2. **The tools we will use for ongoing learning and support are:**

____

____

Tips and Examples

- ❑ Create a tracking system.
- ❑ Dedicate time during each meeting to coach and adjust.
- ❑ Incorporate ongoing learning and skill building (guest speakers, facilitators, book readings).
- ❑ Keep perspective.
- ❑ Keep initial momentum, goals, and motivation alive.
- ❑ Create tools to track team results, team member results, and linkage to overall business results.

(continued)

WORKSHEET 3.4: The Leader and the Team (*continued*)

COMPETENCIES

On a scale of 1 to 5 (1 = nonexistent; 5 = outstanding), rate yourself on each competency for this step:

1. **Interdependence** **1 2 3 4 5**

   Two specific ways I will demonstrate this competency in this step:

   a. ______________________________

   b. ______________________________

2. **Willingness to Risk** **1 2 3 4 5**

   Two specific ways I will demonstrate this competency in this step:

   a. ______________________________

   b. ______________________________

3. **Execution** **1 2 3 4 5**

   Two specific ways I will demonstrate this competency in this step:

   a. ______________________________

   b. ______________________________

4. **Reinforcement** **1 2 3 4 5**

   Two specific ways I will demonstrate this competency in this step:

   a. ______________________________

   b. ______________________________

Tips and Examples

- ❑ Look for opportunities for the team to collaborate.
- ❑ Acknowledge early efforts.
- ❑ Reinforce the desired behaviors when you see them.
- ❑ Analyze performance and help the team to make midcourse corrections.
- ❑ When stuck, ask, "What's the worst that could happen?"
- ❑ Use critical thinking!
- ❑ Learn by trying it out!
- ❑ Keep explaining why you are doing this.
- ❑ Describe the business results you expect.

WORKSHEET 3.5: The Leader and the Team

Step 5: Evaluating Your Progress

DEFINING THE DESIRED OUTCOMES

1. **We will evaluate the team's progress in the following ways:**

   ____

   ____

2. **We will make our progress public by:**

   ____

   ____

Tips and Examples

- ❑ Measure the effectiveness of each action you took.
- ❑ Review the results in context. Look at the edges, the handoffs.
- ❑ Refine processes as necessary around the seams.
- ❑ Celebrate the team's successes!
- ❑ Discover what is contributing to your successes and leverage it.
- ❑ Measure success not only in terms of coaching leadership but also in terms of linkages to business success.
- ❑ Look at how the team members are taking their learning out into their own departments.

QUESTIONS TO CONSIDER

1. **What is our evaluation of our progress?**
2. **Where have we made the greatest headway? How do we know?**
3. **Where are we hitting barriers?**
4. **What will it take to overcome them?**
5. **How can we help each other?**
6. **How are we a stronger team because of our actions?**
7. **How are we a stronger organization because of our actions?**
8. **What are our next steps?**

Tips and Examples

- ❑ Make performance, not nonperformance, the standard.
- ❑ Measure your progress on your action plan regularly and often.
- ❑ Publicize the results.

(continued)

WORKSHEET 3.5: The Leader and the Team *(continued)*

- ❑ Measure the impact of your actions on you, others, and the organization.
- ❑ Reward performance as agreed.
- ❑ Make rewards visible.
- ❑ Help everyone understand the benefits.
- ❑ Hold everyone accountable.
- ❑ Show courage in delivering consequences as promised.
- ❑ Continue to ask the team for new ideas and suggestions for improvement.
- ❑ Reset the standards and begin the cycle again.

RESOURCES AND TOOLS

1. The tools we will use to measure our progress are:

____

____

2. The process we will use to review results is:

____

____

Tips and Examples

- ❑ Examples of measurement tools are team ratings on agreed-on elements using scales of 1 to 5, peer evaluations, surveys, interviews, performance indicators such as turnover, exit interview data, sales numbers, and production targets.
- ❑ Document action conversations and events that demonstrate success or failure.
- ❑ Extract lessons learned from every action.
- ❑ Share what is learned throughout the team.

COMPETENCIES

On a scale of 1 to 5 (1 = nonexistent; 5 = outstanding), rate yourself on each competency for this step:

1. Measurement 1 2 3 4 5

Two specific ways I will demonstrate this competency in this step:

a. ____

b. ____

(continued)

WORKSHEET 3.5: The Leader and the Team (*continued*)

2. Learning Mind-Set 1 2 3 4 5

Two specific ways I will demonstrate this competency in this step:

a. ______________________________

b. ______________________________

3. Follow-Through 1 2 3 4 5

Two specific ways I will demonstrate this competency in this step:

a. ______________________________

b. ______________________________

4. Recognition 1 2 3 4 5

Two specific ways I will demonstrate this competency in this step:

a. ______________________________

b. ______________________________

5. Future Focus 1 2 3 4 5

Two specific ways I will demonstrate this competency in this step:

a. ______________________________

b. ______________________________

Tips and Examples

- ❑ Link actions and consequences.
- ❑ Communicate progress within and outside of the team.
- ❑ Continually improve systems.
- ❑ Analyze contributions.
- ❑ Create a culture that is biased toward action.
- ❑ Develop yourself and those around you.
- ❑ Learn from your mistakes and move on.
- ❑ Look toward the future and what comes next.
- ❑ Be committed to learning as a way of life.

part 4

From Traditional to Coaching Organization

Coaching is destined to be the leadership approach of the twenty-first century.

—James Belasco,
Foreword to M. Goldsmith et al.,
Coaching for Leadership

This chapter ties the previous two chapters together—the leader and self, the leader and the team, and now the leader and the entire organization. To make your organization a coaching organization, you, as the committed leader, must redefine the traditional hierarchical paradigm that exists in your organization and convert it to a coaching partnership.

When you attempt to establish a coaching culture, you are grappling with all the issues of communication, discovery, and change that have been discussed in the previous chapters—but now compounded 100-fold. Your organization, with all the many individuals making up the whole, has evolved over many years and is subject to its own barriers, mind-sets, culture, defensive routines, blocks to learning, and frames of reference. We all have heard too many times phrases like "We don't do things like that here," "It can't be done," "You can't say things like that," or "You'd better go through the appropriate channels."

The momentum of an organization is like a stampede of elephants, a 10-ton semi speeding down the highway, or a steam locomotive rolling down a mountain without brakes. How do you, as the leader, harness that energy? How do you focus, motivate, and inspire hundreds and sometimes thousands of individuals into becoming a unified group—more important, a unified group that is working toward mutually reinforced goals and that is fulfilled, fully informed, synergistic, continually learning and improving, and successfully outperforming itself and the competition?

Ironically, although this kinetic energy is present in most organizations, there also exists a monumental inertia—a resistance to changing, learning, opening up to new approaches and options, and thinking and acting in new ways. Many organizations are stuck. This is a marvelous dilemma that leaders must tackle. Traditional leadership approaches no longer seem effective; or, if they are effective, they achieve success in only one situation or for a limited period of time.

This chapter establishes that a coaching environment embraces the necessary characteristics that today's workers demand. An organization that is built on the basis of a coaching mind-set is able to capture the human spirit—and it is this ingredient that aligns personal and organizational goals and results in high performance. This is not total quality management, participative management, reengineering, or process improvement. This is a "way of being" for you and the entire organization. A coaching organization is an embedded culture in which carefully chosen tools—whether they are teams, quality initiatives, or open-book management—can be successfully implemented.

Working with your own coach and then coaching your top team give you the appropriate skills, focus, and positioning. You begin to make coaching your very own. It becomes part of who you are, and your style can be identified as that of a "coaching leader." But now what? As a leader of a company, your goal is to lead—to lead an entire organization toward fulfilling the corporate mission and vision. This is a destiny that you must shape so that it becomes the fabric of the organization on many levels—monetarily, personally, culturally, individually, environmentally, and socially. How the hell are you supposed to do that?

Many leaders have been able to achieve incredible goals—Gandhi, Mother Teresa, Hitler, Jack Welch, Saddam Hussein, John Kennedy, and Bill Gates. In this context, however, we are talking about a leader who is able to build an organization that upholds certain values, displays certain characteristics, practices well-defined behaviors, and achieves specific results. We are talking about a coaching organization in which a leader practices a coaching style and the entire organizational infrastructure supports coaching behaviors and results.

Given that we are going to try to encompass the entire organization, this chapter covers a lot more ground than the previous ones. We are going to discuss the philosophy and basics of a coaching organization before going into the mechanics of how to lead and develop one. First, there will be a discussion of what constitutes a coaching organization and why a coaching style of leadership is necessary in today's world. Issues of bottom-line results and goal alignment are addressed. We then present the coaching system, a model that will help you assess an organization and plan coaching strategies. Last, a comprehensive case study is shared that follows the steps for building a coaching organization. As in all of the chapters, specific competencies are outlined. Worksheets for each step are at the end of the chapter. You can use and adapt these job aids to assist in your journey toward a coaching organization.

The What and Why of a Coaching Organization

A Couple of Scenarios

So what is a coaching organization? A definition might go something like this: an organization based on a coaching mind-set, supported by a coaching infrastructure, with the aim of achieving organizational strategy, individual goals, and bottom-line results.

So what is it really? Let's look at a couple of scenarios. In which organization would you like to work?

Scenario 1: You get up on a Monday morning and groan. You dress, drive to work, and enter your windowless cubicle. Coworkers halfheartedly greet you with a "Hey, Joe, welcome to another stinking week." You spend an hour filling out endless forms that don't seem to have any meaning. Midmorning, you attend a grueling 2-hour staff meeting in which the boss drones on about competition and declining sales and makes cliché threats like "heads will roll." One brave employee makes a few suggestions that could actually improve things. The boss explains that such actions are against company policy.

You gulp down a sandwich at lunch in order to have time to run a few personal errands. You know you have to work late to meet a deadline, and flexibility is not part of your company's lexicon. Your excitement for the afternoon is your yearly performance appraisal. You have actually prepared and outlined your accomplishments, areas for improvement, and goals for next year. You rarely see your boss, and you want to make the most of this event. However, you soon learn that your efforts are wasted. Sure, your boss listens for the mandatory 10 minutes, but then he shifts into gear and basically says, "You're doing a great job, keep up the good work, try to improve your attitude with the secretaries, and let's hope business will get better next year so we all can get a bigger bonus."

You smile and shake your head as you leave the boss's office. You pass the vapid plaque on the wall, "Our Company Values." You know you will continue to do a good job because of your own internal drive and sense of accomplishment but certainly not because of anything having to do with the company. The company pays well. There are good benefits and stock options. But let's face it, boring is boring. In another 6 months, once you've mastered the new programming system, you'll move on to another organization. Maybe you can figure out how to work only 4 days a week.

Scenario 2: It's Monday morning, and you jump out of bed. You decide to jog, play with your toddler for an hour, and relax at the nearby coffeehouse before heading off to work. You know you need to be at the office for a meeting at 10:00, so you plan around it. You know you'll be putting in a lot of hours this week, so you want to be appropriately energized and focused. You worked at home for a few hours over the weekend because you have home access to all of your electronic files. You discovered a solution to the client's request that you can't wait to share with your team.

When you enter your work site, there is a hubbub of excitement. Work groups are talking intensely in "dialogue centers," complete with noise modifiers, whiteboards, sofas, and computer terminals. You are waved over by your own team as they make room for you at the center table. John, the team leader, displays a project flow chart (with focused goals, milestones, updated measurements, and notes) on the overhead screen and sits back. The group immediately attacks the information, noting discrepancies, brainstorming alternatives, and coaching one another on assumptions and more creative approaches. John jumps into the conversation as a working member, providing support and guidance: "What has gone well? Why? Where is there room for improvement?" He tells Lisa, "Great suggestion. The obstacles you point out are challenging, but I expect you to tackle them successfully." The meeting wraps up in the agreed-on 40 minutes.

You run off to a production meeting. During this 3-hour work session, you and your colleagues hash out several sticky problems and develop the second phase of plans for the customer. This requires an incredible amount of collaboration and buy-in as you all question assumptions, break through personal mind-sets, and develop a solution that surpasses everyone's expectations.

You grab a quick lunch at the on-site café and then meet with one of your junior team members. You are coaching her in two areas: how to frame discussions with clients and how to use a new cost accounting program. After the coaching session, you take 20 minutes to review your personal vision, mission, goals, and tasks. You have your quarterly review with your own coach, and you've gained some insights since your last dialogue. Basically, you've streamlined one of your work processes, and you think others might benefit from your model. Given what the company president had to say at the recent strategy update meeting, you've also refined one of your goals. The company has decided to expand its product line, and you want to be a part of the pilot. Your team leader comes by and suggests that you talk while walking outside because it's a beautiful day.

So which company would you like to lead? You have a choice. You claim that companies as described in Scenario 2 are hard to find? Perhaps. But they do exist. Some companies come very close to achieving this kind of rich environment. Other companies are struggling to get there, but they are definitely on the path. You can find pockets of such cultures at Lucent Technologies,

Hewlett-Packard, Patagonia, Southwest Airlines, Springfield ReManufacturing, Disney, Hallmark, 3M, Johnson and Johnson, FedEx, Sears, IBM, and AT&T. Countless others are not recognized by name because they are small but peacefully flourishing. The examples you find may not be perfect, and their efforts may come under a variety of names. However, all these companies are striving for basically the same thing, namely a coaching organization that

- Captures the human spirit
- Involves people in all aspects of work
- Connects each person's individual vision and goals with those of the organization
- Provides flexibility, learning, creativity, and continuous improvement
- Creates aligned structures and processes for dialogue, support, and focused results
- Achieves bottom-line success through cooperation and energy, not compliance

The Evolution From Control to Coaching

Why are organizations trying to create coaching cultures? Let's revisit the example in Scenario 1. The old company paradigm that grew out of the industrial revolution—and that many companies today still follow—is based on hierarchy, control, specialization, and job security. Evered and Selman (1989) described this as the "control-order-prescription," which fosters "being in charge, controlling others, prescribing behaviors and events, maintaining order, gaining and exercising command and control, and discarding the noncompliant" (p. 3). Senge and Wheatley, in a recent interview (McLeod, 2001), supported this further and pointed out that people are living systems. Consequently, "when we ask people to obey and they do obey, they become lifeless. They shut down. They disappear. They become automatons" (Senge, quoted in McLeod, 2001, p. 32).

But, you may point out, some companies are successful despite confining cultures. You are right—but the key word is *despite*. Most people inherently want to succeed, and they manage to produce despite the obstacles of inefficient processes, meaningless or conflicting goals, organizational politics, and oppressive procedures. They often create systems "within the system." Furthermore, these people may produce, but at a great price that includes high turnover, mediocrity, waste, and lost potential. Think of what could be achieved if these obstacles were removed. Think of the motivation, competitive advantage, and profits.

From their research and work, Evered and Selman (1989) concluded that

> a management paradigm based on building an organizational context for "coaching" can readily out perform the existing paradigm based on "control." . . . A leader must create an organizational environment in which coaching and being coached can occur continuously. You cannot generate high performance by managing by the numbers. Coaching allows you to get in touch with the human spirit. (p. 2)

Such a coaching system puts people at the center of all practices and decisions. As a leader, you have access to the same tools, technology, and consultants as everybody else (Shaffer, 2000, p. 4). People are what make the difference. Lawrence Bossidy, the exemplary leader who turned AlliedSignal around, makes a similar argument:

> The traditional bases of managerial authority are eroding. In the past, we used to reward the lone rangers in the corner offices because their achievements were brilliant even though their behavior was destructive. That day is gone. We need people who are better at persuading than at barking orders, who know how to coach and build consensus. . . .
>
> Don't get me wrong. We're not looking for backslapping nice guys. . . . Today we look for smart people with an added dimension: they have an interest in other people and derive psychic satisfaction from working with them. (Tichy & Charon, 1995, p. 76)

The Bottom Line

James Belasco (2000) boldly stated that "coaching is destined to be the leadership approach of the twenty-first century" (p. xiii). A culture of coaching nurtures leadership in every employee. The coaching leader lives in a world supported by dialogue. This kind of interactive style attracts free agents (high-performance employees) who are less likely to respect positional power as a motivator. Coaching reaches these people. They come. They stay. They outperform the competition.

That last point is an important one. We are not advocating that you build a coaching organization because "it's the nice thing to do." We are not claiming that you need to become a "coaching guru" who walks the halls of corporate America in flowing robes preaching harmony, fulfillment, and well-being. As a leader, it is understood that you must seek earnings, sales volume, productivity, and market share. You must create a coaching system, not to put smiles on faces, but to obtain solid business results from engaged, passionate people. Let's face it. The bottom line is the bottom line.

You should not build a coaching organization for the mere sake of building a coaching organization. If you do, you will go the way of those companies in the 1980s that embraced TQM, won the Baldridge Award, and then went bankrupt the following year. A coaching organization enables you to create an environment—through dialogue, vision, learning, and stretch goals—in which people develop and through which obstacles to obtaining business results are eliminated (Belasco, 2000, p. xiii). A coaching organization empowers individuals. They feel good about themselves, and when they feel good about themselves, they strive toward high performance. In a review of the book *Unlock Behavior, Unleash Profits* by Braksick, BIZNews made the point that "if the effect of leadership behavior is to encourage people to feel good about themselves, their contributions, and their potential to perform better, then increased profits will follow" ("Leadership Behaviors," 2000, p. 7).

As we saw in previous chapters, as coaching spreads down and across an organization, employees develop into more effective contributors. Basically, coaching is a strategic process that adds value to the people being coached and to the bottom line of the organization.

Goal Alignment

We have stated that a coaching organization creates a system that engages people and captures the human spirit. This can only happen by helping employees align their personal goals, vision, and operations with those of the organization. Coaching helps people understand when they are out of alignment and can put them back on track.

Are we suggesting that every organization must be a coaching organization? No, we are not. A coaching environment is not the answer for every business endeavor. However, we do believe that organizations must be true to themselves and what they are. A company that claims to be a "participative organization that believes in people" but behaves like a hierarchical "do as I say" kind of company inevitably produces cynicism, sabotage, mediocrity, game playing, and lackluster performance. It's this disconnect between the "talk" and the "walk" that demotivates and forces employees to essentially retire on the job.

A highly successful international consulting firm in the United States is very open about its culture. When hiring people, company representatives say,

> We are known to burn our employees out. The travel is constant, and the work is all encompassing. Though some folks have been with us for 10 years, the average retention rate is 3 to 5 years. However, you will be working with high-powered executives in highly visible companies. You will be certified in our coveted management processes, and you will make a lot of money.

The result of this kind of orientation? The company hires very talented people who want to cram 10 years of experience into 5, make a large sum of money in a short period of time, and then leave for high-level jobs in other organizations. When faced with the truth, employees can make a clear, educated choice and align their goals with those of the organization.

This was not the case of a recent college graduate who decided to join a Web design company that gave sports cars to employees who met performance goals:

> But last November, just three months after he reported to work—and before he was able to collect any of the corporate perks—Jones' first job ended on a less splashy note. He and 75 colleagues were led into a conference room, given cardboard boxes to pack their belongings and shown to the door. "One of the big things built up was the corporate culture and the value of employees," said Jones, who sued . . . for $1700 in severance pay he said he is owed. "I went there because of the way they treated employees. It was such a disrespectful exit." (Johnson, 2001, p. 1)

You must walk the talk and give prospective employees a realistic picture of what it is like to work there. If you are building an organization and are in it only for the money, say so. If you are merely growing an organization in order to sell it, explain what you are doing, what you need from people, and what's in it for them if they want to participate in your endeavor. People will join you if your goals match their goals, given a certain time in their career and personal growth.

However, we have found that noncoaching cultures cannot sustain themselves over time. Unless the very basic human needs of involvement, respect, interesting work, goal alignment, learning, recognition, and continuous improvement are nurtured and allowed to flourish, success is temporary—it lacks momentum and a foundation. A coaching environment engages and renews itself so that today's high-speed world can be navigated.

A coaching organization creates an entire "performance community," providing a creative framework that helps people navigate their personal and professional lives—bringing them closer to the values of the organization. A marvelous example of this is Vitra, a furniture company in Basel, Switzerland. The founder and CEO, Rolf Fehlbain, has spoken about the campus atmosphere he created:

> A company's strength comes from the love and respect that it has for the creative people who work for it and with it. . . . We have a common project that we give part of our lives to and for which we are compensated in one way or another. We live in a state of interdependence. . . . A good leader helps give cultural meaning to work and creates a place where people can be themselves and grow. (quoted in Rosenfeld, *Fast Company,* 2000, p. 233)

The Coaching System

As a leader, do you want your company, department, or business unit to be a coaching entity? A coaching organization needs to be supported by an entire coaching system, consisting of key levers and drivers that sustain the culture. You can use the coaching system model (Figure 4.1) to assess your organization and develop action plans to move toward the desired state.

- Is a coaching mind-set pervasive throughout the organization?
- Is there a leadership-driven vision that is clearly understood and aligned with all actions and structures?
- Do skilled dialogue and coaching practices guide all conversations?
- Is the intent and desire for learning and continuous improvement in all interactions and structures?
- Are stretch goals embedded in measurements and plans in order to foster breakthrough thinking and high performance?
- Are all formal and informal policies, procedures, structures, processes, tools, techniques, technology, functions, and supportive mechanisms aligned and reinforced through a coaching infrastructure that links and tracks the entire system?

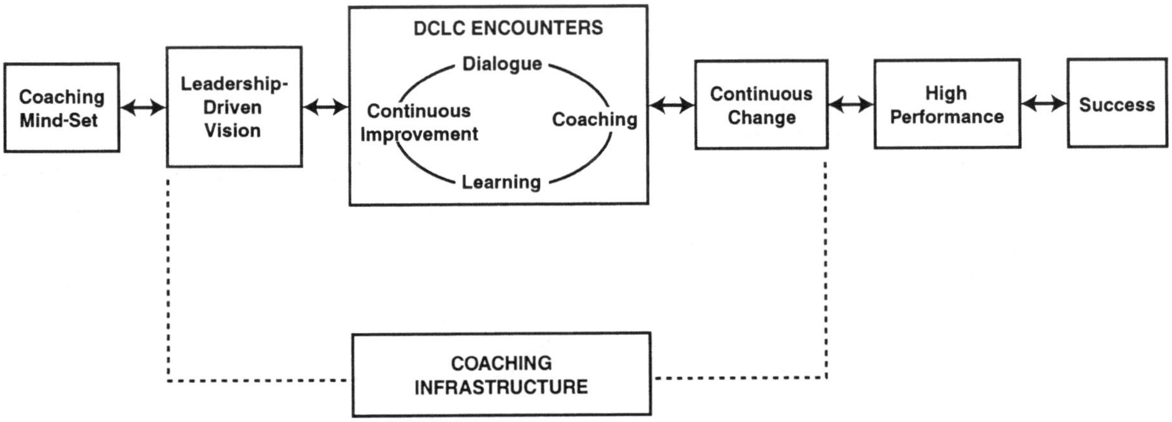

Figure 4.1. The Coaching System Model

- Can results be measured in terms of bottom-line success, goal achievement, and/or profits?

Like most system models in organizational behavior and management practice, all components are interdependent. If you tweak one element, it will have a cascading effect on the others. If you eliminate or neglect a particular driver, the entire system will suffer. Studies have shown not only that supporting drivers are interdependent within a system but that a change effort or continued success is proportionally related to the attention and effort given to each driver (Bianco & Roman, 1994; Industry Week, 1993). For example, using the coaching system model, a change effort that balances all seven components will be more successful than a change effort that uses only two or three of the components. If you try to perpetuate a leadership-driven vision without a coaching infrastructure, the vision will merely be empty statements on a plaque on the wall. If you try to have dialogue sessions without the intent of learning or high performance, you will have a very aware organization that doesn't accomplish anything. And if you create a coaching mind-set without an eye on results or profits, you will end up with a cult, not a business entity.

Now you can see why many leaders revert to the traditional "do as I say" mentality. It's easier. Deliberate, mindful, and coordinated effort must be exerted to build and sustain a coaching culture. Leaders that have started on the path of a coaching organization agree that there is no clear recipe or magic wand.

It takes discipline and passion. It also takes time. Just as you have to be patient with yourself when working on your own personal development, you need to be patient with the entire organizational process. You need to celebrate step-by-step progress and remember that even though you might not be totally successful, you are continuously "on the path"—or, as the saying goes, the organization is a "work in progress."

The Coaching Mind-Set

The previous chapters of this book emphasize that coaching has to become more than just your leadership style. You need to become so adept at the principles, language, and practice of coaching that it becomes your focused and purposeful way of being. As Lyons (2000) explained:

> Coaching facilitates success and is congruent with the way we want to work and the way we have to work. It is relevant to the modern world of business because it is holistic and adaptive. Coaching is also a method that respects people as individuals, not merely cogs in the business machine. Rooted in conversation, coaching is evolving as a natural form of leadership. (p. 11)

As stated earlier in this chapter, this is not TQM, participative management, reengineering, open-book management, management by objectives, or any of the other many fads, programs, tools, or initiatives that have come down the pike. There's nothing wrong with any of these tools—in fact, they can be useful and powerful when embedded within a coaching organization. A coaching organization is the entity itself, not a program that is introduced into a company. The coaching mind-set is what allows programs, such as TQM or open-book management, to take hold and be successful. It is the fertile ground that nurtures openness, creativity, and the ability to choose effective management tools and make them work.

According to Evered and Selman (1989), old beliefs have to be rethought and replaced with "aligned purpose, commitment to accomplishment, collaboration, involvement, mutual support, individual growth—enabling people in a group or team to generate results and to be empowered by the results they generate" (p. 3). This is a coaching mind-set.

Vision

In his film *The Power of Vision*, Joel Barker (1993) says, "Vision without action is a dream. Action without vision is merely passing time. Vision and action can change the world." He goes on to describe vision as "dreams in action." Barker is joined by other experts in emphasizing that a vision must be powerful, must be explained in terms that everyone understands, and must also include a path or strategy for how to get there—something that employees can hold on to, follow, and embed in their own work and goals.

We believe that a successful vision must have three characteristics: It must be driven by a leader, it must be shared and supported by the top team, and it must be compelling and comprehensive enough to provide a pathway to action.

Driven by a Leader

The leader can be anywhere in the organization but must be in a position to influence others. The leader you need to be must talk about the vision, listen, get input, and sharpen the vision even further. You must create conversations around the vision to foster a common understanding. Dialogue allows a vision to become real. Dialogue teases out the explicit and subtle meanings. If you, as the coaching leader, don't champion the effort, it won't be perceived as important and it won't get done. You must demonstrate, through your actions, what is acceptable and unacceptable.

Shaffer (2000) stressed that unless a leader is passionate about linking people and what they do to the business goals and strategy, the dots won't connect (p. 46). To test yourself, Shaffer suggested, look at your actions over the past month. Look at your calendar. Can you point to specific events, conversations, or actions where you have shared and perpetuated the vision? Similarly, in discussing successful change efforts, Kotter (1995) explained that a leader must use every possible avenue to get the message across:

> Executives who communicate well incorporate messages into hour-by-hour activities. In a routine discussion about a business problem, they talk about how proposed solutions fit (or don't fit) into the bigger picture. In a regular performance appraisal, they talk about how the employee's behavior helps or undermines the vision. In a review of a division's quarterly performance, they talk not only about the numbers but also about how the division's executives are contributing to the transformation.
>
> In a routine Q & A with employees at a company facility, they tie their answers back to renewal goals. . . . They consciously attempt to become a living symbol of the new corporate culture. (p. 64)

Shared and Supported by the Top Team

Part 3 of this book emphasized the importance and techniques for coaching your top team. The top team must understand and agree on the direction of the organization and how that is going to happen. However, we are using a broad definition of *top team*. We are referring to a group of people throughout the organization who have the ability to inspire, role-model, and drive the vision. Senge (1999) called this group a "leadership community." Kotter (1995) referred to it as the "guiding coalition." Barker (1993) called it a "vision community." Whatever the label, this group has a clear picture of the focused message. With the focused message in mind, they can connect people and what they do (through dialogue, structures, and actions) to the greater purpose, strategy, and vision. Because of this alignment, people are more apt to make the right decisions at the right moments.

So what do you do when a member of the vision community displays actions, makes decisions, or exhibits behaviors that go against the vision and strategy? Remember, the entire organization is looking for consistency, something they can trust and around which they can shape their own goals and actions. Will you, as the leader, be strong enough to reprimand and even let go a high performer who doesn't support the vision and culture?

Nothing undermines a vision more drastically than inconsistent messages and actions. As a coaching leader, your conviction has to be demonstrated by more than words. Through careful coaching and involvement, you can slowly bring nonbelievers into the fold. However, if after a designated period of time, these folks do not or cannot align their goals and actions around the organization's vision, then it's time for them to seek a more compatible workplace.

Compelling, Comprehensive, and a Pathway to Action

Kotter (1995) emphasized that a successful vision must be easy to communicate and must clarify the direction in which an organization needs to move. When we refer to vision in this book, we are talking about a vision that encompasses both the business initiatives and the coaching culture needed to make it happen. Your company's vision must paint the picture of the organization reaching competitive success, navigating mergers and acquisitions, conquering financial threats, outsmarting foreign pressures, increasing market share, achieving environmental initiatives, or reinventing itself to survive—all within the context of a coaching organization. The relationship is symbiotic and must be inherent and felt within the vision.

Without a compelling vision, efforts can dissolve into a series of disruptive and incompatible projects that lead the organization in the wrong direction or in too many directions. Without a focused vision and three or four explicit strategies, the performance appraisal process will be incompatible with the structure, the accounting process will conflict with the decision-making protocol, or the marketing efforts will conflict with engineering initiatives. Nothing will add up.

Though simple, the vision must be comprehensive enough so that focused strategies and actions can easily follow. This component allows employees to see their own role in the process. As a coaching leader, you must have a vision that is tangible. It must tell a story. As Shaffer (2000) pointed out (p. 4), most organizations don't fail for lack of vision. Vision statements abound. Where they fail is in the execution. Success is a result of down-and-dirty execution. This happens through walking the talk, aligning all strategies, conducting dialogue sessions, and constant coaching. Would any coach of a major league team neglect to share the strategy with the entire team—talk about it, practice it, and analyze it through video playback?

Dialogue, Coaching, Learning, and Stretch Goals

Dialogue, coaching, learning, and stretch goals (DCLS) are drivers so interrelated that it is hard to tease out where one begins and another ends. Together, they provide a force that is the heart of a coaching organization.

Dialogue

As previously discussed in other sections of this book, we define dialogue as a form of communication based on intense listening, mutual understanding and learning, testing of assumptions, and alignment with a purpose—not on arguing, taking sides, convincing, controlling, politicking, or manipulation. Once a higher level of understanding is reached, powerful insights and solutions can evolve. Conducting true dialogue sessions requires an entirely different set of skills and mind-set (a coaching mind-set) than most people use. Simply practicing new skills would be imposing a new game onto the old model. Only through the addition of a coaching mind-set can the very intent of conversations change. Let's look at an example:

Mike Long is president of a high-tech firm. He is conducting an executive retreat with his top 12 directors. First, Mike congratulates the team for a great year. The company made more money and accomplished more goals than ever before. It was a very successful year. After a period of appropriate acknowledgment and recognition, Mike flips on a slide and says, "However, as successful as we were, we are still $3 million short of our overall goal. I want you each to take 15 minutes and think through how you and your people are going to help close this gap. We're going to go around the table and each person is going to share his or her ideas. We are not going to stop the conversation until we have an action plan and commitment for making up the $3 million."

The conversation lasts for 3 hours. It's very intense. A segment of this dialogue is shown in Exhibit 4.1. Later, Mike explains how powerful such a discussion is:

> We may never reach that additional $3 million. On the other hand, we might exceed it. The point is that we will never even have a chance if I don't push our thinking through creative discussion. Most things don't get done because people don't work through all the options, possibilities, constraints, and alternative actions. Through effective questioning and support, the possibility becomes more tangible. Through dialogue, we can pave the way to higher achievement.

Let's look more closely at Mike's session. During the dialogue, Mike does not accept "yes, but" or other defensive routines. He listens and then says, "Good point. That's a challenge. What are some creative ways to deal with that barrier?" There is no blaming or controlling. Mike and the team use effective questions (Krug & Oakley, 1994, p. 138) to elicit thoughtful responses that lead to focused actions.

By asking effective questions, Mike empowers his group and creates a willingness on their part to pursue solutions with minimal resistance. Mike also knows that it is through the process of answering that each team member learns and embraces action. Consequently, through his questions, Mike probes, frames, motivates—and gets commitment:

- What are you doing now that is working very well?
- Why is it working well?
- How can you apply what you are doing well to achieve this objective?
- What are the benefits of achieving this objective?
- What can you/we do to move closer?
- What can you do differently?
- What aspect of what you are doing needs additional work?

Exhibit 4.1 Dialogue Session

Larry, the East Coast division director, is sharing his thoughts. Mike and other directors jump in during the dialogue.

Larry: I have an idea, but I'm almost afraid to bring it up. When I raised the topic 18 months ago, you all didn't want to pursue it.

Mike: Larry, I'm sensing that you still feel strongly about this idea?

Larry: Absolutely. I think the economy and business arena has changed and that the idea now makes more sense than ever.

Donna: Sounds logical. Let's hear it.

Larry: I'm talking about ABS software development. Originally, most of you felt that the technology was only a passing fad and was going to be replaced by the emerging TDS. As it turns out, TDS has moved in another direction, and ABS is gaining momentum and strength in the marketplace.

Tom: Yes, I just read an article about that, and I must admit I was surprised. I was one of the ones that believed it was going to die. But I'm still apprehensive. Larry, I'm concerned about the size of the opportunity and how much it would cost us to build a viable team.

Rich: Exactly. We've been down this road before. Just because there's now a market for ABS doesn't mean it's feasible for us.

Donna: Rich, I'm sensing that you are against this idea, just as you were last year. Are you willing to hear more facts so you can assess whether your doubts are still valid?

Rich: Point well taken, Donna. Larry, have you done any research or run any numbers?

Larry: Yes. As a matter of fact, Nancy and I have almost finished a cost-benefit analysis. The preliminary numbers look very good.

Mike: Larry, this sounds like a potential moneymaker. What factors led you to pursue this further?

Larry: Good question. First, I got suspicious when I heard that TDS had morphed into something different than originally planned. I checked this out with the designers. Second, I heard through our contacts that two industry giants had hired our direct competitor to develop ABS systems. Of course, they are typically slow and expensive.

Mike: Wow! So I assume you will lay out the market share opportunity. Can you give us a ballpark number?

Larry: Yes. I'll be giving you all specifics, including a game plan. But I think we are looking at $3.5 million in 2 years.

Mike: Fantastic. This is what I'm talking about in terms of stretch goals.

Tom: Larry, a concern I have—which I hope you address—is start-up and expertise. Right now, at least to my knowledge, only you and Jose are competent in ABS. Is that correct?

Larry: You're right, Tom. And that's a significant concern. However, I think I can share some concrete ideas on how to overcome that. Definitely, there are some tough hurdles, but I think we can do it.

Mike: Good. Add $3.5 million to the chart.

- How will that lead to the right result?
- What would that look like? Let's paint a picture.
- What key things need to happen in the next 6 months?

The magic happens through the dialogue. What if Mike said, "We didn't make the goal. How many contracts were lost? I want to know what went wrong. What's the matter with you guys? What's the problem?" What kind of reaction would such questions foster? Team members would become defensive, disempowered, and unproductive. Their focus would be on saving face, failure, and avoidance. As a leader, Mike would also be establishing a way of behavior that would become embedded in the culture. He would be perpetuating a culture of blame and avoidance, not openness and action.

As a leader, you have a choice. You can guide the company's attention to the results that need to be accomplished or to the reasons why goals can't be achieved. Mastering these skills takes practice. This is not a technique; it's intent. Krug and Oakley (1994, pp. 162-164) explained that empowerment is a place to come from, not something we do. It is not just words but a feeling. People can tell whether you are tying to "get them" or help them. Krug and Oakley emphasized that you need to internalize this paradigm and demonstrate a new way of thinking. Such an approach supports the very essence of a coaching organization: ownership, alignment, innovation, involvement, trust, risk taking, reconditioning.

We have been using an example of a leader and his top team. Obviously, this dialogue approach should be used in one-on-one coaching sessions, small groups, and large groups, and in all written communications as well.

Parts 2 and 3 of this book discussed Chris Argyris and his work around defensive routines. Argyris (1986, 1994) also gave many examples of how entire companies develop defensive routines ("we can't do that because . . .") and mental models that prevent learning and result in mediocre performance. Argyris discussed how leaders and companies can have conflicting "espoused theories" and "theories in use." For example, a leader may claim that she is very open and available yet always keep her door closed. A company may claim that it supports teamwork yet reward people only for individual contributions. This is why consultants can come in, talk to employees, and pinpoint problems. Employees know what is wrong. They even know how to solve the problems. Unfortunately, the existing mental models and espoused theories prevent pointing out errors or confronting faulty reasoning because it is "unacceptable" to get others in trouble for the sake of correcting problems. It's an interesting catch-22. The result is that no one takes on the responsibility for fixing things. It always becomes someone else's responsibility. No accountability, no change.

Returning to our example, Mike uses questions to learn, not to blame. Team members try to draw out the truth, not to embarrass, but to clarify and reach an even better alternative. Mike explains his motives, not to protect and defend himself, but to gain understanding and spur further thought. The results: Everyone feels respected, and $3 million is added to the bottom line.

Coaching, Learning, and Stretch Goals

Through coaching, vague strategy statements are connected to the jobs that people do every day: What do I need to do? Is my work purposeful and connected? What might I do differently? How do I align myself with the organization? How do I continuously get better and better?

If we return to the traditional sports analogy, the job of a coach is to help the performer see blind spots and enable the performer to excel beyond those limits:

> Without a coach, the person just keeps honing the prevailing level of play. Coaching makes possible a reinterpretation of actions so that a quantum shift in results can naturally occur. Coaching generates new possibilities . . . and allows for breakthroughs in performance. (Evered & Selman, 1989, p. 8)

Coaching uses dialogue to point out frames of reference that keep individuals, groups, and the entire organization from being effective. When used in one-on-one coaching sessions and group meetings, coaching encourages reflection, learning, and totally new ways of performing. Employees can "try on" new behaviors and get unstuck.

As a coaching leader, you create an environment that fosters learning within the context of getting the job done. Success depends on your organization constantly learning, adapting, and capitalizing on sudden shifts in the marketplace. If you make coaching and dialogue "the way things are done around here," you have built-in continuous improvement.

When you confront me, I can trust that you are pushing me to think beyond my existing paradigms, not trying to blame or hinder me. When you ask me to explain my reasoning, I can trust that you will not use my answer against me but will help me seek higher levels of performance. In a coaching organization, my mistakes will be treated as learning opportunities—steps on the path of accomplishment, not failures.

Let's return once again to Mike and his strategy session. Pretend you are Mike. You ask your team to stretch themselves to obtain another $3 million. Through dialogue, you question, coach, and guide. Through coaching, you help them break through one level of thinking and enter an entirely different realm—a series of actions and behaviors that leads to even higher performance. You do this in such a way that they are energized. You grab their inner spirit. Hargrove, in his book *Masterful Coaching* (1995), claimed that if you don't demand something out of the ordinary, you won't get something out of the ordinary (p. 86).

Coaching Infrastructure

Let's go back to the coaching system and the concept of a linking system. As a coaching leader, you must align all of the drivers, and you do that through the infrastructure. The infrastructure connects the "say" with the "do," the "walk" with the "talk," the vision with the everyday action. Because of the

Exhibit 4.2 **Infrastructure Examples**

1. A 360-degree inventory that assesses coaching behaviors. Leaders and team members receive feedback twice a year and develop action plans for improvement during one-on-one coaching sessions.
2. A leader who conducts small group dialogue sessions throughout the company for the purpose of discussing vision, values, and the top three goals for the year.
3. Weekly huddles where teams review performance spreadsheets and make on-the-spot decisions.
4. Cross-functional teams that work together and hash out issues that cross over departmental boundaries.
5. Cash awards for individuals or teams that creatively solve a problem or pursue an opportunity that moves the organization forward.
6. Promotions or growth opportunities for individuals that embody a coaching mind-set and walk the talk. Exit discussions with those that merely perform without the appropriate mind-set.
7. Training sessions with intact groups where new skills are immediately practiced and implemented into real-time behavior.
8. Open-book management practices, where employees and leaders track the business.

infrastructure, coaching comes alive—in the hallways, communication vehicles, performance evaluation system, strategic planning, human resource policies, financial protocols, and measurements. The infrastructure is the underpinning that makes it possible for people to translate the bigger picture issues into their own behavior.

The infrastructure consists of tools, programs, vehicles, structures, and processes that are created to reinforce the right messages and mind-set. These vehicles are not meant to be rigid. They should be fluid and flexible—created and re-created to support and evolve, not to become barriers themselves.

It is through the infrastructure that you take many of the theories laid out in this chapter, attach a specific program, and make them come alive. Exhibit 4.2 lists some examples.

Leaders have said, "Just give us a list of things we need to do." Such a list can be easily developed. The problem, of course, is in the execution. Without the components of the coaching system model, leadership actions fall flat—they are sporadic, confusing, random, and disconnected.

If you want something to happen, it must become a part of the language, action, and structures. It cannot be a program or idea that is merely "plopped" into the organization. Any such "new program" will be at odds with other systems and structures. Kotter (1995) has talked about the need to create a linking infrastructure and remove obstacles that will thwart new behaviors:

> Renewal also requires the removal of obstacles. Too often, an employee understands the new vision and wants to help make it happen. But an elephant appears to be blocking the path. . . . Sometimes the obstacle is the organizational structure. Narrow job categories can seriously undermine efforts to increase productivity or make it very difficult

> even to think about customers. Sometimes compensation or performance appraisal systems make people choose between the new vision and their own self-interest. Perhaps worst of all are bosses who refuse to change and who make demands that are inconsistent with the overall effort. (p. 64)

John McBeth, former president of Century Computing, uses a unique strategic planning process for aligning vision, values, strategic goals, and actions. On separate walls in the room, he places the company's vision, key strategic goals, values, and action plans. He then spends hours with his top team making sure that all components fit the overall vision, are mutually aligned and consistent, and lead to the desired goals. If something doesn't fit, it is discussed, and alignment is adjusted across all four walls:

- What do we mean by that?
- Will this action get the results we want?
- We say this is a value, but I don't see anything leading to it. Do you?
- Is that the right strategy, or do we need to look at it differently? Maybe we are going after the wrong thing.

The meeting doesn't end until all members of the team are prepared to pledge unqualified support to all components of the plan.

Communication Systems

Communication is an important part of a company's infrastructure. All communication systems within a company must support, align, and link vision to action. Like many other executives, you may believe that there is "a lot of communication" in your organization—newsletters, e-mails, memos, intranet, presentations, and meetings. Often, however, the problem isn't the amount of communication but the kind of information that is shared. Most employees don't have the basic information they need to perform their jobs well. How does this proposal relate to the vision? How does this piece of research tie in to the strategy? How does all of this paperwork support our values? How does this report take the company to a higher level? Shaffer (2000) and others have called this "connecting the dots" (p. 96).

Phillips Corporation, a machine manufacturer and distributor in Maryland, uses a relevant communication tool. The sales force uses "spreadsheet meetings" to track progress, coach, and guide decisions. On a weekly basis, work teams "huddle" and review the status of key goals. Each person must explain his or her progress with specific examples and action plans. Team members coach each other. Glitches are noted and immediately remedied before they become problems. This is truly a DCLS encounter. Employees see not only how their actions are linked to business goals but how they can personally affect the outcomes. Colleagues share tips for success. The team sharpens its decision-making power. Furthermore, within a group setting, each person commits and becomes accountable.

The example above is an example not only of aligned communications but also of the concept of open-book management—sharing business and financial information so that the entire company participates in the running of the company (Case, 1995). Every entrance and common area within America Online is filled with computer terminals so that guests and employees can freely go online and check e-mail or the company stock price. The same is true at AlliedSignal: "People's mindsets have changed. Employees are interested in our stock price now. You go into the lobbies where we've installed monitors, and people are tracking AlliedSignal. . . . People are thinking differently about their jobs" (Tichy & Charon, 1995, p. 77).

Development and Education

Another significant area of alignment within a coaching infrastructure is development and education. As already discussed, learning must include stretch goals and be continuous, pertinent, and measurable. Every employee should have a "learning plan" that outlines a wide range of development activities—all tied to visible and stated results.

Development in a classroom setting has taken on many new forms. Given that organizations are now global, training and education must also be global—online, videoconferencing, chat rooms, and satellite. The dynamics of today's world has made education, training, and learning a necessity—not an "extra benefit" that is cut during lean times. Learning is not only essential for future growth. It's mandatory for just staying in the game.

Then there's the process of coaching itself as a development tool. As pointed out in Part 1 of this book, coaching is a form of development that meets the needs of today's workforce. It's real time, personal, value driven, tailored, measurable, and portable. If you are clearly communicating a leadership-driven vision, pertinent learning points should emerge during coaching discussions. Is the company going global? Are certain products dying out and others taking hold? Is there going to be a new emphasis in marketing or research? Is the company going to reorganize to better serve the customer? These kinds of strategic issues must be discussed in coaching sessions because they pose implications for learning and career shifts.

Coaching is flexible and can be done one-on-one or in groups. Internal employees are being trained to be coaches, and external coaches are being put on retainer. Internal coaching networks and certification programs are being formed in hospitals, Fortune 500 companies, government agencies, and associations. At Phillips Corporation, there are no project managers, only team coaches. One interesting company eliminated the role of vice president of human resources and substituted the title of "head coach."

Another example of building a learning infrastructure is the trend to offer innovative training programs to intact work teams in order to foster "high-performance" teams. Team leaders are developed so they can coach project teams toward success. America Online has launched a "team kickoff" program for cross-functional teams. The purpose is to create a "coaching entity" with defined vision, objectives, schedules, interpersonal agreements, conflict resolution, escalation, and mutual support across functional areas. The team learns to cut through organizational barriers and get the product out faster than the competition.

Perhaps the most significant development tool that has come along in the last 10 years has been the 360-degree feedback tool. You can make a 360-degree feedback tool a part of your overall process to align corporate values and individual behavior. It can be used for hiring, orientation, training, development activities, and coaching. The parameters within a 360-degree instrument should measure the behaviors that support the corporate vision and culture. You can develop these parameters using teams and groups throughout the organization. This increases buy-in and further links personal goals with those of the organization.

- Does this leader consider the customer when making decisions?
- Does this team leader conduct regular coaching sessions?
- Is there open dialogue within this leader's department?

You must remember, however, that 360-degree tools are development vehicles, not formal appraisal documents. Feedback results should be used for coaching and action planning, not appraising or making personnel decisions. If you try to use a 360-degree instrument as an appraisal tool, you will break down trust. The system will be manipulated and sabotaged and will become yet another "trend" that bites the dust. People should not be measured using 360-degree feedback results. What they should be measured on is movement and progress along the course of their development action plans. What have you done in the past 6 months to improve your project management skills? What benchmarks have you reached along the course of your action plan? What specific outcomes can you point to that demonstrate improvement in this area? When feedback is used in this way, people openly accept it because you are giving them support and control to do something about it.

Building a connected infrastructure with an emphasis on learning further supports the need for "knowledge management." Bonner (2000) defined and explained knowledge management as follows:

> Senior managers are realizing that the success factors for aggressive business growth in today's highly competitive marketplace are what their employees know and how capable they are at learning the newest solutions and technologies. In this knowledge era, an organization's intangible assets—employees' collective intelligence of skills, experience, and work ethic—is crucial to business advantage. . . . Once a firm has a grip on what knowledge it has and how to manage it, then it will be able to more effectively assess its organizational learning capabilities, maximize learning at the individual level, and use knowledge capture and sharing as ways to enhance organization-wide learning. (p. 36)

When people leave your company—with all of their learning, experiences, trial-and-error discoveries, insights, and contacts—they walk away with your

Exhibit 4.3 **Knowledge Exchange**

1. *Project follow-up reports.* Key findings from projects that are recorded and filed in a special database, coded for easy access and reference.
2. *Lessons learned meetings.* Meetings where employees share significant experiences, work processes, interactions, and implications for ongoing projects.
3. *Performance improvement audits.* Audits of projects or teams that are studied and analyzed in small groups.
4. *Project fairs.* Employees/teams highlight and share significant projects; organized like a convention where attendees roam the booths.
5. *Online communities.* Widely dispersed groups that have common interests in terms of work topic/discipline or work-related issues, meet online for knowledge transfer.
6. *Electronic polling and voting.* The use of electronic tools to solicit candid, rapid feedback for strategy, problem solving, reports, and project plans.
7. *Organizational debates.* Organized debates on controversial topics in order to surface all facets of a topic.
8. *Expert exchange and experience finder.* Database of identified experts in the organization that can provide information and guidance on key topics and issues, and/or a system that users can search for others who might have relevant knowledge. (KnowledgeMail, by Tacit Knowledge Systems, Palo Alto, is such a system.)
9. *Acknowledgment bulletins.* Special screen on the company intranet where employees can acknowledge each other for sharing and providing guidance.
10. *University Web site.* A site where employees can find papers, reports, or mini-lessons on pertinent topics.

greatest resource and hand it over to your competition! Even when employees stay, work is often duplicated, or the same mistakes are continually made because teams don't sit down and exchange lessons learned. Chief knowledge officers, learning officers, and technology officers often join forces to hardwire organizational learning so it can be easily referenced and shared.

Exhibit 4.3 lists examples of knowledge exchanges that leading companies have built into their infrastructures. As you can see, these knowledge structures resemble the natural elements one would find in a coaching organization.

Appraisal, Recognition, and Rewards

In a coaching environment, people need to be recognized—they need tangible signs that their work is valued and is making a difference. Such recognition is embedded within the very tenets of a coaching organization—coaching sessions, support in personal development, open dialogue and involvement, "discussable" communication, a connection to the whole, a certain amount of control over projects and work assignments, an inner spirit that is passionately engaged through enlightened leadership, and a learning environment.

More means of providing direct recognition are also required. To emphasize the importance of vision, continuous improvement, and making a difference, Phillips Corporation (a machine tool company in Columbia, Maryland) has instituted the "Virtuoso Star Award." This award is periodically given to employees who make a significant contribution to the company. Another meaningful symbol they use is the "Torch Award." This gold flame is given to employees who complete the internal coaching class: "Go out and spread the light of continuous learning." In some organizations, these awards might come off as simplistic or trite. However, when implemented within an organization that has aligned all systems behind a coaching mind-set, these symbols significantly reinforce the right behaviors.

Building an aligned infrastructure also requires a more creative implementation of compensation and benefits. Government agencies have developed and expanded their pay levels to foster more flexibility, movement, and pay options. Government agencies and many private companies have also taken the lead in implementing very innovative benefit programs—telecommuting, flexible benefit plans, shared vacation arrangements, and special employee buying capabilities. Private companies are using stock options, equity, variable pay, bonuses, and profit sharing to tie individual performance to overall corporate performance.

Once again, just "plopping" these kinds of programs into a company will not work. Many executives say, "Gee, we have stock options, big bonuses, and flexible benefits, and still people are leaving and saying they are not happy here. What else are we supposed to do?"

What you are supposed to do is tie all of these things together within a coaching mind-set. Unless connections are made, even the most innovative and exciting programs lose their power to influence and guide the culture. A good example is Premium Standard Farms, a pork-processing plant in Missouri (Balu, *Fast Company*, 2000, p. 74). The company was suffering from 100% turnover, low morale, and total disengagement among staff. The company implemented a gain-sharing plan that turned the company around. A design team was formed to create involvement and buy-in. Everyone was educated in how the plan worked, how it related to every job in the company, and how to track and monitor results. Everyone became a partner in running the business. Not only were there bottom-line results, but also retention rates improved by more than half, production errors and overtime hours were greatly reduced, and employees' attitudes changed. Employees explained that they gained dignity and a greater sense of purpose. Employees felt "in control," and they even reached out and decided to give a portion of their gains to neighborhood charities—they connected the value of their work with the surrounding community. Performance, learning, participation, respect, and dialogue became a way of being.

In this example, profits and success are the outcomes, along with engaged spirits and a committed workforce. This is not just the touchy-feely stuff. Everyone is accountable and must be held accountable. Ironically, that's one reason why certain people choose not to belong to a coaching organization. There is nowhere to hide. There are no systems to blame. There is no "us" versus "them." You either do it or you don't and you deal with the consequences.

Some people don't like being accountable for behaviors and accomplishments other than those that are financial. "Hey, leave me alone. I brought in $1 million this year. Don't bug me about stretch goals, continuous improvement, dialogue, or coaching. I do my job better than anybody else." Such people need to be led to the door. Their way of achieving results is only temporary and will not help the company reach long-term goals. Their success resides within themselves. They are not helping to build a team, foster commitment, pass on knowledge, or ignite passion.

In the "old" system, you looked at measures and performance in a linear fashion. In a coaching organization, you need to look at performance through a different frame—breakthroughs, dialogue, working around obstacles, continually improving, forming goals around possibilities. Remember our example of Mike and his executive team. Even if the team did not meet the stretch goal, they were still doing better than the competitors because of the stretch goals. In a coaching organization, success is reframed in terms of linkages and being continually "on the path." This won't feel right for everyone. Some folks, like our $1 million financial person above, can deal with performance and goals only in a linear way. In a coaching organization, performance, goals, and measures are tied more directly to what and who we are.

Appraisal mechanisms within coaching organizations must be based on achieving defined benchmarks on the path toward far-reaching goals. It's a continuum of success. It's a range of achievement with clear markers and rewards attached along the way.

- How did you overcome obstacles?
- How did you turn losses into opportunities?
- How did you make a marvelous 50% gain in profits over the past 6 months?
- How are you going to continue to achieve beyond that 50% gain in order to achieve an overall 75% gain?

Rewards are tied to how the organization does as a whole, how individuals and teams influence that success, and how far people have moved along their growth paths. Goals and objectives must include tangible measures and meaningful results—not just actions. What is important is not that you conducted 20 coaching sessions but that your team feels involved and productive as a result.

FedEx is a good example of a company that has aligned measures and success to daily work—and also directly to the customer. Every FedEx delivery person carries a monitor that logs all activity and gives up-to-the-minute measures on key corporate drivers. How are you doing? Where is the company today? Push a button and look. Whether a company is using a hand-held monitor, computer screen, weekly spreadsheets with dialogue sessions, or posters on a wall, there must be measures, discussions, adjustments, and leaps forward.

Benchmarking tends to be a major activity of coaching organizations. By benchmarking other companies, processes, programs, or even tasks, you and your people gain valuable insights into trends, best practices, competitive practices, and gaps in your own systems. Benchmarking data are food for thought and dialogue—and the basis for vision and stretch goals. Benchmarking allows objectives to be developed based on "what is possible," not on "what we've done before."

Environment and Financial Management

Final alignment areas that organizations frequently overlook include environment and financial management. Obviously, environment is an easy one. Either the work areas, cubicles, windows, sounds, colors, structures, light, and space foster teamwork, openness, creativity, and learning or they don't. Though architectural firms and design consultants have made a business out of ergonomically correct environments, it doesn't take a genius to sense whether a workplace supports or hinders a coaching environment. Walk the space. How does it feel? If you, as the leader, are standing up there preaching dialogue and openness, yet the hallways are dark and long, the offices are formal and cold, and the cubicles are stacked and unattractive, what kind of behaviors do you think you're going to get? Remember, consistent messages.

Financial systems tend to be silent contributors or inhibitors. One large organization had a system where departments would submit a yearly budget. If the department did not use that money by the end of the year, the department was docked that amount going into the next year. The message? Inflate your budget and make sure you spend every cent. The behavior? In the fourth quarter of every year, the organization experienced frenzied spending.

Another financial trap that many organizations fall into is the yearly allocation of funds for salary increases and hiring. First of all, the hiring numbers are based solely on "amount of money we can give you next year," not on any systematic recruitment study of what kinds of people are actually needed. Second, what drives salary increases is "amount of money left in the pool," not actual performance. Basically, managers guess, "Well, Paul will probably have another good year, so I'll budget him for an 'outstanding,' and Mary will probably move along adequately, so I'll budget her normal 'average' rating." What each person actually receives in pay has little to do with actual performance. This practice is not aligned with vision or stretch goals and can never motivate.

So the job of a leader is intense. Your radar must continually scan the organization searching for misalignment and inconsistent messages. Whenever you sense a problem, go through the coaching system model and assess the status of coaching mind-set, leadership-driven vision, DCLS encounters, and coaching infrastructure. Then check out the results of continuous change, high performance, and success (goal achievement, profits, market share, etc.).

Keep the system balanced.

Results

The results of a coaching organization—continuous change, high performance, and success—are self-evident in this system. They naturally evolve. They are embedded in how the organization thinks and acts.

For example, let's look at what the gurus say about implementing change. According to Lance Berger (1998, p. 61), a "change-ready" culture must be based on change-responsive people, leadership, vision, risk taking, and optimism. Peter Senge (1999) claimed that you need the following: time, support, relevancy, assessment, strategy, purpose, governance, true believers, and walking the talk (p. 28). Bianco and Roman (1994) found that you need six drivers: leadership, infrastructure, training and communication, techniques and measurements, recognition and rewards, and customer and supplier focus (p. 29). Finally, Kotter (1995) outlined eight factors: establishing a sense of urgency, forming a powerful coalition, creating a vision, empowering others, creating short-term wins, consolidating improvements and producing still more change, and institutionalizing new approaches.

Do you notice anything about these factors? They all have been mentioned as being a necessary part of a coaching organization. In a coaching organization, change happens because learning and stretch goals are constant. A blip on the screen is folded into that day's spreadsheet, that afternoon's dialogue session, and tomorrow morning's coaching session. The status quo is not acceptable.

When you are a coaching leader, change and success are what you are about. You drive them. You support them.

> In the final analysis, change sticks when it becomes "the way we do things around here," when it seeps into the bloodstream of the corporate body. Until new behaviors are rooted in social norms and shared values, they are subject to degradation as soon as the pressure for change is removed. (Kotter, 1995, p. 67)

You work with a coach on your own strengths and weaknesses. You coach other executives. You coach your top team. They, in turn, coach across and down the organization. In building a coaching organization, you are leaving a legacy—an organization that can sustain itself as a coaching entity, with or without you.

Applying the Model

Case Study Overview

So how do you make all of this happen? To illustrate how you can use the five steps within the coaching model to create a coaching organization, we will use a case study that represents a combination of leaders and organizations that we have worked with over the years. By tracing the journey of "Joe Ryan" and his company, we can demonstrate the steps and competencies required to move from a "traditional company" to a "high-performance coaching organization."

Keep in mind the point that has been made in previous chapters: Despite the definitive five steps, this is not a linear process. Change evolves and can be quite messy. One step forward is usually followed by several steps backwards. However, by having a model with steps, a coaching leader can more easily plan and manage. A plan enables you to appropriately analyze and refocus the often haphazard events of a change. As we will see in the Ryan case study, this is an essential ingredient for success.

Another advantage of the steps within the model is the synergy among all of the components. No task, competency, or behavior is isolated. A communication vehicle can guide and educate. An involvement and buy-in exercise can help to create a vision and develop corporate stories. As we have already seen in coaching oneself and coaching the team, no single event, memo, speech, or experience can cause lasting change.

This case study is going to describe the efforts that Joe Ryan undertakes to create a coaching organization. Let's remember that creating a coaching organization is creating an organization that can more readily grasp and reach high performance and bottom-line business goals. The coaching organization is not an end in itself. Joe must create a coaching organization within the context of a vision that will help the company reinvent itself and survive the trends that are happening in his industry.

We have already discussed the efficacy of undertaking major change efforts. Obviously, there are ways to get bottom-line results "in spite of" the culture, people, trends, and systems. But in these cases you get compliance, not commitment. You get a drop in the bucket, not continuous success. You allow yourself to proclaim victory when you might be leading your company to the brink of disaster.

One leader shared the pain of what it takes to make intrinsic organizational change—the diligence, patience, and time. He wanted to be able to take his entire executive team on a special cruise whereupon they would "transform" in 2 weeks and be able to return as coaching leaders. That would be convenient and easy—and this kind of wishful thinking explains why change efforts often are aborted, fail, or remain merely cosmetic. Constancy of purpose—interrelated and focused behaviors again and again—is needed to get lasting change. Are you ready?

The Case: Building a Coaching Organization

Joe Ryan was driving up Highway 95 to Philadelphia. He had just visited his manufacturing plant in eastern Maryland and was headed back to headquarters in Pennsylvania. He was switching radio stations and began to listen to a talk show. The guest speaker was Jim Wiltens, author of *Goal Express*. The author was talking about teaching children how to set meaningful goals and the positive results of defined outputs, confidence, continued performance, and inner motivation and energy.

Joe was enthralled. "How powerful it would be if every employee in my company felt this way." Joe, who keeps a running journal of thoughts and notes, began to integrate these ideas with those he had been contemplating for the past year. As a member of an international group of fellow presidents, he had been exposed to a series of leadership concepts. In particular, he was fascinated with Peter Senge and his five disciplines: shared vision, personal mastery, team learning, systems thinking, and mental models. He also felt strongly about the work of Laurie Beth Jones and the ideas in her book *The Path:* personal vision and passion, alignment of one's personal and professional life, and creation of a lifelong path.

Joe felt he was on the verge of something different and exciting, but he couldn't get his mind around it. Ryan Manufacturing, Inc. (RMI) was a 32-year-old plastic molding manufacturer and distributor. The company had tripled in size since his father started the business with one plant and one distribution center. There were now 600 employees, six locations, and partnerships with several European manufacturers. There were the usual ups and downs of the economy, but there was certain continuous growth.

RMI's culture was positive, with an emphasis on community, problem solving, respect, communication, and feedback. Turnover was low—something unusual for the industry. The performance appraisal process included a team approach where "partners" (not employees) received feedback from four to six coworkers. There were frequent celebrations, a folksy newsletter, a monthly e-mail from Joe Ryan, and a true open-door policy. So why was Joe reaching for something "different and exciting"?

> I began to envision something more: A company where both profits and spirits are high . . . where partners keep on learning and getting better at what they do . . . where everyone has a personal vision and mission that's in line with the company goals . . . a place where vision is not a plaque on the wall but a reality . . . an environment where people are excited about coming to work. Frankly, I began to feel that just running and growing a company was—in and of itself—quite boring. I began to feel that if I was putting this much work, energy, and spirit into leading a company, then I wanted it to be something above and beyond just a place to work and make money. I wanted a company that could keep reinventing itself and where people could not only make money but also feel fulfilled. From the books I was reading, I began to realize that it was only by capturing people's passion that you could go above and beyond the norm.

Joe began to solidify his thoughts through discussions with his support group of presidents and a couple of expert consultants. He refined a list of "key concepts" that he wanted to further explore and make real within RMI: passion, vision, high performance, continuous learning, stretch goals, and coaching.

It was at this point that Joe started a close relationship with a personal coach. He chose someone who challenged him and his mental models. Joe remembers that this was perhaps the most difficult element in the entire process—becoming a consistent role model and putting himself out there as a "work in progress."

> It was difficult to establish a balance between being a strong visionary and coaching leader on the one hand and yet a vulnerable human being trying to deal with my own strengths and weaknesses on the other. I remember being at one meeting and asking for feedback on something I had done. It was hard to listen, ask questions, and not become defensive. I still struggle with this. But now it is acknowledged and managed—not swept under the rug as a company "undiscussable."

However, as Joe was attacked or teased about becoming a "touch-feely guru," he began to look more seriously at the company's strategy and 5-year plan. He carefully studied a recent marketing report. Through the lenses of a coaching framework, he began to see RMI in a new light. Competition was getting tougher. Sales were slumped in Europe. The plastic molding industry needed to be revitalized in terms of approach and technology in order to survive the next 50 years. Joe looked at RMI's vision. It seemed flat and uninspiring. He reviewed the top six strategic goals. They were too simple and easily achieved. He realized that he might be the company's biggest barrier. Was he listening to his customers and salespeople? Did he really understand the competitive landscape? Was he getting too comfortable leading the company in a steady growth pattern year after year? Joe put a series of charts together and began to shape a new message for the next executive meeting:

> This is us. This is our competition. These are the trends in the industry. I see some major gaps. Over the next 5 years, I want us to transform RMI into the top plastic molding company in the industry. In fact, I want us to redefine the plastic molding industry. I want us to achieve this by becoming a learning organization, where we are all supporting each other and moving forward. I want us to question everything—even me and my ideas. I suspect that we're going to look and act differently. I want us to begin by trashing our vision and strategic goals and starting over. I want a vision and plan that takes us to a new level. I want passion . . . and I want every person involved and excited.

Joe began to distribute relevant books, articles, and tapes to key leaders throughout the company. He had guest speakers come in and talk about other companies that had become learning organizations with coaching leaders. The human resource director incorporated several of the key concepts into the existing performance management system: Everyone was given a "team coach," stretch goals were developed, learning goals were added, and performance "dialogue sessions" were scheduled four times a year. Tom Nutley, one of the division presidents, recalls this phase of the process:

> I remember thinking that this stuff was interesting, but I wasn't sure where Joe was trying to go. We had in-depth discussions and some of us shared ideas, but nothing really changed in the daily work. I remember thinking that Joe could better spend his time and money on "real company business" instead of this philosophy stuff. I must admit, it took me a good 2 or 3 years to "get it" and realize the incredible benefits—in terms of both personal satisfaction and overall company profits.

Joanie Smith, a finance director, remembers when she began to "get it."

> At a meeting, Joe turned to me and said, "So Joanie, how are you going to reinvent the accounting department to support a coaching organization?" I just stared at him. It was one thing to talk about all of this stuff, but it was quite another to actually incorporate the ideas into the daily fabric of our work. I remember being scared and excited at the same time.

This was a turning point in the organization. Joe pushed the idea that the only sustainable competitive advantage was to learn faster than the competition. "Keep learning" became his motto.

Joe began to work more closely with his executive team. He painted a picture of what the organization should strive for and encouraged everyone to give an example of how this picture could be translated into the individual divisions and departments. Mike Peters, a division president, remembers one of the more powerful exercises:

> With the help of an outside facilitator, Joe divided us into groups and had each group draw a diagram, write a newspaper article, and outline key parameters of the company 5 years ahead. We were forced to think outside of our narrow viewpoints and incorporate the key vision, culture, and bottom-line goals that Joe kept putting in front of us. The results were amazing. Many of those early ideas have definitely become part of what we are today.

Joe kept hammering home the idea of true dialogue, questioning assumptions, advocating ideas, and reaching higher levels of understanding. The top team made a list of communication agreements and got better at talking through issues. Every objective, measure, strategy, and desired outcome was questioned and pushed further. "How are you going to get there?" "What mechanisms are you going to put into place to support these ideas?" "What has to happen now that hasn't happened in the past to make this come about?"

It was the job of every executive to leave each meeting and "take the message forward." Similar vision and strategy meetings were held throughout the company. Joe made sure he visited at least one meeting per site. Joe remembers how difficult this was:

> This required a real paradigm shift. My first reaction was "I can't do this. I have other things to do. I need to be running the company." It took me a while to realize that this was "running the company." What could be more important than spreading the vision and aligning the strategy? How could I not do it?

Janice, an operations manager at one of the plants, recalls her initial experience in one of these vision meetings:

> It really was unusual to see Joe, the company president, sitting down with us and chatting about the future of our division. I remember the exact moment I decided to tell Joe that I thought his quarterly measures were ineffective and that other measures could help the organization better. Joe asked me to expound on my statement and to go to the flipchart and outline what I thought would be more appropriate measures. I learned two things at that meeting. First, it was okay to share what you really think. Two, be ready to be accountable for what you say. I, of course, become the one responsible for developing a new measurement tool. We still use it today.

To accompany the evolving vision meetings, Joe created a Vision Task Force (VTF). The job of the VTF was to develop ways to bring the vision alive throughout the company—in all systems and activities. Joe sat on the task force, which was run by the vice president of human resources, Sandra Pike. Sitting on the VTF were representatives from all levels and different parts of the company. Given distance and timing, some folks attended the meeting through voice conferencing.

Sandra knew she needed to create buy-in. She also realized that anything that came out of the VTF had to align the corporate vision with each partner's vision—and also had to integrate the culture with bottom-line objectives. She remembers her initial thoughts:

> This was scary. I had to make sure this wasn't seen as just another human resource exercise. We needed to initiate very concrete ideas, nothing fluffy. It dawned on me that we were taking on a major change effort, something that was going to take years of integration and work. I wasn't even sure we could do it.

But the system began to move. The VTF, with the help of an outside consultant, realized that data and benchmarking were needed to assess the "present state" at RMI, compare it to a "desired state," outline gaps, and develop appropriate action plans. Joe was really behind this idea, and he charged every single partner in the company with the assignment of going out and benchmarking his or her own job. An internal survey was conducted to establish baseline data in terms of culture, measures, and blocks to performance. Data were also gathered on industry trends, marketing, customers, distribution systems, sales, the economy, employment, technology, and competitive analysis.

Joe orchestrated three major trips for the entire executive team. They visited three companies that were "on the path" to becoming coaching organizations. They videotaped the visits and shared these examples throughout RMI. As it turned out, top performers from other companies were more than happy to come to RMI and give presentations, explaining their successes and failures as they moved toward becoming high-performance organizations.

As data came in, Joe reminded everyone that this was a process and that everyone had to keep his or her eyes on the goal. Some folks became defensive or even depressed with certain findings. However, through open communication, partners began to see that they weren't going to be "punished" or blamed for the findings. At meetings, in the company newsletter, in his monthly e-mail to the company, and through the special VTF Updates, Joe made it clear that the data findings were merely "points in time" and that the emphasis had to be on action and growth.

With the help of consultants, the VTF worked very hard to sort through the data, define the emerging themes, and develop a plan for engaging different parts of the organization in action planning. Dramatic changes began to take place as data were shared and partners became involved in action planning. People had to actually get involved and become accountable for implementing actions. Division presidents and other key leaders were trained in action planning and appropriate dialogue techniques. The action planning process became a vehicle that forced leaders and managers to become facilitators and role models for the kind of behaviors that the new culture required.

Each division president conducted an action planning meeting to work through issues. The VTF collated all action items, listed one accountable contact person, and provided updates every 3 months in a VTF Update publication. Joe was very active and made sure all action items were prioritized and explained why certain things were being done and why other things had to wait. Everyone became involved in running the company.

Joe pushed hard and made it very clear that actions had to be measurable. "What will that look like? How will we know that has been achieved?" Partners slowly became comfortable with new behaviors and expectations. Some were more willing than others to take the plunge. José Rodriguez, an East Coast salesperson, felt that this was a significant initiative:

> Attitudes were positive. There was an electric energy. There had been other changes and trends in the past, but this was significantly different. The entire company was involved. Joe was everywhere and obviously committed. But not only that—Joe seemed to be actually changing. He listened. He often asked for feedback. Yet he also held our feet to the fire. By watching Joe, I was able to see and better understand what he was talking about. He became what he said. That was powerful. That gave me permission to try these things out for myself.

Each major department/division took part in four action planning sessions. By the third session some conversations were breaking down, and it became evident that partners needed a more focused lesson in dialogue. Sandra created a pool of "dialogue coaches" (some internal partners and some external consultants) to visit and conduct short booster lessons within the existing action planning sessions. The dialogue coaches facilitated in "real time" during the meetings:

Sandra realized the importance of such real-time coaching:

> I really underestimated the amount of learning and coaching that was necessary in the area of dialogue. People are just not taught to talk in an open way. In fact, after years of conditioning in traditional organizations, it's a slow process to move toward trusting conversations and higher levels of understanding. I also realized that the coaches were able to acknowledge and recognize those partners that tried out new behaviors. The coaches became cheerleaders. That idea of creating a pool of internal coaches was something we formally continued over the years.

Joe and Sandra timed the collation of all action plans to coincide with the next formal strategic planning process. Joe and his executive team were able to incorporate the action plans into the vision and supporting strategy. It became obvious that some significant changes were needed to support new goals. Some were more sensitive and personal than others, and Joe realized that this would be a real test for the new culture. Supporting strategies included a restructuring of leadership responsibilities, an expansion into the company's European market, research and production in more advanced technologies, two acquisitions, the development of a more aggressive marketing team, and one divestiture. Joe was excited and concerned:

> This was the most aggressive strategic plan in our history. I found myself wondering if I had the leaders who could do it. I wondered whether I could do it. I explored this deeply with my coach and realized that my role as champion was essential. My coach helped me to keep the big picture in mind, move steadily forward, and trust the process. I began to shift my view. At first I saw this as a huge combination of actions that I needed to balance—the old "balls in the air" syndrome. I grew to understand that my job was not that of a juggler but of someone who needed to provide focus and alignment. With this more streamlined role in mind, I was better able to coach and guide. I was also able to combat my own fears and plunge into business areas that I had been comfortably avoiding. Ironically, I became a better leader when I allowed myself to be coached by those I was coaching.

Joe continued to use the VTF as the point of focus for the continued change effort. Sandra made sure that results were publicized and celebrated:

> The VTF Update was distributed online and in hard copy. We videotaped action teams, celebrations, and program results and showed the video at various summer picnics across the company. In his monthly e-mail, Joe commented on major successes. I wanted to make sure partners saw the connections between their actions and results. In other companies, I had seen too many good efforts killed by falling into a black hole, never to be heard of again. I was determined that this wouldn't happen at RMI.

The large number of changes put stress on the company. To keep the vision alive, Joe hired an outside consultant team to come in and conduct a series of half-day "change seminars." Partners discussed the "pain of change" and revisited the ultimate culture and goals they were trying to achieve. They learned ways to deal with stress, reframe daily work, create mechanisms for mutual support, and just relax and enjoy the roller-coaster ride. They drew time lines on the walls, charting out progress and changes over the past 2 years.

Perhaps one of the most significant outcomes of this process was the development and implementation of a revised performance system. The VTF targeted the existing performance system as a way to align personal and organizational goals. The implementation went through several stages, three name changes, and 2 years of revisions. When it was first implemented, the system was met with much moaning and groaning. Though based on all of the right drivers, the process was cumbersome and long. Furthermore, it required skill sets that were not yet embedded in the culture.

Over a 2-year period, the total process was revised. The system was put online, and trust was so high that everyone had access to everybody else's plan—even Joe's. Called the Guide to Exceleration Program (GTEP)[1], it linked everything throughout the company, from hiring, coaching, and development to performance assessment, continuous improvement, and bottom-line success (see Figure 4.2).

The yearly strategic planning process was coordinated with the beginning of the performance management cycle. The key strategic drivers and actions for the year were clearly publicized and discussed. While strategic meetings were taking place, individual partners were developing or revising their role descriptions and personal vision, mission, and value statements. Though traditional job descriptions were written and kept on file for legal purposes, it was role descriptions that guided performance. Role descriptions described work

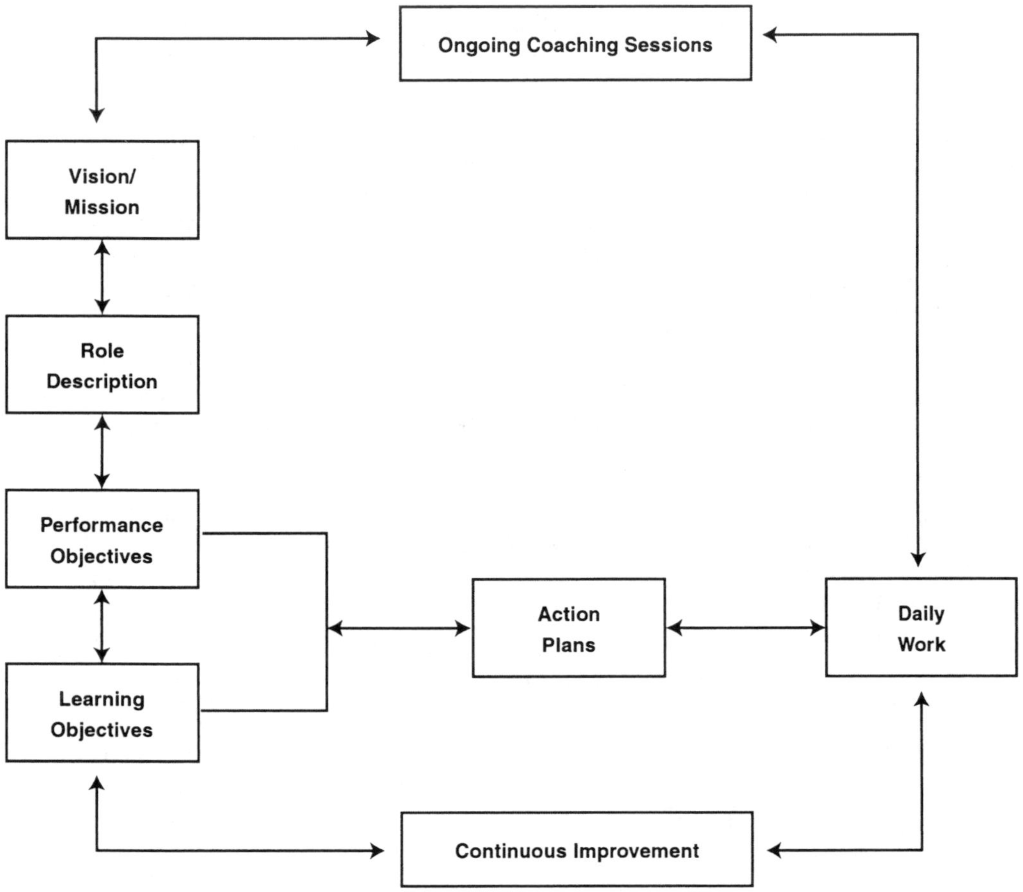

Figure 4.2. Guide to Exceleration
SOURCE: Developed by Virginia Bianco-Mathis for Phillips Corporation, Inc., Columbia, Maryland.

and tasks in a "continuous improvement" format (Thayer, 2001). Each major activity was written within the context of "what would this look like if it were done by a world-class performer" (see Exhibit 4.4). The role description put each job within the frame of possible opportunities. Yearly discussions of the role description enabled partners to think outside the box.

The role description was also used during the hiring process. Any candidate reading a role description would immediately realize that this was a different kind of company. Discussions of the role description ensured the right kind of hires—the right attitude, spirit, commitment, and vision for a high-performance organization.

During coaching sessions, a partner's personal vision, mission, and values were also revisited. Am I still on the path? Does working at RMI still support my vision? Is there a connection between my personal vision and corporate vision?

Then the team coach and partner would mutually develop performance objectives, learning objectives, and action plans. There would be four coaching sessions a year to ensure progress, goal alignment, and support.

However, in the second year of implementation, Joe felt that the GTEP was not being appropriately followed. Parts of the company were still merely filling in the blanks, and certain division and team leaders were just going through the motions. The system seemed to break down with the action plans. People

Exhibit 4.4 **Sample Role Description Components**

For a vice president/business area leader:

- Modeling, and demanding from all others, performance consistent with our values of integrity and ethics—of always doing the right thing.
- At all times having someone ready, willing, and able to take over my job and capable of doing it better than I do.
- Making sure that our strategic partners, suppliers, customers, and the telecommunications industry view me as a key leader in the field.
- Creating and involving every key person in business strategies that will ensure our company's health and growth both short term and long term, thereby providing an endless succession of opportunities for the company and for every member of the company.

For a company president:

- Becoming the leader I need to be to seduce people to our mission and to put our mission first in their hearts and minds at work. Nurturing the sort of culture that will make it necessary for them to demand of themselves, of others, and of their tools and resources whatever it takes to make the company the best in the business by any measure.
- Creating the kind of culture that keeps everyone focused on accomplishments, not activities.
- Being the exemplary question asker in the organization. Being a world-class example of a person who is always in the learning mode, and making it necessary for everyone I come in contact with to be in the learning mode.

For a human resource manager:

- Ensuring that we hire only people who are on the path to virtuosity.
- Knowing at all times how to provide the most current resources to further our partners' personal and professional development.
- Creating a culture such that it is necessary to be the best. This includes creating methods of measurement that benchmark individual and team performance against the best. It includes creating a learning organization where it is necessary to be dedicated to a lifetime of creating greater and greater accomplishments.

SOURCE: From selected role descriptions provided by Alan Phillips, President, Phillips Corporation; and John McBeth, former President of Century Computing. Used with permission. Based on the work of Lee Thayer.

were not seeing the connection between overall goals and the daily work. With the help of consultants, Sandra was able to connect the dots:

> The action plans were not carefully thought through or followed. Consequently, during coaching sessions, partners weren't seeing the connection to the whole. We revised the online guidelines and demonstrated how to develop meaningful action plans—how to take an objective, look 6 to 12 weeks out, and outline tasks with tangible milestones that would lead to the stretch goals.
>
> Then we developed a series of dialogue sessions for key leaders and team coaches at every location. Believe it or not, Joe attended at least one session at each division. The results were amazing. Leaders began to see how they had to coach and guide through the action plans and milestones. Once they saw the connection to the daily work, they were able to modify their coaching dialogues, and many gaps throughout the organization began to close. The interesting thing is that all of these programs and approaches

> were only tools that enabled the right conversations to emerge. Once the right conversations were reinforced, magic happened.

In the third year, the compensation system was modified to reinforce teamwork, successful milestones, and a combination of personal and company growth. An equity program was added once open management was incorporated into the culture. Every partner attended workshops and learned how to track company drivers, read financial statements, note patterns, and proactively make financial decisions. Joe's commitment was constant:

> I had to be visible and engaged—otherwise, partners would think, "Oh good, this is fading away," and they would return to old behaviors. I also had to continue to role-model, hold the torch, celebrate successes, and question, challenge, and reinforce. As tough as this was, it wasn't as tough as having to face the fact that certain leaders and partners were not going to be able to function in this new culture. I had to come down hard on a couple of key leaders. One didn't think I was serious, and she just kept giving lip service. However, I put her in charge of the open management workshop and she turned around. Unfortunately, one division president didn't believe in the underlying concept of coaching and continuous improvement. He was stuck in an old hierarchical paradigm, and no amount of coaching could shake him loose. However, the coaching process did make it easier for us to reach a mutual agreement that he had to leave. It was respectful. It also sent the right message to the rest of the company.

Because Joe stressed continuous improvement, evaluation was incorporated throughout the change effort. Every action plan had an accountable contact and a meaningful measure—a measure based on results, not just activity. Within the open-book management system, a series of top-down and bottom-up reports highlighted key drivers and tracked milestones. The GTEP continuously aligned individual performance with organizational goals. Quarterly dialogue sessions fostered down-board thinking so that actions could be redirected and adjusted.

During difficult times, Joe was there to listen, provide focus, and make any tough decisions that needed to be made concerning alignment. Sandra felt that the strongest evaluation technique they used was the process of building a "continuous change cycle":

> Every year, an organizational survey and focus groups collected data on a wide range of key dimensions. As part of the strategic planning process, there were updated studies on competition, environment, and trends. We got better and better at focusing on the right things so we weren't collecting data for the sake of collecting data. We built a seamless evaluation system. Evaluation was not a discrete activity—it was built into the infrastructure. We incorporated a 360-degree development tool and actually put it online so folks could get more instantaneous results.

Joe continued to be passionate about learning. He brought in a high-level planner to help the executive team get more sophisticated and global in their strategic thinking. At the same time, he created a "High Jump" award for those partners who demonstrated leaps in their thinking and approach. In the third year of their metamorphosis, people began to notice that it wasn't just Joe anymore—all of the leaders were demonstrating powerful coaching behaviors.

It was also around this time that Joe had a discussion with his coach and decided that it was time to move on to another coach:

> I found that my coach helped me discover myself, expand my thinking, define my goals, and put structure around my passions. He kept me on track and gave me exercises to practice and modify my behaviors. However, because I was serious about my leadership, I began to internalize a new way of being. My conversations with my coach began to be mostly sharing. I found that I was learning more through my interactions with other consultants and readings. In one of the books I was reading, I discovered that it is normal to "outgrow" one coach and move on to another. My coach agreed. I met with a few coaches before choosing a new one. This time my focus was different. I now wanted to explore and concentrate on organizational behavior and becoming more skilled in implementing programs, building infrastructures, and influencing groups. I also wanted to become more adept in working with partners outside the organization. In all honesty, my first coach could have helped me through my new goals, but psychologically I wanted the experience of working with someone else—like moving on to a new teacher in a new grade. It was an enriching change.

During all this time of change, RMI gained 50% more market share and successfully moved into the European and Asian markets. They developed and successfully marketed an innovative molding process that was making them a forerunner in the industry. Unfortunately, RMI also had to struggle through an 18-month economic downturn. Many other companies folded, and a lot of people lost their jobs in major cities. Even RMI had to cut back. However, because of the excellent infrastructure and planning, only a minimum number of factory workers had to be let go. They were treated respectfully, given good severance and outplacement—and an open option to come back when the economy improved. Critics wanted to know why a "coaching organization" wasn't able to escape hard times. Joe was quick to answer:

> No culture, leader, program, or approach can provide protection from industrial, national, or international trends. However, companies that are tied closely to their people, with aligned personal and organizational goals, can better manage the tough times. First, because of our aggressive tracking and dialogue sessions, we were able to plan ahead and we were more prepared for the downturn. Our people were mentally ready. In fact, they are the ones that developed the plan for minimizing the effects of the downsizing. There was respect and support. When folks are seeing the numbers, studying trends, and making decisions, there is no game playing. Everything is aboveboard and understood. I laugh at leaders who say, "We can't tell the people that." Who do these leaders think they are kidding? It's your people who know what is going on and what has to be done.

Competencies

For the first step, establishing the coaching relationship, you must demonstrate six key competencies to raise awareness and begin movement toward a coaching organization. Through commitment, vision, a sense of urgency, collaboration, self-knowledge, and teaching, you can educate your organization, create a picture of the vision, and get employees involved in the process. Table 4.1 outlines these competencies and provides supporting examples from the case study.

Table 4.1 Demonstrated Competencies for Step 1: Establishing the Coaching Relationship

Competency	*Demonstrated Actions From Case Study*
Commitment: Demonstrating dedication and the ability to establish trust and buy-in	■ Joe made his own strengths and weaknesses discussible and allowed himself to be challenged. ■ He took on a personal coach, thereby role-modeling a coaching relationship. ■ He developed and shared concrete examples and vision in charts and presentations. ■ He bombarded his organization with learning materials. ■ He created dialogue sessions and meetings to explore new approaches.
Vision: Being able to paint a purposeful and inspirational picture of the future that motivates others to action	■ Joe clearly defined business results and culture expectations. ■ He challenged the top group to reinvent the business. ■ He invited everyone to participate in the building of a new organization. ■ He painted a picture and provided a path.
Sense of Urgency: Being able to take risks, demonstrate dramatic action, and apply the tools of change management	■ Joe charted the market and the competition and created a sense of opportunity. ■ He set a challenge to revolutionize the business. ■ He outlined new skills, a new market, new relationships, and new technology.
Collaboration: Demonstrating patience, being involved and present, and creating means for others to participate	■ Joe asked for people's thoughts and participation. ■ He set the stage for the vision to become everyone's vision. ■ He inquired about and discussed learning materials—created awareness. ■ He asked employees to join and share in the dream—did not demand compliance.
Self-Knowledge: Possessing emotional awareness, continually learning and adjusting, and asking for feedback	■ Joe discussed ideas and progress with a coach and a group of outside peers. ■ He challenged himself and his own mind-sets. ■ He demonstrated continuous learning. ■ He actively struggled with behavior changes and asked for feedback.
Teaching: Showing the ability to facilitate learning, listen, and role-model new behaviors	■ Joe facilitated dialogue sessions and reached higher levels of understanding. ■ He practiced advocacy and inquiry. ■ He transferred his own learning to others through example. ■ He demonstrated an alternative "way of being." ■ He challenged others to try out new roles.

Table 4.2 Demonstrated Competencies for Step 2: Collecting and Analyzing Data

Competency	*Demonstrated Actions From Case Study*
Participation: Being involved and creating vehicles for collaboration and accountability	■ Joe created intense meetings with the executive group. ■ He challenged leaders to infuse meaning into the vision and strategically move forward. ■ He challenged each leader to become a role model. ■ He created cascading meetings to carry the message down and across the organization. ■ He personally attended at least one field meeting at each location. ■ He created a Vision Task Force. ■ He had every employee benchmark his/her own job. ■ He discovered information, gaps, themes, and needed actions in collaboration with others.
Establishment of Trust: Demonstrating integrity and honesty	■ Joe involved his own people in strategy, vision, data gathering, and planning. ■ He demonstrated faith in his people, and they stepped up to the plate—which in turn created momentum, high expectations, and motivation. ■ He put his own ideas on the table to be discussed, explored, challenged, and changed. ■ He took part in the frustrating task of sorting and analyzing the data. ■ He did not sugarcoat data or hide sensitive data.
Courage: Demonstrating the ability to face one's own fears and be accountable for one's own actions; creating tools for others to do the same	■ Joe allowed his own mental models to be challenged and pushed. ■ He demonstrated the ability to be flexible and to grow. ■ He diminished fears through dialogue and support. ■ He fostered the sharing of ideas without attack or blame. ■ He demanded accountability and follow-up actions.
Persistence: Demonstrating constancy of purpose and providing continual focus and goal alignment	■ Joe forced agreement on meanings. ■ He worked issues to the point of alignment with vision and increased performance. ■ He demonstrated that this was a process—ongoing refinement and forward movement. ■ He created plans for aligning strategy with tangible actions. ■ He supported the purpose of the Vision Task Force to create an infrastructure—themes and actions to drive the vision. ■ He accepted negative feedback and data as an opportunity to move closer to virtuosity.

(continued)

Table 4.2 Continued

Competency	*Demonstrated Actions From Case Study*
Education: Showing the ability to coach others and demonstrating new behaviors for learning	■ Joe created pockets of learning in activities and conversations. ■ He led the executive team through exercises to "draw the future." ■ He encouraged thinking "outside the box." ■ He made his own learning visible and discussible. ■ He created communication agreements so that all leaders became role models. ■ He distributed articles and books. ■ He provided consultants and presenters, as needed. ■ Through involvement, he transferred the skills required to conduct benchmarking, surveys, data analysis, focus groups, and interviewing. ■ He created a self-perpetuating "learning system" within the organization.

The data collection and analysis step also uses five competencies that open the doors of an organization to scrutiny and careful planning—while also keeping an eye on the overall goal of coaching and high performance: participation, establishment of trust, courage, persistence, and education. Collaboration and involvement are key in ensuring a total systems approach. Everyone must be involved in the process of collecting data and creating plans for how to get closer to the vision. In this way, the effort becomes everyone's agenda, not just that of leadership, human resources, or "them." Table 4.2 outlines these competencies with specific examples from the case study.

Three powerful competencies drive Step 3, processing feedback and planning actions: focus on the vision, provision of a challenge, and the ability to act as a change agent. Key actions for you during this step are to keep employees focused on the vision, push for creative ideas, and encourage accountability for actions. Table 4.3 outlines example behaviors from the case study.

After all of the dialogue and action planning, things have to be implemented. The coaching leader must still provide vision and learning, but he or she must also provide acknowledgment, alignment, and follow-through. Some leaders drop out during this stage, believing that now "it's up to them." A coaching leader realizes there is no "them."

During the step of taking action, you should begin to see the fruits of your commitment and persistence. When you link systems to vision, more of the right things get done. You have built coaching leadership into the culture, and leadership doesn't fall solely on your shoulders. As Table 4.4 demonstrates,

Table 4.3 Demonstrated Competencies in Step 3: Processing Feedback and Planning Actions

Competency	*Demonstrated Actions From Case Study*
Focus on the Vision: Being a cheerleader in guiding others toward the vision; demonstrating courage in dealing with new directions and behaviors	■ Joe involved everyone in the action planning process and demanded alignment with the vision. ■ He incorporated action plans into the yearly strategic planning process. ■ He demanded tangible measures and outputs: leading-edge products, increased market share, total restructuring. ■ He defined his role as "focused radar," not "juggler." ■ He transformed himself in front of others—entered "unsafe" territory. ■ He fostered communication, negotiation, and decision making through the action planning meetings. ■ He instituted a cadre of "dialogue coaches" who provided "just-in-time" feedback. ■ He empowered employees to reach for stretch goals by providing the right kinds of tools.
Provision of a Challenge: Confronting and questioning personal agendas; setting expectations beyond old paradigms	■ Joe fostered commitment and a sense of responsibility through participatory action planning meetings. ■ He questioned personal agendas and turf issues and encouraged problem solving and stretch goals that went beyond old paradigms. ■ He kept the pressure on through the Vision Task Force: communicating status updates, naming accountable parties, and tracking progress toward goals.
Ability to Act as a Change Agent: Modeling new behaviors and provide supporting structures to guide change	■ Joe encouraged people to experiment and try new behaviors by role-modeling his own changes. ■ He supplied stronger support tools (dialogue coaches) when action planning meetings broke down. ■ He required action plans that were bold and moved each person and the organization toward virtuosity.

your key competencies during this step are alignment with the vision, follow-through, facilitation of continuous learning, and acknowledgment of others' contributions.

Evaluation tends to be a neglected step because most leaders assume it is expensive and time-consuming. In the case study, Joe demonstrates that evaluation can be embedded in normal work practices and does not have to be something imposed. The three major competencies for effectively evaluating your progress are decision making, passion, and rewarding of others' contributions. Table 4.5 provides valuable ideas from the case study.

Table 4.4 Demonstrated Competencies in Step 4: Taking Action

Competency	*Demonstrated Actions From Case Study*
Alignment With the Vision: Linking all actions and structures to the vision	■ Joe built a coaching infrastructure, aligning personal vision with the organizational vision, coaching sessions, and continuous improvement. ■ He created a linking performance management system, the Guide to Exceleration Program (GTEP). ■ He instituted open-book management, aligning daily work with business decisions. ■ He made tough decisions about behavior and goals: you either were aligned or moved on. ■ He connected daily tasks to employees' personal vision, role description, objectives, and specific action plans. ■ He broke down stretch goals into meaningful action plans and tasks that were modified and supported through ongoing coaching sessions: a concrete walkway to high performance. ■ He tied communications to specific tasks, meaningful information, key decisions, and results, thereby linking action to results.
Follow-Through: Being able to plan, organize, and track measurable results	■ The Vision Task Force communicated status and results of action plans on a regular basis: It kept the pressure on, created momentum, inspired high performance, and acknowledged movement along the path. ■ Joe provided the Change Seminars to foster creativity, deal with losses and difficulties of change, and inspire and motivate to action. ■ He instituted "quarterly strategic checkups" as part of the open-book management system to provide acknowledgment, measurement, accountability, and focus.
Facilitation of Continuous Learning: Demonstrating a dedication to learning and providing structures for continuous development	■ Joe provided supportive workshops when certain programs began to lose momentum or required high-level skills—open-book management techniques, change seminars, strategic planning skills; he raised the bar. ■ He built structures that made continuous learning a way of life: stretch goals, coaching sessions, strategic checkpoints, open-book management analysis, and learning action plans as part of the GTEP. ■ He provided dialogue coaches and internal consultants to individuals or groups that got "stuck" along the way; this was viewed as part of the learning process, not as a mistake or problem. ■ He offered seminars on coping strategies, mutual support, stress, and reframing the daily work.
Acknowledgment of Others' Contributions: Recognizing others and creating structures that support and celebrate the right behaviors.	■ Joe videotaped and showed examples of teamwork, programs, learning, and celebrations that supported the coaching environment. ■ He utilized internal communications (newsletter, emails, reports from the Vision Task Force) to acknowledge achievements and "stretch successes." ■ He implemented a revised compensation system that rewarded team effort, ownership, and continuous improvement. ■ He participated in the advanced training and internal consulting himself.

Table 4.5 Demonstrated Competencies in Step 5: Evaluating Your Progress

Competency	*Demonstrated Actions From the Case Study*
Decision Making: Being able to make tough choices that support the vision, foster accountability, and align consequences	▪ Joe built evaluation into existing programs: quarterly coaching sessions, quarterly strategic updates, tracking reports (key drivers and milestones, not just activities). ▪ He made tough decisions—within a trusting and open framework—that kept actions on course and supported overall vision and goals. ▪ He established consequences: higher standards, continuous growth, more supportive coaching, learning activities, or a decision to leave the organization and seek alignment with personal goals that could not be attained within RMI. ▪ He utilized an internal radar system to plan ahead and mitigate effects of an economic downturn.
Passion: Possessing and showing strong enthusiasm and energy toward a vision; providing focus and learning through one's energy and excitement	▪ Joe provided continuous momentum and revitalization through an updated data collection process, yearly surveys, and focus groups. ▪ The Vision Task Force scanned the environment yearly; data collection and analysis was ongoing, not a one-time event. ▪ Joe personally used the data collection process as a way to establish future stretch goals, always reaching for higher performance. ▪ He provided internal and external coaches. ▪ He moved on to a new coach in order to explore new horizons and approaches.
Rewarding of Others' Contributions: Openly recognizing those who role-model desired behaviors; sharing the benefits of a rewarding culture	▪ Joe implemented the High Jump Award for accomplishment of stretch goals—out of the ordinary. ▪ He communicated the mind-set of companywide rewards of low turnover, increased market share, and overall financial success.

Another Look

Obviously, the case study provides a dramatic example of building a coaching organization and linking all of the concepts from the previous chapters. Joe Ryan was committed to his vision. What is important was not just what went right but what went wrong—and how it was handled. By using the worksheets at the end of this chapter, you can incorporate the lessons from the case and adapt them to your own organization.

In Part 1, we provided a table that compared traditional leaders to coaching leaders. Table 4.6 compares a traditional organization to a coaching organization. Study the chart and assess the basic philosophies that you might need to begin to change—for yourself and for your organization.

Table 4.6 Conventional Versus Coaching Organizations

Dimension	*Conventional Organization*	*High-Performance Coaching Organization*
Assessment of our own capabilities	Based on past experience and therefore self-limiting	Expects more than indicated by past experience
Our habits and standard approaches	If they work, use them	We must change our habits regularly to improve
Performance improvement	Assumes people will naturally improve	Makes it necessary to change and improve
What is possible?	Determined through past experience and benchmarks	The only way to know what's possible is to do it
Approach to planning	Sometimes considered unnecessary; "winging it" is okay if it works	Planning is critical to success
Goal setting	Sets achievable goals	Sets audacious stretch goals
Performance measurement	Often views personal metrics as difficult and ineffective	Sees personal performance metrics as crucial
Work focus	Focuses on activities	Focuses on accomplishments
Long-term goals	Focuses primarily on short-term goals	Sees that long-term goals are crucial to mastery; uses role descriptions to define them
Plan for mastery	No focus on mastery	Uses role descriptions, performance goals, learning plan, and coaching sessions to define the plan
Level of mastery	Pays little attention to level of mastery, so contributes to long periods of plateaus	Uses coaching and practice to advance to higher levels of performance
Ownership of results	Often uses excuses and blames others	Takes 100% ownership
Mode of operation	In the knowing mode	In the learning mode
Conversation	Purpose is to convince and persuade	Purpose is meaningful dialogue leading to understanding and higher levels of performance
Mistakes	Opportunity to blame	Opportunity for learning

SOURCE: Developed by Don Link, from *The Journey to High Performance*, internal publication, Adapted and used here with permission.

Note

1. The Guide to Exceleration Program was developed by the Phillips Corporation, Columbia, Maryland, and is being adapted here with permission.

WORKSHEET 4.1: From Traditional to Coaching Organization

Step 1: Establishing the Coaching Relationship

DEFINING THE DESIRED OUTCOMES

1. **My vision of a coaching organization is:**

 ____

 ____

2. **My reasons for creating a coaching organization are:**

 ____

 ____

3. **The values, characteristics, and key components of my coaching organization are:**

 ____

 ____

4. **The role I expect to play in building a coaching organization is:**

 ____

 ____

5. **Building a coaching organization supports my vision as a leader by:**

 ____

 ____

6. **Personal and organizational challenges I need to overcome when building a coaching organization are:**

 ____

 ____

Tips and Examples

- ❑ Consider how building a coaching organization coincides with your leadership goals.
- ❑ Stay mindful of the fact that a "coaching organization" is a mind-set, not a program.
- ❑ Remember that the vision must connect to the human spirit: It must inspire, be easily understood, and incorporate both business goals and cultural goals within the same framework.
- ❑ Make your vision of the coaching organization tangible: something you can show, talk about, explain, and enhance through dialogue.
- ❑ Build off any methods and structures that were established in creating a coaching mind-set within the executive team (Part 3).
- ❑ Outline the components (make a list) of the coaching organization that you want to establish. Brainstorm, using many levels, categories, behaviors, outputs, structures, roles, and so forth. Embed the coaching systems model: coaching mind-set, leadership-driven vision, dialogue, continuous improvement, coaching, learning, coaching infrastructure, continuous change, high performance, success.

(continued)

WORKSHEET 4.1: From Traditional to Coaching *(continued)*

- ❑ Examine your self-awareness: how your strengths and weaknesses play into this goal.
- ❑ Totally embrace the time commitment and role modeling that you are going to have to demonstrate.

QUESTIONS TO CONSIDER

1. **What do I want to create that is bigger than me and my organization?**
2. **What am I passionate about?**
3. **Why do I want to build a coaching organization at this time?**
4. **How does my vision as a leader coincide with the development of a coaching organization?**
5. **What's my vision of the amount of time and commitment that this is going to take?**
6. **What outputs and results do I believe can be achieved through a coaching organization?**
7. **As I look at my leadership strengths and weaknesses, what challenges do I need to overcome?**
8. **As I look at the organization in its present state, what challenges do I have to overcome to build a coaching organization?**

Tips and Examples

- ❑ Leading a coaching organization is a calling beyond starting and sustaining a business or business unit.
- ❑ Get in touch with your inner passion. Do you believe that a coaching organization is the best way for you to lead and the best way for an organization to function?
- ❑ Think in terms of both tangible and intangible benefits/outputs to you and the organization.
- ❑ Realize that you will be taking a risk and that your business judgment and approaches may be questioned.
- ❑ Realize that this is something you must do yourself; it cannot be delegated.
- ❑ Your list of personal and organizational challenges should lead to concrete methods, approaches, tools, and helpful mechanisms.

RESOURCES AND TOOLS

1. **Internal structures that I will use to involve and educate the organization toward becoming a "total coaching organization" are:**

   ____

   ____

(continued)

WORKSHEET 4.1: From Traditional to Coaching *(continued)*

2. **Methods I will use to share and inspire the organization toward the vision of a coaching organization are:**

___

___

3. **Specific things I will do and say in the establishment of a coaching organization are:**

___

___

Tips and Examples

- ❑ Have dialogue sessions with colleagues/sources outside the organization that support your belief in a coaching organization.
- ❑ Visit coaching organizations to create your own vision and picture.
- ❑ Create dialogue structures within the organization to educate, create buy-in, and build momentum: focus groups, surveys, cascading meetings.
- ❑ Develop and share a vision that addresses business goals and culture within the same picture.
- ❑ Develop and share a vision that connects to each person's internal mission, values, and spirit (something that is inherent in every person).
- ❑ Share pertinent articles and books.
- ❑ Collect and share preliminary data from organizations that are on the path of becoming coaching organizations (videos, policies and procedures, vision statements, cultural descriptions).
- ❑ Create a Vision Task Force to begin investigating, communicating, and developing components of a coaching vision and total coaching organization.
- ❑ Role-model a coaching relationship by having your own coach.
- ❑ Role-model coaching relationships through your top team and by participating in dialogue sessions.
- ❑ Place "establishing a coaching organization" on meeting agendas.
- ❑ Invite guest speakers/experts on the topics of coaching, continuous learning, stretch goals, high performance, and other supporting themes.

COMPETENCIES

On a scale of 1 to 5 (1 = nonexistent; 5 = outstanding), rate yourself on the following competencies for this step:

1. **Commitment** 1 2 3 4 5

   Two specific ways I will demonstrate this competency in this step:

   a. ___

   b. ___

(continued)

WORKSHEET 4.1: From Traditional to Coaching (*continued*)

2. Vision **1 2 3 4 5**

Two specific ways I will demonstrate this competency in this step:

a. ______________________________

b. ______________________________

3. Sense of Urgency **1 2 3 4 5**

Two specific ways I will demonstrate this competency in this step:

a. ______________________________

b. ______________________________

4. Collaboration **1 2 3 4 5**

Two specific ways I will demonstrate this competency in this step:

a. ______________________________

b. ______________________________

5. Self-Knowledge **1 2 3 4 5**

Two specific ways I will demonstrate this competency in this step:

a. ______________________________

b. ______________________________

Tips and Examples

- ❑ Allow yourself to be challenged.
- ❑ Give away control in order to gain control.
- ❑ Develop and share examples and vision of a coaching organization through presentations and through the facilitation of dialogue sessions.
- ❑ Bombard the organization with learning materials.
- ❑ Make your own strengths and weaknesses discussible. Ask for feedback.
- ❑ Clearly define business results and culture expectations.
- ❑ Invite everyone to participate.
- ❑ Provide a path.
- ❑ Demonstrate and outline the possibilities.
- ❑ Demonstrate and outline the dangers of not revitalizing the business and focusing on a coaching vision.
- ❑ Exhibit patience. People will move at different paces.
- ❑ Practice advocacy and inquiry in all conversations. Demonstrate high levels of understanding.
- ❑ Challenge others to try out new roles.

WORKSHEET 4.2: From Traditional to Coaching Organization

Step 2: Collecting and Analyzing Data

DEFINING THE DESIRED OUTCOMES

1. **The data collection process will support my vision of a coaching organization by:**

   ____

   ____

2. **The kinds of data I will gather concerning coaching organizations include:**

   ____

   ____

3. **My purpose for collecting data about coaching organizations is:**

   ____

   ____

4. **Coaching organization themes and trends that I will look for from data analysis are:**

   ____

   ____

5. **The results of the data collection and analysis process will provide focus for building a coaching organization by:**

   ____

   ____

Tips and Examples

- ❑ Develop a list of exploration areas and themes to focus the data collection process and ensure that it supports your vision.
- ❑ Provide guidelines that keep the research realistic and meaningful given the organization's resources, time, money, and product/service.
- ❑ Utilize the exploratory findings from Step 1 to focus more in-depth research.
- ❑ Seek out not only factual information but also feelings, benefits, thoughts, and philosophies that connect to the human spirit.

QUESTIONS TO CONSIDER

1. **What specific results am I seeking from the data collection process?**
2. **How will the information gained be used to build a coaching organization?**
3. **What guidelines and ideas can I provide that will narrow the search and result in more focused information?**
4. **How will the vision drive the data collection and analysis?**

(continued)

WORKSHEET 4.2: From Traditional to Coaching (*continued*)

Tips and Examples

- ❑ You want results that lead people to action, provide guidance in the actual building of a coaching organization, further paint a picture that employees can identify with, and build momentum.
- ❑ Don't let the vision get lost in the details.
- ❑ Design the research process around how you ultimately want to present the findings to the rest of the organization.

RESOURCES AND TOOLS

1. **The internal structures that we will create to collect and analyze the coaching organization data are:**

   ____

   ____

2. **The methods that we will use to collect data concerning coaching organizations are:**

   ____

   ____

3. **The methods that we will use to analyze data and summarize/sort the data into appropriate coaching organization themes are:**

   ____

   ____

4. **My participation in the data collection and analysis process will be:**

   ____

   ____

5. **We will ensure participation in the data collection and analysis process through:**

   ____

   ____

6. **The skills and attitudes that we will demonstrate throughout the data collection and analysis process include:**

   ____

   ____

Tips and Examples

- ❑ Form a committee or task force to conduct research and analysis. The committee can become a permanent entity to guide the coaching organization process.
- ❑ Provide updates to the process through internal communications and continually tie to the ultimate goals and vision.

(continued)

WORKSHEET 4.2: From Traditional to Coaching *(continued)*

- ❑ Consider the use of benchmarking, interviews, the Internet, guest speakers, material from other organizations that are becoming coaching organizations, pertinent books/journals, and expert consultants.
- ❑ Consider internal surveys, focus groups, and dialogue sessions.
- ❑ Create a picture of "here we are" and "here is where we want to be."
- ❑ Utilize themes and trends that make sense given your resources, goals, and vision.
- ❑ Demonstrate openness and creativity toward the data. Some internal findings may be difficult to hear. Some external ideas may sound too difficult to achieve.
- ❑ Remind everyone that the process is "a work in progress." It will take time to achieve goals. It is important to chart the path.
- ❑ Create cascading meetings for total involvement.
- ❑ Have everyone benchmark his/her own job.
- ❑ Take groups to visit other coaching organizations.
- ❑ Use internal or external facilitators to assist in the process of data collection and data analysis.

COMPETENCIES

On a scale of 1 to 5 (1 = nonexistent; 5 = outstanding), rate yourself on each competency for this step:

1. **Participation** **1 2 3 4 5**

   Two specific ways I will demonstrate this competency in this step:

   a. ____________________

   b. ____________________

2. **Establishment of Trust** **1 2 3 4 5**

   Two specific ways I will demonstrate this competency in this step:

   a. ____________________

   b. ____________________

3. **Courage** **1 2 3 4 5**

   Two specific ways I will demonstrate this competency in this step:

   a. ____________________

   b. ____________________

4. **Persistence** **1 2 3 4 5**

   Two specific ways I will demonstrate this competency in this step:

   a. ____________________

   b. ____________________

(continued)

WORKSHEET 4.2: From Traditional to Coaching *(continued)*

5. Education **1 2 3 4 5**

Two specific ways I will demonstrate this competency in this step:

a. ____________________

b. ____________________

Tips and Examples

- ❑ Take on some aspect of the research and data analysis yourself. Seek out colleagues and experts and share the experience.
- ❑ The more employees participate in the process, the more trust, buy-in, and enthusiasm will develop.
- ❑ Challenge every leader to become a role model.
- ❑ Embrace all data openly.
- ❑ Keep the vision out in front.
- ❑ Allow your own mental models, ideas, and behaviors to be challenged.
- ❑ Diminish fears through dialogue and support.
- ❑ Work issues to the point of alignment with vision and increased performance.
- ❑ Demand that accountability accompany ideas.
- ❑ Provide learning activities and thinking "outside the box."

WORKSHEET 4.3: From Traditional to Coaching Organization

Step 3: Processing Feedback and Planning Actions

DEFINING THE DESIRED OUTCOMES

1. **Specific outcomes from the data findings that I expect to share with the organization are:**

   ____

   ____

2. **Our purpose for developing an action plan to build a coaching organization is:**

   ____

   ____

3. **My purpose in being involved in the feedback and action planning process is:**

   ____

   ____

4. **Measurements that we should embed in our action plans for building a coaching organization are:**

   ____

   ____

Tips and Examples

- ❑ Consider outputs of creativity, innovation, alignment, and excitement. How can these be fostered during the data feedback process?
- ❑ Determine ways that the feedback can lead people to focused action.
- ❑ Resources, actions, and vision need to be aligned through an action plan.
- ❑ Consider the unique contributions you can make as a leader in this step.
- ❑ Begin to brainstorm on the kind of measurements that make sense given the research, the gap analysis, and the kind of coaching organization that you are trying to build.

QUESTIONS TO CONSIDER

1. **Why do I want to share the data findings?**
2. **How will I use the action plan to build a coaching organization?**
3. **What value does this action plan have for those inside the organization?**
4. **What can I see myself doing and saying during this step?**
5. **What measurements would be most meaningful to include in the action plan?**

Tips and Examples

- ❑ People become committed when they are involved.
- ❑ The spirit of continuous improvement, being "on the path," and stretch goals must be emphasized.

(continued)

WORKSHEET 4.3: From Traditional to Coaching *(continued)*

- ❑ Carefully developed action plans provide a path.
- ❑ You are in a position to provide vision on the one hand and a dose of reality on the other.
- ❑ Defining measurements up front leads to more effective action plans.

RESOURCES AND TOOLS

1. **Techniques that we will use to share data findings and themes are:**

   ____

   ____

2. **Methods that we will use to involve others in the action planning process will be:**

   ____

   ____

3. **Guidelines (process and attitude) that we will use for developing our "coaching organization" action plan are:**

   ____

   ____

4. **Different components (categories, dimensions) of these action plans will include:**

   ____

   ____

5. **Final decisions on the action plans for building our coaching organization will happen through:**

   ____

   ____

6. **My involvement in the action planning process will be:**

   ____

   ____

Tips and Examples

- ❑ Utilize a variety of communication tools to share the data.
- ❑ Implement an inclusive action planning model that moves up, down, and across the organization.
- ❑ Provide an action planning template with components of objectives, measurements, tracking, resources, and ownership.
- ❑ Different categories of information will require action plans: perpetuation of the vision, coaching activities, stretch goals, leadership role, ongoing learning, support infrastructures, operation guidelines, strategic plans, resource allocation, reorganization of staff and work, new products and business approaches, innovative market ideas, etc.

(continued)

WORKSHEET 4.3: From Traditional to Coaching (*continued*)

- ❑ Provide a template/checklist that will ensure a systems approach toward the building of a coaching organization (use the coaching systems model).
- ❑ A clear decision-making process (with criteria) needs to be understood and accepted.
- ❑ Provide guidelines—in line with the vision and resources—for determining what can and cannot be done.
- ❑ Supply job aids that can guide the dialogue, process, and decision.
- ❑ Provide internal and external facilitators/coaches as needed.
- ❑ Continue or create a task force or committee that coordinates, communicates, and keeps the momentum going.

COMPETENCIES

On a scale of 1 to 5 (1 = nonexistent; 5 = outstanding), rate yourself on the following competencies for this step.

1. **Focus on the Vision** 1 2 3 4 5

   Two specific ways I will demonstrate this competency in this step:

   a. ______________________________

   b. ______________________________

2. **Provision of a Challenge** 1 2 3 4 5

   Two specific ways I will demonstrate this competency in this step:

   a. ______________________________

   b. ______________________________

3. **Ability to Act as a Change Agent** 1 2 3 4 5

   Two specific ways I will demonstrate this competency in this step:

   a. ______________________________

   b. ______________________________

Tips and Examples

- ❑ Personal and organizational resources are at stake. Be a role model in sorting through wants and needs.
- ❑ Push for involvement, fairness, action, stretch goals, and support structures.
- ❑ Incorporate action plans into a yearly strategic planning process.
- ❑ Transform yourself in front of others.
- ❑ Empower employees to reach for stretch goals by providing the right kinds of tools.
- ❑ Encourage problem solving and stretch goals that go beyond old paradigms.
- ❑ Keep the pressure on through your constant involvement.
- ❑ Supply stronger tools when the process or activities break down.
- ❑ Encourage people to experiment and try new behaviors.

WORKSHEET 4.4: From Traditional to Coaching Organization

Step 4: Taking Action

DEFINING THE DESIRED OUTCOMES

1. I expect the results of implementing the "coaching organization" action plans to be:

____

____

2. I will know that the action plans are successfully implemented when:

____

____

3. Possible roadblocks in this step that I will guard against are:

____

____

4. The specific role I intend to play in the implementation of these action plans is:

____

____

Tips and Examples

- ❑ Concentrate on execution of the action plans.
- ❑ Success indicators can be planned or unplanned: the formation of innovative product teams or your newsletter's winning of an award from an outside association.
- ❑ This is new territory. Consider personal and organizational challenges that you will need to overcome.
- ❑ Use the coaching system model as a template for envisioning successful outcomes for each component. Consider specific activities and structures that will exist to support leadership-driven vision, the coaching mind-set, dialogue, stretch goals, high performance, learning, and a coaching infrastructure. Make a list.
- ❑ Consider your role and the purpose of your actions during this step.
- ❑ There must be alignment of personal and organizational vision.
- ❑ There must be alignment of daily work with the vision and organizational goals.

QUESTIONS TO CONSIDER

1. How will I know that the implementation process is going well?

2. What positive signs will I see in the staff, myself, and the organization?

3. What components/actions will ensure that a coaching organization is being built?

4. What will I actually say and do in this step to support the overall purpose and vision?

(continued)

WORKSHEET 4.4: From Traditional to Coaching (*continued*)

Tips and Examples

- ❑ Don't lose sight of the ultimate goal: a coaching organization.
- ❑ Encourage coaching attitudes and activities as the plans roll out.
- ❑ Create a list of "success indicators": tangible examples that can be shared when people get stuck.
- ❑ Develop a list of themes, goals, and guidelines that you need to reinforce in this step.

RESOURCES AND TOOLS

1. **Tools that we will use to track "coaching organization" action plans are:**

   ____

   ____

2. **Methods that we will use to manage and administer the implementation of the action plans are:**

   ____

   ____

3. **Ongoing learning in coaching organization skills, knowledge, and approaches will be ensured through:**

   ____

   ____

4. **We will acknowledge and share our learning during the implementation of a coaching organization by:**

   ____

   ____

5. **We will ensure involvement and communication during the implementation of action plans through:**

   ____

   ____

6. **The tools we will use to acknowledge and celebrate implementation results are:**

   ____

   ____

Tips and Examples

- ❑ Provide implementation guidelines that address not only process but also behavior.
- ❑ Continue to use the existing task force or committee as coordinator, monitor, and communicator of the implementation process.
- ❑ Provide a job aid based on the coaching systems model to ensure an aligned approach.
- ❑ Provide ongoing learning, coaching, and dialogue.

(continued)

WORKSHEET 4.4: From Traditional to Coaching *(continued)*

- ❑ Strive for continuous improvement and realign activities with goals, as necessary.
- ❑ Create mechanisms for celebration.

COMPETENCIES

On a scale of 1 to 5 (1 = nonexistent; 5 = outstanding), rate yourself on the following competencies:

1. **Alignment With the Vision** **1 2 3 4 5**

   Two specific ways I will demonstrate this competency in this step:

   a. ____

   b. ____

2. **Follow-Through** **1 2 3 4 5**

   Two specific ways I will demonstrate this competency in this step:

   a. ____

   b. ____

3. **Facilitation of Continuous Learning** **1 2 3 4 5**

   Two specific ways I will demonstrate this competency in this step:

   a. ____

   b. ____

4. **Acknowledgment of Others' Contributions** **1 2 3 4 5**

   Two specific ways I will demonstrate this competency in this step:

   a. ____

   b. ____

Tips and Examples

- ❑ Build a coaching infrastructure.
- ❑ Institute systems that align performance, vision, and goals, such as the Guide to Exceleration Program.
- ❑ Institute open-book management.
- ❑ Make tough decisions when people can't align.
- ❑ Break down stretch goals into meaningful action steps.
- ❑ Communicate the right information.
- ❑ Provide support and resources to foster creativity and nurture new skills.
- ❑ Create dialogue and knowledge sharing.
- ❑ Build structures that make continuous learning a way of life.
- ❑ Align compensation and benefit systems with the overall vision and goals of a coaching organization.
- ❑ Highlight successes.

WORKSHEET 4.5: From Traditional to Coaching Organization

Step 5: Evaluating Your Progress

DEFINING THE DESIRED OUTCOMES

1. **The purpose of evaluating the building of our coaching organization is:**

   ____

   ____

2. **Outcomes that I expect from evaluating the building of our coaching organization are:**

   ____

   ____

3. **Areas/dimensions for which I expect to see evaluation outputs include:**

   ____

   ____

4. **My role in evaluating the building of our coaching organization is:**

   ____

   ____

Tips and Examples

- ❑ The results of evaluating the building of a coaching organization should be used for learning, alignment, and focus.
- ❑ Evaluation efforts should include all levels of the organization.
- ❑ Evaluation results should cover a variety of dimensions, both tangible and intangible. Utilize lists and job aids from this chapter.
- ❑ Your role in the evaluation effort can inspire and motivate.
- ❑ Evaluation dimensions can follow the coaching system model and success factors outlined in Step 4.

QUESTIONS TO CONSIDER

1. **What do I plan to do with the evaluation results?**
2. **What do I plan to say and do in this step that will support the coaching organization?**
3. **How can I tie the evaluation process to the goals of the coaching organization?**

Tips and Examples

- ❑ Evaluation categories should mirror the tenets of a coaching organization.
- ❑ In considering evaluation outcomes, determine what you intend to do with the results: Cycle back into the process.
- ❑ Your participation in evaluation efforts strengthens the process and perpetuates the "leadership-driven vision."

(continued)

WORKSHEET 4.5: From Traditional to Coaching (*continued*)

RESOURCES AND TOOLS

1. **The methods/tools that we will use in evaluating the building of our coaching organization are:**

   ____

   ____

2. **We will manage the evaluation process through:**

   ____

   ____

3. **Pertinent evaluation questions to consider are:**

   ____

   ____

4. **We will ensure involvement and participation in the evaluation process by:**

   ____

   ____

5. **We will ensure ongoing exploration and research in how to build and maintain coaching organizations through:**

   ____

   ____

Tips and Examples

- ❑ Coordinate and reinforce evaluation, and link it to existing coaching structures. It does not have to be a discrete activity.
- ❑ Utilize some of the same methods used for data gathering, but explore outcomes and results: focus groups, interviews, surveys, data analysis.
- ❑ Create evaluation tools where none exist.
- ❑ Develop job aids that provide appropriate questions to assess alignment and the building of a successful coaching organization.
- ❑ Utilize the efforts of an existing task force or committee to manage and communicate the evaluation effort.
- ❑ Ensure that the evaluation effort is used for learning, coaching, and adjusting.
- ❑ Distribute guidelines on the evaluation and renewal process so there is understanding of how it is done.
- ❑ Provide communication and involvement to promote understanding, fairness, and continuous input.
- ❑ Make changes and adjustments to the coaching organization to reflect organizational goals, values, and vision.
- ❑ Involve employees in the evaluation process and incorporate into dialogue sessions.

(continued)

WORKSHEET 4.5: From Traditional to Coaching (*continued*)

COMPETENCIES

On a scale of 1 to 5 (1 = nonexistent; 5 = outstanding), rate yourself on the following competencies for this step:

1. **Decision Making** **1 2 3 4 5**

   Two specific ways I will demonstrate this competency in this step:

   a. ____________________

   b. ____________________

2. **Passion** **1 2 3 4 5**

   Two specific ways I will demonstrate this competency in this step:

   a. ____________________

   b. ____________________

3. **Rewarding of Others' Contributions** **1 2 3 4 5**

   Two specific ways I will demonstrate this competency in this step:

   a. ____________________

   b. ____________________

Tips and Examples

- ❑ Provide guidelines for evaluation parameters. Be clear on what you are looking for.
- ❑ Make balanced decisions within a trusting and open framework.
- ❑ Establish consequences: higher standards, continuous growth, more supportive coaching, learning activities.
- ❑ Pinpoint lessons from the evaluation data and use them to improve the process.
- ❑ Push for new findings; don't accept perfunctory assessments.
- ❑ Be actively involved yourself. Take on the evaluation of a particular component.
- ❑ Build vehicles for continued exploration, ideas, and improvement. Keep the program alive and active.
- ❑ Create meaningful rewards that are aligned with coaching values.
- ❑ Communicate companywide rewards of low turnover, increased market share, and so forth.

part 5

Beyond Organizational Walls

A major challenge will be to effectively lead and manage the relationships among the organization's mission and purpose, its interaction and partnerships with other institutions and other sectors, and its statements of its values.

— R. Beckhard,
"On Future Leaders"

What do we mean by leading "beyond organizational walls"? It is common to hear coaching leaders say that their goal is to create something beyond themselves—something that will last and engage the human spirit. It doesn't take long for such leaders to realize that the sense of the community that they are trying to foster reaches far beyond the walls of their companies and organizations. That longing for connection, high performance, engagement, and learning reaches out to the surrounding city or town and even across nations.

When we speak of organizations reaching out to the community, we are not referring to those wonderful nonprofit organizations that are already dedicated to the community and whose missions embrace charity and support—such as the American Red Cross, the American Cancer Society, Goodwill Industries, or the Salvation Army. Rather, we are talking about businesses for profit that realize that continuous growth can happen only by reaching out into the community, creating vehicles for mutual exchange, and enriching the lives of those beyond the company walls. As the social commentator Frances Moore Lappe pointed out, "Our true nature calls us to connect deeply to our community and to find larger meaning in what we do there. . . . Making a contribution becomes a mutual exchange, rather than a one-way transaction" (quoted in McCauley & Canabou, 2000, p. 118).

Continuation of Values and Spirit

One reason coaching leaders find themselves "reaching out" is that community involvement is a natural extension of a coaching lifestyle. If you have really embraced effective questions, continuous learning, dialogue, and mutual support and growth, this does not stop at the corporate walls. When you are at a meeting at the client's site, you continue to test your assumptions. When you are speaking to the local PTA, you ask effective questions and try to establish common goals. When you conduct your professional or personal business at the local bank, you engage others in meaningful dialogue. You—and every leader in your organization—become a role model for coaching behaviors and approaches. It's contagious. Your organization becomes known as "a good company to work for and interact with." Clients, business associates, friends, community leaders, social workers, and political figures all want to be a part of this "spirit" that you seem to ignite and spread.

An effective coaching organization connects business goals with individual goals, establishing a tie to the human spirit within us all. This human spirit does not stop at the company's front door. Your employees live and play in the surrounding community. If you are going to deal with the entire person, you must reach out to the schools that your employees' children attend, sporting events they participate in, small businesses they frequent, and banks where they deposit their paychecks, as well as address local concerns of homelessness, illiteracy, child abuse, or hunger. What might this look like?

- Sponsoring sports teams
- Providing internship programs
- Giving money to community causes
- Conducting charity drives
- Giving people time off to represent the company in nearby schools or neighborhood boards
- Joining surrounding companies in larger endeavors—supplying computers to inner-city schools, funding a playground, or renovating a halfway house

Such endeavors produce pride in your employees and a positive reputation within the community.

When you spread the concept of a coaching environment to those you interact with, you bring them into the fold. You partner with them. You share your programs, interventions, philosophy, and standards.

When you conduct a meeting with a client or partner organization, you use the same coaching approach that you would with any department within your own company. You establish the same concept of mutual goals and continuous improvement. Your high standards and example rub off. Your organization becomes the company of choice to work with—a company that cares about business and its people.

Sense of Responsibility

A second reason leaders reach out beyond organizational walls is a sense of responsibility. They feel they have an obligation to leave a legacy beyond themselves and just their one company. They want to make a difference in the larger community. They possess a sense of social responsibility and a social consciousness.

Hargrove (1995) called this concept "stewardship" (p. 18). He chastised many of today's leaders, saying that they are merely on "voyages on the road to personal and corporate success" with a lack of "a foundation of socially constructive values deeply embedded in our society, communities, and schools." He asserted that leaders who embody coaching begin to realize that "stewardship is taking a stand for the future of the people, communities, complex social systems, and the world we care about" (p. 18).

As you can see, this is not just "charity" or obligatory philanthropy. Rather, it is something best referred to as "servant-leadership." This is a concept that is taught and perpetuated at the Robert K. Greenleaf Center for Servant-Leadership in Indianapolis, Indiana. In his article on the topic, Spears (1998) explained that the servant-leader is a servant first. One begins with the natural feeling that one wants to serve; then a conscious choice brings one to aspire to lead. The underlying behaviors of servant-leadership are like those of a coaching leader: ethical and caring behavior; enhancement of personal growth of workers and simultaneous improvement of the quality of many institutions; teamwork; joint decision making; and the primary motivation of helping others. Spears further pointed out that servant-leadership emphasizes "increased service to others, a holistic approach to work, the promotion of a sense of community, and a deepening understanding of spirit in the workplace" (p. 43).

The servant-leadership approach is based on the purpose of creating a positive impact on employees and the surrounding community, rather than using profit as the sole motive. The view of servant-leadership is that all leaders play significant roles in holding their institutions in trust for the greater good of society (p. 46). Block (1996) emphasized this same concept when he stated that "stewardship is to hold something in trust for another. . . . We choose service over self-interest most powerfully when we build the capacity of the next generation to govern themselves" (p. xx). Hesselbein (1996) further supported this idea when he described the kind of leader that is needed for the future: "The wise leader embraces all those concerned in a circle that surrounds the corporation, the organization, the people, the leadership, and the community" (p. 123).

Keppel (1999) pointed out the need for organizations to pick up the slack that government programs can't handle. We live in an age of complicated social needs, and government agencies cannot reach every community or deal with every issue. Coaching leaders have a responsibility to step up to the plate. According to Lyle Estill, a leader at EMJ America, which took on the task of wiring the majority of schools in Chatham County, North Carolina, for access to the Internet,

> EMJ America has always believed that we cannot have a healthy business without a healthy community. We are a merchant in the village, and although business is our domain, our lives are dependent on schools, the arts, the environment, and every other aspect of village life. (quoted in "Enterprising Philanthropists," 1999)

So what are examples of this stewardship, servant leadership, or social responsibility?

- Ben and Jerry's—dedicated to making the best ice cream but also to issues of peace and justice
- The Body Shop—dedicated to offering cosmetics and body products that are not tested on animals
- Pear Transmedia Inc. (Web design and development company)—every quarter, it chooses a pro bono project so it can give back to the community
- Fresh Fields Whole Foods Market—dedicates 5% of a designated day's profits to Healthy Families, a community-based support program
- Bill Gates—formed the William H. Gates Foundation and the Gates Learning Foundation, which has given $100 million to a children's vaccine program and has become the sixth largest grant-making private trust (Keppel, 1999)
- IBM—created a "Reinventing Education" program and has given millions in cash awards, technology, and volunteer time to various school systems (Fischer, 1999)
- Frontline Group—mentors at-risk youth and helps them find meaningful work after graduation (McCauley & Canabou, 2000, p. 112)

Good for Business

Reaching out into the community is good for business and the bottom line. Obviously, if you become known as an organization with an involved and enriched culture, you are going to attract clients and top performers. It becomes self-perpetuating. As Jonathan Tisch, president and CEO of Loews Hotels, has said about his own philanthropy:

> You really can do good and do well at the same time. . . . You'll differentiate yourself from the competition. . . . A client may choose you over the company down the road, because she appreciates the fact that you're a good neighbor. . . . At the same time, you'll send your employees an important message. (quoted in McCauley & Canabou, 2000, p. 116)

When you interact with the community, you network and create more business opportunities than would otherwise come about. You create better relationships between your employees and customers, and this boosts profits. And because corporate giving has tax implications, it gives you proactive control over where that money gets spent. If planned well, your profit and nonprofit endeavors will build off each other.

You want to make sure that all outreach programs are in line with your organizational values and mission, and you can do this by incorporating the sense of "community" into your vision and mission statements. As Marguerite Sallee, chair and CEO of Frontline Group, commented on the connection between vision and community involvement:

> To create real change in this world, you have to have vision. . . . When you fuse your giving back with your company's objectives, you'll find that it's good for business as well. . . . Businesses that provide opportunities for employees to give back create balance—for the company and for its employees. (quoted in McCauley & Canabou, 2000, p. 112)

How to Make a Difference

This idea of a leader interacting with his or her community is called many things: social entrepreneurialism, charity, philanthropy, giving back, volunteerism, social development, venture philanthropy, charitable giving, social responsibility, corporate philanthropy, citizenship, civic entrepreneurialism. There is an entire support industry dedicated to helping leaders and their organizations engage in community efforts.

As Table 5.1 demonstrates, there are many resources to assist "reaching out" efforts. Research at the library or on the Internet will uncover focused publications on community interaction and giving. There are consultant organizations that provide guidance in matching organizational values with specific causes and endeavors. The Internet also provides lists and sites that outline a range of possibilities.

Consultants and coaching leaders who have been involved in this process for some time can give "lessons learned." Large companies have created departments dedicated to outreach programs and can serve as a resource for information and guidance.

Several key tips can guide your research and decisions.

Programs Should Be Value Driven

Peter Karoff, founder and president of the Philanthropic Initiative, has stressed the importance of aligning personal values with giving efforts

Table 5.1 Outreach Resources

Resource	*Examples*
Journals/ Newsletters	■ Philanthropy Magazine ■ Philanthropy Today ■ Philanthropy News Digest ■ Chronicle of Philanthropy ■ Corporate Giving Watch
Books	■ High Impact Philanthropy: How Donors, Boards, and Nonprofit Organizations Can Transform Communities (Grace & Wendroff, 2000) ■ The Cathedral Within: Transforming Your Life by Giving Something Back (Shore & Shore, 2001)
Internet Sites	■ Charitable Choices, <www.charitablechoices.org> ■ Community Foundation's Data Base, <www.siliconvalleygives.org/homepage1930/index.htm> ■ AllCharities.com, <www.allcharities.com> ■ GuideStar, <www.guidestar.org> ■ Helping Organizations, <www.helping.org>
Consulting Organizations	■ Family Philanthropy Resources, San Diego ■ Silicon Valley Social Venture Fund, San Jose, CA ■ Foundation Center, New York ■ Family Philanthropy Resources, San Diego, CA ■ National Commission on Philanthropy and Civic Renewal, Indianapolis, IN ■ Social Welfare Research Institute, Boston College
Corporate Departments	■ First Union Bank, Manager of Corporate Contributions and Community Involvement ■ LCC International, Vice President of Investor and Corporate Relations ■ Hallmark, President of Hallmark Family Foundation; Volunteer Program Manager ■ Gannett, Manager of Gannett Foundation/Manager of Community Relations ■ Marriott, Vice President of Corporate Relations

(McCauley & Canabou, 2000, p. 138). He believes that your community values should be based on what you truly care about. Why give to university scholarships when what you really care about most is homelessness?

You need to believe in what you are doing and why you are doing it. This centered approach leads to mutual gain—you can give to others while also learning about yourself. In terms of an entire organization, the giving effort must align with the corporate vision and values. In this way, charitable efforts will be aligned with each person's individual spirit and goals.

This kind of giving, however, is not about you. There can be no ego, arrogance, or status. You may be president of a company, but you are not president of your chosen effort or program. What you are doing is acting as a fellow human being or as a fellow organization within the community—connecting with that deep social nature that is within all of us but is often forgotten and buried.

Programs Should Connect With the Resources You Have to Offer

If you want to connect with your cause, it should be an extension of yourself—something you like to do, a skill or resource that comes easily, an effort that makes sense and provides a balance in your life. If you are a good corporate coach, you might want to coach a community sports team. If your organization produces machine tools, you might want to create an internship program with local technical schools. This might seem obvious, but some leaders or companies feel they have to do something huge or totally different to give back to the community. This assumption is incorrect. You don't have to move mountains. If your effort is too big, you may miss out on the joy and may not be able to sustain the effort over time.

It is helpful to decide on a certain level of involvement that can be integrated in your personal or organizational life. Taking on too much can result in false promises or half-baked efforts. You might also want to choose an effort that has a human face. It's tough to get your arms around "world peace."

Table 5.2 outlines five "emphasis areas" that can help you zero in on a cause, idea, approach, or audience that more readily connects with the resources you have to offer. In reviewing these emphasis areas, remember that you can combine areas and choose varying levels of size and intensity. For example, the same "idea" can be practiced in any of the following ways:

- Every day after school, provide peanut-butter-and-jelly sandwiches to 10 kids in an impoverished neighborhood and tutor them on school assignments.
- Sponsor a shelter where neighborhood kids can convene after school for sandwiches and tutoring.
- Create a partnership with area businesses to donate a percentage of profits to community efforts that deal with hunger and tutoring in impoverished areas.

Here's another example:

- Spend 1 hour a week assisting in a school reading program.
- Donate your company software program (an educational reading game) to several impoverished school systems.
- Create a corporationwide program that gives all employees paid time off to assist in school reading programs.
- Provide special incentives, training, and awards to teachers who demonstrate excellence in the teaching of reading.

Table 5.2 Sample Efforts

Emphasis Area	*Example*
Education/Children	■ Providing computers to schools and libraries ■ Volunteering assistance and mentoring to schools or impoverished children ■ Sponsoring programs for food, medical care, clothes, or special efforts ■ Providing grants for playgrounds, libraries, hospitals, vaccines, or enrichment activities
Business Growth/ Business Based	■ Sharing skills and knowledge with small businesses ■ Providing assistance to start-ups ■ Donating seed money to minority business efforts ■ Campaigning for the buying and use of certain products/services ■ Engaging in business practices that donate a percentage of profits to meaningful causes ■ Providing training to other businesses or institutions: strategic planning, quality, coaching ■ Providing your service/product free of charge to certain causes
Global Causes	■ Providing technology to a remote or impoverished area in the world so it can communicate with the rest of society ■ Leading large-scale efforts against poverty, hunger, or illiteracy ■ Developing programs to fight drunk driving, drug addiction, teenage pregnancy, unemployment, or a particular injustice
Improvement of Lives/Community	■ Partnering with neighboring businesses to improve a community situation: welfare to work, halfway house, health issue, immigrant concerns ■ Donating funds for a wildlife center, zoo, or community center ■ Providing training for local efforts: violence, drugs, career development, job skills ■ Volunteering for classroom assistance, homework help, renovating a neighborhood, coaching a team, mentoring the homeless
Partnering	■ Joining forces with neighboring organizations or like organizations and forming a coalition to provide grants, services, or programs for any of the causes listed above ■ Creating symbiotic relationships among organizations, such as schools or community organizations with businesses

- Provide a large grant to an educational campaign to combat illiteracy in your community, state, or an impoverished international site.
- Offer to train school administrators and teachers in strategic planning and program management so they can plan, design, and implement stronger reading programs.

Programs Should Be Focused and Action Oriented

It is deflating to work toward a goal that accomplishes nothing or gets lost in the system. It is wise to direct your efforts (time, energy, skills, knowledge, money) toward an effort that involves tangible actions—no matter how small.

This doesn't mean that you should choose only efforts that are reliable and boring. However, it does mean that you need to appropriately research your cause and test for authenticity, measurements, results, ethical behavior, and accountability. Mistakes will be made. Certain results may not be possible. However, it is important to track programs, make adjustments, and be realistic about what can be achieved and what can't. Sometimes it's necessary to redefine your purpose and outcomes.

You also need to test yourself. Even though you really may want to mentor drug addicts so they can turn their lives around, can you realistically give that much time and assistance? Perhaps you need to be content with just assisting in the process and offering a weekly dinner, activity, and conversation.

You must educate yourself. Your company must become educated. You need to set limits and make informed decisions. You want to make sure that your resources are focused, not haphazard or misdirected.

Yet you also want to add the magic of your coaching mind-set. Create new models and ways to reach out and approach your corporate giving. This kind of creativity and teamwork might allow you to make a difference where others have failed. By using the same vision and perseverance you have used to build a coaching organization, you can now create similar benefits within a larger community. Here is a real-life case study provided by John McBeth (personal communication, July 26, 2001), former president of Century Computing.

> The top management and founders of Century had several meetings with my top group, grappling with how we wanted to do give back to the community. We were very excited about the high-performance efforts we were attaining within the company, and we all felt the need to interact with the community and make a difference. We brainstormed on a range of possibilities, including "adopting a disease," giving money to a cause, or supporting schools in some way. After much discussion, we concluded that we wanted to support the local public school system.
>
> Coincidentally, I was invited to attend a task force established by the local government that was trying to improve technology in local public schools. The task force had obtained a "wish list" of items that various schools within the local system needed—miscellaneous wiring, printers, and software. I looked over the list and said to the group, "You are thinking too small. We need to think bigger. How about asking for help in designing and building leading-edge technology classrooms within each school?" Folks were skeptical. Working with a subset committee, we developed plans for "classrooms of the future" and a strategic business approach for how to get there.
>
> We developed an interactive presentation that demonstrated the classroom of the future with lessons that came alive, teacher and student chat rooms, and special software. Instead of the original request for $10,000, we outlined a $4 million program. We introduced the concepts of "bold and audacious goals," step-by-step accomplishments, creativity, relentless pursuit, and "seducing" others into the vision. As we made the presentation to other companies and school administrators, we gained momentum and overwhelming support. Company representatives actually pledged money during our presentations.

Our vision caught the fancy of the entire county. Why not classrooms of the future for the entire county? That was fine with us. We were willing to share our ideas and plans. However, we also realized that we had to remain focused on our goal—improvements for our school district. This was an important lesson for us. We could have gotten lost in the process.

As time went on, the response was incredible. The idea caught the attention of the state governor's office. The governor's office assembled a room full of big players—Apple, Dell, Microsoft, and other major technology firms. Our school district got everything it needed. Computer manufacturers donated hundreds of computers. Telecommunications companies donated networking services. The schools started winning state and federal grants because, as one school official stated, "This was the most thought-out, comprehensive plan I have ever seen."

Employees of Century enthusiastically volunteered by going into the schools to teach various technology courses and provide technical support. The resulting technology in our local public school system is now better than that of most companies. The school system now offers evening computer courses to parents in the community. A local school district, the county, the state, politicians, businesses—all wrapped into a cooperative effort to achieve a vision.

Applying the Coaching Model

If you are involved in building a coaching organization, dialogue and planning vehicles already exist within your organization for discussing community involvement. Brainstorming and implementation efforts for community outreach can be embedded in the existing vision and agenda.

However, if you are just beginning to think about creating a coaching organization, you can actually use the topic of community outreach as a way to kick-start your efforts. Reaching out and helping the community touches the human spirit. By having discussions, mobilizing efforts, and celebrating community involvement, you can begin to raise the organization's awareness toward a higher level of thought, purpose, and vision. You can parlay this into deeper discussions concerning dialogue, coaching, and high performance—in other words, the creation of an internal coaching community. Consequently, either way, community efforts reinforce coaching organizations.

Step 1: Establishing the Coaching Relationship

In this step, you are establishing a relationship on two levels—with your organization and with your surrounding community. Four core competencies help to create a strong foundation for moving a coaching mind-set outward into the community: investigation, vision, brainstorming, and education.

Investigation is the competency to employ in order to explore outside relationships and contacts. With the help of a few key leaders in your organization, you can gather initial information:

- What are other coaching leaders doing in the surrounding community?
- What ideas do your contacts have? Are they interested in your ideas?
- What kind of initiatives are already in progress?
- What are similar organizations in your industry doing?

- What information can be found through a quick Internet search?
- What information can be obtained through a couple of philanthropic or social foundations?

This is the time to be curious and open. Consider the multitude of options. Listen to the experiences of others. You must also investigate internally. Many employees and leaders within your organization are already involved in community service. They are coaching teams, sitting on boards, delivering meals to shut-ins, and coaching students in nearby high schools. Some of them are also dedicating time to clubs, associations, or grassroots efforts involving the environment, diabetes, AIDS, crime, technology, or health care.

- What ideas do they have?
- What do they think would work from a total company perspective?
- How do they think such efforts should be organized and supported?

As you are investigating, you must share your vision of expanding the coaching "way of being" beyond the company walls. You need to paint the picture and share scenarios of the company being involved outwardly—taking the concepts of teams, continuous improvement, coaching, stretch goals, learning activities, and high performance—and broadening the playing field. Your community vision must be tied to the underlying purpose and values of the company and embedded in the yearly goals. It must build off and enrich your existing vision. By sharing your community vision with an outside contact or an internal employee, you begin to build momentum and focus your exploration.

This is the time for brainstorming possibilities. In discussions with your top team and other designated groups, begin to compose lists, scenarios, and various levels of ideas. You may want to conduct a couple of focus groups.

You need to be an educator to get people thinking in the right direction—whether that is social entrepreneurialism, corporate philanthropy, citizenship, volunteerism, or whatever term best meets the vision of the organization. Pertinent articles and professional learning materials should be distributed. Helpful checklists or tips from the Internet can be shared. Philosophical pieces on servant-leadership, the role of organizations in the community, and obligations to society can be a topic at staff meetings. Dialogue needs to happen.

Step 2: Collecting and Analyzing Data

In this step, three competencies should be used to gather appropriate information that can be analyzed and lead to meaningful actions for your organization. These competencies ensure employee inclusion and communication: research, involvement, and focus.

On the basis of initial data gathered in Step 1, you can now conduct research that is directed in areas that make sense for your company, resources, and interest. You might want to form a committee or task force here to steer and oversee the effort. This "outreach committee" should coordinate a combination of research efforts: Internet searches, summary of themes from publications and writings, internal interviews/surveys, external interviews/surveys, and benchmarking of other companies. Finding out what has worked and not worked in other companies is extremely important. Throughout the process, the committee should conduct thematic analysis and provide summaries of the findings.

Many activities during the research stage provide opportunities for employee involvement. Internal surveys and focus groups can be used to match ideas with the values of the employees and the organization as a whole. It is also wise to use these efforts to distinguish and explore different levels of connection and outreach: organizational, departmental, and individual. Many companies like to use a tiered approach. Obviously, involvement keeps dialogue alive and continues to strengthen knowledge, creativity, and vision.

Focus is essential during this stage so that participants don't lose the big picture—which is easy to do when one is inundated with research findings. The outreach committee is in and of itself a focus vehicle. The committee can distribute a periodic newsletter or e-mail that summarizes key findings to date. This would also be the time to provide guest speakers who can provide real case studies and live examples.

You might want to use your existing communication system to highlight outreach efforts that are already being accomplished through community-oriented employees—the kinds of activities that often go unrecognized. Another powerful idea during this stage is to initiate a pilot. One department or group of employees can take on one or more outreach programs. The tracking and communicating of the pilot can provide ongoing focus, lessons learned, energy, vision, and goodwill.

Step 3: Processing Feedback and Planning Actions

As in previous chapters, Step 3 is where the rubber meets the road. You and your employees are faced with themes from the research, and it is time to sort through the data, ask questions, reach conclusions, make decisions, and develop action plans that are going to make the process work. Three competencies are key during this step: negotiation, drive, and training.

Negotiation is an essential ingredient during this process because personal and organizational resources are at stake. As you sort through the data and make decisions, it is going to be important that you, your key leaders, and the outreach committee clarify criteria for making decisions and establish limits in terms of what is doable or not. Obviously, some of that will be challenged, tested, and negotiated. You may be able to provide an overall approach or model and leave it to employees—through team meetings—to fill in the specifics, make final choices, and personalize the options.

You might want to establish cost-benefit guidelines to structure the action planning process. In this way, employees can work through their wants within established goals. Besides the actual programs that will be implemented, it is important to talk through and decide upon an overall yearly process, tracking and coordination mechanisms, ongoing guidelines, assessment and measurement tools, and communication processes. Because the action planning for these kinds of initiatives involves both internal and external people, tasks and responsibilities need to be clearly outlined.

The beauty of this process is that it is not necessary to reinvent the wheel. As a coaching organization, you already have many support structures within which you can readily insert the community outreach program—it becomes yet another systemwide project that needs to be supported through your existing coaching organization. It should add value to your vision and can be embedded within your yearly standards and stretch goals.

During the data analysis and action planning, you must exhibit drive, constantly pushing for involvement, fair decision making, reality testing, and forward action. You want to highlight infrastructures that will be needed to support outreach activities and make sure they are included within action plans. You also want to remind participants to integrate the vision of community involvement into existing structures: personal goals and success, reward systems, newsletters, dialogue sessions, learning discussions, and coaching sessions. Internal or external consultants may be necessary to guide action planning meetings, educate, or assist in the design of support processes.

Training and learning are, of course, essential in ensuring that employees have the skills and knowledge to work through the issues, choose valid community programs, and build strong underlying procedures. This can happen through the use of consultants, guest speakers, clear communication of the research data, and facilitated dialogue sessions. Sharing concrete examples and providing job aids (such as those included earlier in this chapter) can guide the process.

Step 4: Taking Action

Because community involvement deals with both an internal and an external audience, depth in five competencies is required: systems thinking, program management, establishment of relationships, fostering of a vision, and acknowledgment of accomplishments.

The coaching system model described in Part 4 provides an evaluation framework for ensuring that your community outreach initiatives follow a systems approach, and it guides systems thinking. You can take the questions for a coaching organization and apply them to your community outreach plan:

- Is a community outreach mind-set pervasive throughout the organization?
- Is there a leadership-driven community vision that is clearly understood and aligned with all actions and structures?
- Do skilled dialogue and coaching practices guide community conversations?

1. Are the intent and desire for learning and continuous improvement in all community interactions and structures?
2. Are stretch goals embedded in community outreach measurements and plans to foster break-through thinking and high performance?

- Are all formal and informal community outreach policies, procedures, structures, processes, tools, techniques, technology, functions, and supportive mechanisms aligned and reinforced by a coaching infrastructure that links and tracks the entire community outreach system?
- Can community outreach results be measured in terms of bottom-line success and/or goal achievement?

Whether on the organizational, divisional/departmental, or individual level, all community outreach initiatives must be managed as if they were a major work project—with the same checks and balances. The basic skills of program management must be applied. There should be reviews, milestones along the stretch goals, efficiency in execution, accountability, modifications and adjustments, dialogue sessions, team meetings with all internal and external players, and yearly assessments. Furthermore, there should be clear rules concerning integrity, honesty, openness, and ethical behavior—for all parties involved, whether they are down the hall or on another continent. Such rules are a natural consequence of what outreach means within the framework of coaching and learning.

Given the nature of interacting and networking with those outside your company, the competency of establishing relationships is necessary in exploring options, clarifying the scope of the project, bringing diverse groups to the table, establishing levels of involvement, making agreements, setting standards, and contracting with various stakeholders. This is a skill that must be demonstrated by you and by any employee who "goes out there" and participates. It is these relationships that make or break the success of the programs. It must be understood that high standards of behavior and role modeling are to be practiced and transferred.

As a visionary, you must be continually involved and must demonstrate your own initiatives. Not only should you participate in internal monitoring and dialogue, you need to be "out there" taking on a particular community role or goal. Communications should highlight all programs, with pictures, narratives, learnings, and the integration of coaching concepts both inside and outside the company.

Last, acknowledgment of accomplishments should be liberally demonstrated. Again, these acknowledgments should be not only internal but also external—the community paper, a reception at a local community house, a party at the neighborhood orphanage, a ribbon-cutting ceremony at the new playground. These are gatherings and celebrations that emphasize the results of working together and making something significant happen—whether a smiling face, enrichment of lives, or a major improvement in fighting a difficult cause.

Step 5: Evaluating Your Progress

In the evaluation stage of community outreach initiatives, it is important to have clear goals and a mutual understanding of results. In some cases, a result might be a smiling face. In another case, the result might be a computer in every classroom. As was already explained, desired results need to be realistically based on the amount of resources that can be dedicated and the underlying values that are guiding the involvement. Three competencies guide this process: assessment, participation, and exploration.

Using parameters already set within the coaching organization, the act of assessing the program should include tracking outreach initiatives and providing data to make yearly adjustments. This process should assess both internal and external activities. Either the outreach committee or a special meeting of the top team should review progress. Decisions should be made that can then be cycled again through implementation.

- Is the program being managed well?
- Are we within planned parameters concerning resources (time, money, services, products, etc.)?
- Is the program making a difference as outlined in the initial project scope?
- Are adjustments needed concerning conflict of interest, shifting priorities, or changing values or needs of those involved?
- Is it time to shift resources to another initiative? Should certain programs be stopped? Should others be started?
- Do employees feel enriched by the programs?
- Are we spreading the concepts of a coaching organization?
- Are we learning? What are we learning?

As always, assessment doesn't become meaningful until people are involved in the process and understand the results and decisions being made. Participation is essential in reinforcing support, vision, and learning. Yearly assessments should include surveys and focus groups so that dialogue is encouraged both inside and outside the organization. There should be a defined process for making recommendations and asking for new or changed programs and approaches.

Given the continuous improvement aspect of a coaching organization, outreach efforts should include a mechanism for ongoing exploration and research. As a leader, you must continue to network and investigate opportunities or seek improvements in existing efforts. Your top leaders and the community outreach committee should conduct yearly benchmarking and share findings with the entire organization. Pertinent articles, books, and tapes should continue to be distributed and discussed. Community outreach is a goal that stretches each person and the entire company. Continuous exploration fosters creativity, vision, and passion.

Making It Happen

According to Greenleaf,

> All that is needed to rebuild community as a viable life form for large numbers of people is for enough servant-leaders to show the way, not by mass movements, but by each servant-leader demonstrating his (or her) own unlimited liability for a quite specific community-related group. (quoted in Spears, 1998, pp. 46-47)

In his vision of servant-leadership, Greenleaf did not support sweeping change. He envisioned each leader doing his part in making a positive impact on the world.

Obviously, we need the big foundations of Kellogg, Lily, Rockefeller, Carnegie, and Gates. In addition, we need big movements endorsed by government agencies and political forces. However, we also need grassroots efforts—each coaching leader reaching out and providing continuous growth and learning beyond the corporate walls. There's Mac Everett, president of First Union's mid-Atlantic region, who puts on a tall, green-and-white striped stovepipe hat and reads Dr. Seuss for 4 hours a month to school-age children (Fischer, 1999). There's Elayne Bennett, who developed her Best Friends program and successfully persuades young women that motherhood is best postponed until other life goals are met (Joyce, 2000). There are the employees at BTI Telecommunications Services who collect coats every Christmas for underprivileged children ("Enterprising Philanthropists," 1999). And then there is you and your company. The examples are endless. So are the possibilities.

WORKSHEET 5.1: Beyond Organizational Walls

Step 1: Establishing the Coaching Relationship

DEFINING THE DESIRED OUTCOMES

1. **My vision for expanding the concept of a coaching organization beyond organizational walls is:**

   ____

   ____

2. **Specific objectives and outcomes I have for community outreach activities are:**

   ____

   ____

3. **Initial ideas that I have for spreading a coaching organization mind-set into the community are:**

   ____

   ____

Tips and Examples

- ❑ Consider how expanding the coaching organization into the community fits with your leadership goals.
- ❑ Integrate your vision for community outreach with the overall vision and goals of the organization.
- ❑ Base your objectives on a core philosophy of servant-leadership, continuation of values and spirit, and a sense of social responsibility.
- ❑ Determine the benefits to both the company and the community: mutual gain.

QUESTIONS TO CONSIDER

1. **Why do I want to expand the concept of a coaching organization beyond my organization?**
2. **What do I hope to accomplish for myself by reaching out into the community?**
3. **What do I hope to accomplish for the organization by reaching out into the community?**
4. **What initial "outreach" ideas do I have that make sense for me and my organization?**

Tips and Examples

- ❑ Think in terms of both tangible and intangible benefits.
- ❑ Consider key components of a coaching organization and how they can be applied to community outreach: stretch goals, dialogue, continuous improvement, results, vision, coaching, continuous learning.

(continued)

WORKSHEET 5.1: Beyond Organizational Walls (*continued*)

RESOURCES AND TOOLS

1. **Tools and approaches that I'm going to use to explore options for community outreach are:**

 ____

 ____

2. **Actions that I'm going to take to involve and educate the organization about community outreach are:**

 ____

 ____

Tips and Examples

- ❑ Network with professionals, community groups, leadership organizations, partners, and contacts outside the organization.
- ❑ Gather and distribute pertinent articles, newsletters, journals, books, and documents.
- ❑ Explore options on the Internet.
- ❑ Network internally and solicit input on what employees might already be doing.
- ❑ Include your community vision in internal communications, dialogue meetings, coaching sessions, and agendas.
- ❑ Ask key leaders within the company to conduct dialogue sessions on community involvement and gather initial ideas.

COMPETENCIES

On a scale of 1 to 5 (1 = nonexistent; 5 = outstanding), rate yourself on the following competencies for this step:

1. **Investigation** **1 2 3 4 5**

 Two specific ways I will demonstrate this competency in this step:

 a. ____

 b. ____

2. **Vision** **1 2 3 4 5**

 Two specific ways I will demonstrate this competency in this step:

 a. ____

 b. ____

3. **Brainstorming** **1 2 3 4 5**

 Two specific ways I will demonstrate this competency in this step:

 a. ____

 b. ____

(continued)

WORKSHEET 5.1: Beyond Organizational Walls (*continued*)

4. Education **1 2 3 4 5**

Two specific ways I will demonstrate this competency in this step:

a. ______________________________

b. ______________________________

Tips and Examples

- ❑ Commit yourself to exploring options through networking, Internet searches, dialogue, and reading.
- ❑ Keep yourself open to a variety of ideas and approaches.
- ❑ Develop and spread a vision that paints a picture of the end result.
- ❑ Create forums for brainstorming and developing lists of options, levels of interaction, implementation of ideas, infrastructure requirements, and next steps.
- ❑ Get people involved. Make specific requests for information. Form an "exploratory task force."
- ❑ Build momentum and buy-in through coaching and educating.
- ❑ Connect to the human spirit—balancing and integrating work and life.
- ❑ Explore not just the actual activities but the philosophy and meaning behind the activities.

WORKSHEET 5.2: Beyond Organizational Walls

Step 2: Collecting and Analyzing Data

DEFINING THE DESIRED OUTCOMES

1. **The kinds of data I want to gather concerning community outreach include:**

   ____

   ____

2. **Specific community outreach approaches, examples, and areas that I want to focus on include:**

   ____

   ____

3. **Community outreach themes and trends that I will be looking for from data analysis are:**

   ____

   ____

4. **Collecting and analyzing data having to do with community outreach will support the organization's vision and commitment to coaching and learning by:**

   ____

   ____

5. **The results of the data collection and analysis process will provide focus for spreading the concept of a coaching organization by:**

   ____

   ____

Tips and Examples

- ❑ Consider focusing on outreach programs and processes that make sense given your values and those of the organization.
- ❑ Provide guidelines that keep the research realistic and meaningful given the organization's resources of time, money, and product/service.
- ❑ Utilize the exploratory findings from Step 1 to focus more in-depth research.
- ❑ Seek out not only factual information but also feelings, benefits, thoughts, and philosophies that connect to the human spirit.
- ❑ Don't lose sight of the ultimate goal of spreading the tenets of a coaching organization.

(continued)

WORKSHEET 5.2: Beyond Organizational Walls (*continued*)

QUESTIONS TO CONSIDER

1. What specific results am I seeking from the data collection and analysis process?
2. What guidelines and ideas can I provide that will narrow the search and result in more focused information?
3. What do I want to be able to do with the data analysis findings?

RESOURCES AND TOOLS

1. The internal structures that I'm going to create in order to conduct community outreach research are:

   ____

   ____

2. The methods that we will use to collect data concerning community outreach ideas and options are:

   ____

   ____

3. The methods that we will use to analyze data and summarize/sort the data into appropriate community outreach themes are:

   ____

   ____

4. My participation in the data collection and analysis process will be:

   ____

   ____

5. We will ensure involvement and participation in the data collection and analysis process through:

   ____

   ____

6. The skills and attitudes we will demonstrate when collecting and analyzing the data are:

   ____

   ____

(*continued*)

WORKSHEET 5.2: Beyond Organizational Walls (*continued*)

Tips and Examples

- ❑ You want results that lead people to action, support their underlying beliefs, and get them excited about outreach options.
- ❑ Be involved in designing parameters for researching community outreach options.
- ❑ Don't let the cause get lost in the details.
- ❑ Design the research process around how you ultimately want to present the findings to the rest of the organization.
- ❑ Form a committee or task force to conduct the research and analysis.
- ❑ Provide updates to the process through internal communications—and continually tie the process and results to the ultimate goals and vision.
- ❑ Consider use of benchmarking, interviews, the Internet, guest speakers, material from supporting research institutions, pertinent books/journals, and community experts.
- ❑ Consider internal surveys, focus groups, and dialogue sessions.
- ❑ Utilize themes, trends, and categories that make sense given your resources and goals.
- ❑ Demonstrate your own commitment by requiring updates and offering guidance.
- ❑ Be open and honest when confronting the data. Don't hide or rationalize the data away.
- ❑ Some data may be difficult to accept. Embrace them as something to change and improve.

COMPETENCIES

On a scale of 1 to 5 (1 = nonexistent; 5 = outstanding), rate yourself on each competency for this step:

1. Research **1 2 3 4 5**

Two specific ways I will demonstrate this competency in this step:

a. ______________________________

b. ______________________________

2. Involvement **1 2 3 4 5**

Two specific ways I will demonstrate this competency in this step:

a. ______________________________

b. ______________________________

3. Focus **1 2 3 4 5**

Two specific ways I will demonstrate this competency in this step:

a. ______________________________

b. ______________________________

(continued)

WORKSHEET 5.2: Beyond Organizational Walls (*continued*)

Tips and Examples

- ❑ Take on some aspect of the research yourself. Network.
- ❑ Provide dialogue for different levels of giving: self, group, organization.
- ❑ Keep the vision out front: the outreach vision, the company vision, the coaching vision, and both tangible and intangible benefits.
- ❑ Push for innovative and bold examples.

WORKSHEET 5.3: Beyond Organizational Walls

Step 3: Processing Feedback and Planning Actions

DEFINING THE DESIRED OUTCOMES

1. **When I share the data with the organization, I'd like the reactions to include:**

   ____

   ____

2. **The purpose of our outreach action plan is:**

   ____

   ____

3. **My purpose in being involved in processing feedback and planning actions is:**

   ____

   ____

4. **Measurements that we should embed in our outreach action plan include:**

   ____

   ____

Tips and Examples

- ❑ Consider outputs of creativity, innovation, alignment, and excitement. How can these be fostered through feedback?
- ❑ Determine ways that the feedback can lead people to focused action.
- ❑ Resources, actions, and vision need to be aligned through an action plan.
- ❑ Specific action plans lead to specific results.
- ❑ Consider the unique contributions you can make as a leader to this step.
- ❑ Begin to brainstorm on the kind of measurements that make sense given the research, your organization, and the kinds of outreach programs that you are exploring.

QUESTIONS TO CONSIDER

1. **Why do I want to share data findings?**
2. **What do I plan to do with the outreach action plan?**
3. **What value does the outreach action plan have inside the organization?**
4. **What value does the outreach action plan have outside the organization?**
5. **What can I see myself doing and saying during this step?**

(continued)

WORKSHEET 5.3: Beyond Organizational Walls (*continued*)

Tips and Examples

- ❑ Outreach programs affect the organization both internally and externally. Both dimensions need to be included in planning.
- ❑ People become committed when they are involved.
- ❑ The spirit of continuous improvement, coaching, and community must be emphasized.
- ❑ You are in a position to provide vision on the one hand and a dose of reality on the other.

RESOURCES AND TOOLS

1. **Techniques that we will use to share data findings and themes are:**

   ____

   ____

2. **Methods that we will use to involve others in the action planning process will be:**

   ____

   ____

3. **Guidelines (process and attitude) that we will use to develop outreach action plans will be:**

   ____

   ____

4. **Different categories/dimensions that outreach action plans might cover include:**

   ____

   ____

5. **Final decisions on outreach action plans will happen through:**

   ____

   ____

6. **My involvement in the action planning process will be:**

   ____

   ____

Tips and Examples

- ❑ Utilize a variety of communication vehicles to share the data.
- ❑ Implement an inclusive action planning model that moves up, down, and across the organization.
- ❑ Provide an action planning template with components of measurements, tracking, resources, and ownership.
- ❑ Different categories of information will require action plans: the outreach activity itself, supporting infrastructures, management and tracking, measurements, operation guidelines, resource allocation, and so forth.

(continued)

WORKSHEET 5.3: Beyond Organizational Walls (*continued*)

- ❑ Provide a template/checklist that will ensure a systems approach toward action planning.
- ❑ A clear decision-making process—with clear decision-making criteria—needs to be understood and accepted.
- ❑ Provide guidelines—in line with the vision and resources—for determining what can and cannot be done.
- ❑ Supply job aids that can guide the dialogue, process, and decisions.

COMPETENCIES

On a scale of 1 to 5 (1 = nonexistent; 5 = outstanding), rate yourself on the following competencies for this step.

1. **Negotiation** **1 2 3 4 5**

   Two specific ways I will demonstrate this competency in this step:

   a. ______________________________

   b. ______________________________

2. **Drive** **1 2 3 4 5**

   Two specific ways I will demonstrate this competency in this step:

   a. ______________________________

   b. ______________________________

3. **Training** **1 2 3 4 5**

   Two specific ways I will demonstrate this competency in this step:

   a. ______________________________

   b. ______________________________

Tips and Examples

- ❑ Personal and organizational resources are at stake. Be a role model in sorting through wants and needs.
- ❑ You need to push for involvement, fairness, action, stretch goals, and support structures.
- ❑ Provide mechanisms for ongoing learning.
- ❑ New sets of skills and knowledge may be necessary for certain outreach programs.

WORKSHEET 5.4: Beyond Organizational Walls

Step 4: Taking Action

DEFINING THE DESIRED OUTCOMES

1. **The internal results I expect from implementing the outreach action plan are:**

   ____

   ____

2. **The external results I expect from implementing the outreach action plan are:**

   ____

   ____

3. **I will know that the outreach action program is successful when:**

   ____

   ____

4. **Possible roadblocks in this step that I will guard against are:**

   ____

   ____

5. **The specific role I intend to play in implementation of the outreach program is:**

   ____

   ____

Tips and Examples

- ❑ Concentrate on execution of the action plans.
- ❑ Realize that you are managing two dimensions: inside the organization and outside the organization.
- ❑ Success indicators can be planned or unplanned: a planned meeting with city officials or an unexpected article about your efforts in the local paper.
- ❑ Align outcomes/results with coaching values: stretch goals, continuous improvement, vision/picture of the end results, teamwork, energy, learning.
- ❑ This is new territory. Provide a process that includes contingency plans and working around roadblocks.
- ❑ Consider your role and the purpose of your actions during this step.

QUESTIONS TO CONSIDER

1. **How will I know that the implementation process is going well?**
2. **What positive signs will I see in the staff, myself, the organization, and the community?**
3. **What components/actions will ensure that the tenets of a coaching organization are actually spreading beyond the walls of the organization?**

(continued)

WORKSHEET 5.4: Beyond Organizational Walls (*continued*)

4. What will I actually do and say in this step to support the overall purpose and vision?

5. Don't lose sight of the goals of a coaching organization.

Tips and Examples

- ❑ Encourage coaching attitudes and activities as the outreach action plans roll out.
- ❑ Create a list of "success indicators"—tangible examples that can be shared when people get stuck.
- ❑ Develop a list of possible activities that you might engage in to demonstrate your support.
- ❑ Develop a list of possible themes, goals, and guidelines that you need to reinforce in this step.

RESOURCES AND TOOLS

1. Tools that we will use to track outreach action plans are:

____

____

2. Methods that we will use to manage and administer outreach implementation are:

____

____

3. We will acknowledge and demonstrate what we learn in our outreach efforts by:

____

____

4. We will become continually competent in outreach efforts by:

____

____

5. We will ensure a systems approach toward the entire outreach effort through:

____

____

6. We will ensure ongoing involvement and communication concerning implementation of the outreach program by:

____

____

7. Tools that we will use to acknowledge and celebrate outreach actions and results are:

____

____

(continued)

WORKSHEET 5.4: Beyond Organizational Walls *(continued)*

Tips and Examples

- ❑ Provide implementation guidelines that address not only process but also behavior.
- ❑ Create an outreach committee for tracking, program management, and communication.
- ❑ Provide a job aid to ensure a systems approach: mind-set, vision, support structures, dialogue, stretch goals, alignment, measurements.
- ❑ Provide ongoing learning, coaching, and dialogue.
- ❑ Strive for continuous improvement and realign activities with goals, as necessary.
- ❑ Create both internal and external mechanisms for acknowledgment and celebration.
- ❑ Develop a list of criteria for tracking, measuring, and aligning.
- ❑ Structure dialogue and stretch goals, concerning community outreach, to include every member of the organization.

COMPETENCIES

On a scale of 1 to 5 (1 = nonexistent; 5 = outstanding), rate yourself on the following competencies:

1. **Systems Thinking** 1 2 3 4 5

   Two specific ways I will demonstrate this competency in this step:

   a. ______________________________

   b. ______________________________

2. **Program Management** 1 2 3 4 5

   Two specific ways I will demonstrate this competency in this step:

   a. ______________________________

   b. ______________________________

3. **Establishment of Relationships** 1 2 3 4 5

   Two specific ways I will demonstrate this competency in this step:

   a. ______________________________

   b. ______________________________

4. **Fostering of a Vision** 1 2 3 4 5

   Two specific ways I will demonstrate this competency in this step:

   a. ______________________________

   b. ______________________________

5. **Acknowledgment of Accomplishments** 1 2 3 4 5

   Two specific ways I will demonstrate this competency in this step:

   a. ______________________________

   b. ______________________________

(continued)

WORKSHEET 5.4: Beyond Organizational Walls (*continued*)

Tips and Examples

- ❑ Take the question checklist supplied for coaching organizations (Part 4) and apply it to the community outreach program.
- ❑ Embed components of the outreach program into existing infrastructures: dialogue sessions, coaching sessions, stretch goals, continuous improvement strategies, recognition, and so forth.
- ❑ Measure community outreach efforts in terms of bottom-line success and/or goal achievement.
- ❑ Apply program management expertise to the outreach implementation: reviews, milestones, efficiency, team meetings with all players, yearly assessments.
- ❑ Relationships make or break the program. Recognize role models.
- ❑ Establish levels of involvement and standards of behavior.
- ❑ Personally take on a community role or goal.
- ❑ Integrate coaching concepts throughout the process.
- ❑ Participate in internal monitoring and dialogue.
- ❑ Celebrate working together and making a difference.
- ❑ Implement activities to keep the vision and momentum alive.

WORKSHEET 5.5: Beyond Organizational Walls

Step 5: Evaluating Your Progress

DEFINING THE DESIRED OUTCOMES

1. Our purpose in evaluating the community outreach effort is:

____

____

2. Outcomes that I expect from the community outreach evaluation effort are:

____

____

3. My role in the community outreach evaluation effort is:

____

____

Tips and Examples

- ❑ The results of a community outreach evaluation should be used for learning, alignment, and focus.
- ❑ Evaluation efforts should include both internal and external parties and parameters.
- ❑ Evaluation results may cover a variety of internal and external dimensions, both tangible and intangible.
- ❑ Your role in the evaluation effort can inspire or demotivate.
- ❑ All evaluation efforts/outcomes should be tied to organizational goals and the overall goals of the outreach program.

QUESTIONS TO CONSIDER

1. **What do I plan to do with the evaluation results?**
2. **What do I plan to say and do in this step that will support the community outreach goals?**
3. **How can I tie the evaluation process and results to organizational goals: How do these results support the expansion of a coaching organization?**

Tips and Examples

- ❑ In considering evaluation outcomes, determine what you intend to do with the results: Cycle back into the process.
- ❑ Evaluation can motivate when used within a coaching model.
- ❑ Coordinate, reinforce, and link organizational goals, community outreach goals, and the spreading of a coaching organization model.

(continued)

WORKSHEET 5.5: Beyond Organizational Walls (*continued*)

RESOURCES AND TOOLS

1. **Evaluation methods/tools that we will use in this step are:**

 ____

 ____

2. **The process for management of outreach evaluation will be:**

 ____

 ____

3. **Pertinent evaluation questions to consider for the outreach program are:**

 ____

 ____

4. **We will ensure involvement and participation in the outreach evaluation process by:**

 ____

 ____

5. **We will ensure ongoing exploration and research concerning outreach initiatives through:**

 ____

 ____

Tips and Examples

- ❑ Include both internal and external evaluation methods and involvement in the process.
- ❑ Utilize some of the same methods used for research, but explore outcomes and results: focus groups, interviews, surveys, data analysis.
- ❑ Create evaluation tools where none exist: tracking of activities, quarterly reports, financial updates, cost-benefit analysis.
- ❑ Develop job aids that provide appropriate questions to assess alignment with goals, objectives, parameters, and other guidelines (job aids provided in this chapter).
- ❑ Utilize the efforts of an existing community outreach committee or form a separate evaluation task force.
- ❑ Ensure that the evaluation effort is used for learning, coaching, and adjusting.
- ❑ Distribute guidelines on the evaluation and renewal process.
- ❑ Provide communication and involvement in order to promote understanding and fairness.
- ❑ Make changes and adjustments to the outreach program to reflect organizational goals, values, and vision.

(*continued*)

WORKSHEET 5.5: Beyond Organizational Walls *(continued)*

COMPETENCIES

On a scale of 1 to 5 (1 = nonexistent; 5 = outstanding), rate yourself on the following competencies for this step:

1. Assessment **1 2 3 4 5**

Two specific ways I will demonstrate this competency in this step:

a. ______________________________

b. ______________________________

2. Participation **1 2 3 4 5**

Two specific ways I will demonstrate this competency in this step:

a. ______________________________

b. ______________________________

3. Exploration **1 2 3 4 5**

Two specific ways I will demonstrate this competency in this step:

a. ______________________________

b. ______________________________

Tips and Examples

- ❑ Provide guidelines for assessment parameters. Be clear on what you are looking for.
- ❑ Make balanced decisions concerning evaluation findings.
- ❑ Pinpoint learnings from the evaluation data and use them to improve the process.
- ❑ Push for new findings; don't accept perfunctory assessments.
- ❑ Involve employees in the evaluation process and incorporate into dialogue sessions.
- ❑ Be actively involved in the evaluation process yourself. Take on the evaluation of a particular component.
- ❑ Build vehicles for continued exploration, ideas, and improvement. Keep the program active and alive.

References

Abrashoff, D. (2001, February). Retention through redemption. *Harvard Business Review, 79*, 3-7.

Argyris, C. (1957). *Personality and organization*. New York: Harper & Brothers.

Argyris, C. (1986, September-October). Skilled incompetence. *Harvard Business Review, 64*, 74-79.

Argyris, C. (1994, July-August). Good communication that blocks learning. *Harvard Business Review, 72*, 77-85.

Argyris, C., & Schon, D. (1974). *Theory in practice: Increasing professional effectiveness*. San Francisco: Jossey-Bass.

Argyris, C., & Schon, D. (1978). *Organizational learning*. New York: Addison Wesley.

Badaracco, J., & Ellsworth, R. (1989). *Leadership and the quest for integrity*. Boston: Harvard Business School Press.

Balu, R. (2000, December). Bonuses aren't just for the bosses. *Fast Company*, pp. 74-76.

Barker, J. (1993). *The power of vision* [Film]. Available from Chart House Learning Corporation, 221 River Ridge Circle, Burnsville, MN.

Beckhard, R. (1996). On future leaders. In F. Hesselbein, M. Goldsmith, & R. Beckhard (Eds.), *The leader of the future* (pp. 125-129). San Francisco: Jossey-Bass.

Belasco, J. (2000). Foreword. In M. Godsmith, L. Lyons, & A. Freas (Eds.), *Coaching for leadership* (pp. xi-xiv). San Francisco: Jossey-Bass/Pfeiffer.

Belf, T. (in press). *Coaching with spirit: Allowing success to emerge*. San Francisco: Jossey-Bass.

Belf, T., & Ward. C. (1997). *Simply live it up*. Bethesda, MD: Purposeful Press.

Bennis, W. G., & Shepard, H. A. (1956). A theory of group development. *Human Relations, 9*, 415-437.

Berger, L. (1998). *Reengineering the corporation*. Haverford, PA: Haverford Business Publications.

Bianco, V., & Roman, C. (1994). *Change in organizations: Best practices*. Washington, DC: U.S. Department of Agriculture.

Bion, W. R. (1961). *Experiences in groups*. New York: Basic Books.

Birkman, R. (1996). *Birkman Inventory*. Houston, TX: Birkman International, Inc.

Block, P. (1996). *Stewardship*. San Francisco: Berrett-Koehler.

Bohm, D. (1990). *On dialogue* [Transcript]. Ojai, CA: David Bohm Seminars.

Bonner, D. (2000, February). Enter the chief knowledge officer. *Training and Development Magazine, 54*, 36-40.

Breen, B. (2001, October). How EDS got its groove back. *Fast Company*, pp. 106-117.

Bridges, W. (1991). *Managing transitions*. Reading, MA: Addison-Wesley.

Campbell, J. (2000). *Becoming an effective supervisor: A workbook for counselors and psychotherapists*. Philadelphia: Taylor & Francis.

Carkhuff, R. R. (1969). *Helping and human relationships* (Vol. 2). New York: Holt, Rinehart & Winston.

Carlson Learning Co. (1994). *The DISC Personal Profile System*. Minneapolis, MN: Author.

Case, J. (1995). *Open-book management: The coming business revolution*. New York: Harper Business.

Clean Sweep. (1995). *The Clean Sweep Program*. Available from Clean Sweep Program, 2484 Bering Dr., Brandon, FL, phone 1-800-48COACH, fax 1-800-FAX5655, <www.coachu.com>, <info@coachu.com>.

Collins, J. (2001, October). Good to great. *Fast Company*, pp. 90-104.

Conner, D. (1995). *Managing at the speed of change*. New York: Villard.

AUTHORS' NOTE: All quotes from Fast Company magazine are reprinted with permission from the indicated issue. All rights reserved. To subscribe, please call 800-542-6029 or visit <www.fastcompany.com>.

Cooke, R. A., & Lafferty, J. C. (1993). *Group Styles Inventory.* Plymouth, MI: Human Synergistics International.

Covey, S. (1991). *Principle-centered leadership.* New York: Simon & Schuster.

Crane, T. G. (2001). *The heart of coaching* (Rev. ed.). San Diego: FTA Press.

Dahle, C. (2000, December). Natural leader. *Fast Company,* pp. 268-280.

Denison, D. (1995). *Denison Organizational Culture Survey.* Ann Arbor, MI: Aviat.

Denison, D. R., Hart, S. L., & Kahn, J. A. (1996). From chimneys to cross-functional teams: Developing and validating a diagnostic model. *Academy of Management Journal, 30,* 1005-1023.

DePree, M. (1989). *Leadership is an art.* New York: Dell.

Drucker, P. (1999, March-April). Managing oneself. *Harvard Business Review, 77,* 64-74.

Druskat, V. U., & Wolff, S. (2001, March). Building the emotional intelligence of groups. *Harvard Business Review, 79,* 80-90.

Dyer, W. G. (1987). *Team building.* Reading, MA: Addison-Wesley.

Enterprising philanthropists: The new frontier of giving. (1999, December). *Business Leader Magazine.* Retrieved March 26, 2001, from <www.businessleader.com/bl/jan99/bljan99.html>.

Evered, R., & Selman, J. (1989, Fall). Coaching and the art of management. *Organizational Dynamics, 18,* 16-33.

Fiedler, F. (1965). The contingency model. In H. Proshansky & B. Seidenberg (Eds.), *Basic studies in social psychology.* New York: Holt, Rinehart & Winston.

Fischer, S. (1999, December). Business helps build better schools. *North Carolina Magazine.* Retrieved March 26, 2001, from <www.nccbi.org/philantropy1299.htm>.

Folkman, J. (2000). Coaching others to accept feedback. In M. Goldsmith, L. Lyons, & A. Freas (Eds.), *Coaching for leadership* (pp. 299-306). San Francisco: Jossey-Bass/Pfeiffer.

Fortgang, L. B. (1998). *Take yourself to the top.* New York: Warner.

Goldsmith, M., Lyons, L., & Freas, A. (Eds.). *Coaching for leadership.* San Francisco: Jossey-Bass/Pfeiffer.

Goleman, D. (1998a, November/December). What makes a leader? *Harvard Business Review, 76,* 92-102.

Goleman, D. (1998b). *Working with emotional intelligence.* New York: Bantam.

Goleman, D. (2000). *Emotional Intelligence Inventory.* Arlington, VA: Hay Group.

Grace, K. S., & Wendroff, A. (2000). *High impact philanthropy: How donors, boards, and nonprofit organizations can transform communities.* New York: John Wiley.

Green, P. (1984). *More than a gut feeling* [Film]. Available from LearnCom Group, 1-800-262-2557. Urbandale, IA.

Hargrove, R. (1995). *Masterful coaching.* San Francisco: Jossey-Bass.

Hargrove, R. (2000). *Masterful coaching fieldbook.* San Francisco: Jossey-Bass.

Hay Group. (1995). *Targeted culture modeling.* (1995). Arlington, VA: Author.

Hesselbein, F. (1996). The "how to be" leader. In F. Hesselbein, M. Goldsmith, & R. Beckhard (Eds.), *The leader of the future* (pp. 121-124). San Francisco: Jossey-Bass.

Hudson, F. M. (1999). *The handbook of coaching.* San Francisco: Jossey-Bass.

Hudson, F. M., & McLean, P. D. (1995). *Life launch* (2nd ed.). Santa Barbara, CA: Hudson Institute Press.

Industry Week. (1993). TQM forging ahead or falling behind? A study of quality practices. Pittsburgh, PA: Development Dimensions International, Productivity Management Association, and Industry Week.

Isaacs, W. (1999). *Dialogue and the art of thinking together.* New York: Currency.

Johnson, C. (2001, June 31). In dot-com crash, parachutes are scarce. *Washington Post,* p. A1.

Jones, L. (1996). *The path.* New York: Hyperion.

Joyce, M. (2000, March/April). The virtues and vices of philanthropy today. *Philanthropy Magazine.* Retrieved March 26, 2001, from <www.philanthropyroundtable.org>.

Juhnke, G. A. (1996). Solution-focused supervision: Promoting supervisee skills and confidence through successful solutions. *Counselor Education and Supervision, 36,* 48-57.

Katzenbach, J., & Smith, D. (1993). *The wisdom of teams.* Boston: Harvard Business School Press.

Keppel, B. (1999). Bill Gates follows philanthropical tradition. *Washington Journal.* In Weekday Magazine: Analyses and Features by the Staff of Radio Free Europe/Radio Liberty. Retrieved March 26, 2001, from <www.rferl.org/nca/features/1999/03/F.RU.99o312143339.html>.

Kolb, D. (1984). *Experiential learning: Experience as the source of learning and development.* Englewood Cliffs, NJ: Prentice Hall.

Kotter, J. (1995, March). Leading change: Why transformation efforts fail. *Harvard Business Review, 73,* 59-67.

Kouzes, J., & Posner, B. (1993a). *Credibility.* San Francisco: Jossey-Bass.

Kouzes, J., & Posner, B. (1993b). *Leadership Practices Inventory.* San Diego, CA: Pfeiffer.

Krug, D., & Oakely, E. (1994). *Enlightened leadership: Getting to the heart of change.* New York: Simon & Schuster.

Kübler-Ross, E. (1969). *On death and dying.* New York: Macmillan.

LaBarre, P. (2000, March). Do you have the will to lead? *Fast Company,* pp. 222-230.

La Monica Rigolosi, E. (1980). *La Monica Empathy Profile.* Palo Alto, CA: Consulting Psychologists Press.

Landsberg, M. (1997). *The tao of coaching.* Santa Monica, CA: KnowledgeExchange.

Leadership behaviors can lead to profits or disaster. (2000, Summer). *CBIZ Business Solutions Inc., 4,* 1-8.

Leonard, T. (1998). *The portable coach.* New York: Scribner.

Link, D. (2001). *The journey to high performance.* Pleasanton, CA: Commerce One Operations, Inc.

Lipman-Blumen, J., & Leavitt, H. (1999). *Hot groups.* New York: Oxford University Press.

Lombardo, M., & Eichinger, R. (1992). *The career architect.* Minneapolis, MN: Lominger.

Lyons, L. (2000). Coaching at the heart of strategy. In M. Goldsmith, L. Lyons, & A. Freas (Eds.), *Coaching for leadership* (pp. 3-20). San Francisco: Jossey-Bass/Pfeiffer.

Manz, C. (1992). *Mastering self-leadership.* Englewood Cliffs, NJ: Prentice Hall.

Marrow, A., Bowers, D., & Seashore, S. (1967). *Management by participation.* New York: Harper & Row.

Maslow, A. (1970). *Motivation and personality* (2nd ed.). New York: Harper & Row.

McCauley, L., & Canabou, C. (2000, December). Giving back, what's the best way to do good? *Fast Company,* pp. 105-142.

McClelland, D. (1961). *The achieving society.* New York: Von Nostrand.

McGregor, D. (1960). *The human side of enterprise.* New York: McGraw-Hill.

McLeod, M. (2001, January). Changing how we work together: Interview with Peter Senge and Margaret Wheatley. *Shambhala Sun, 9,* 29-33.

Myers, K. (1998). *Myers-Briggs Type Indicator, Form M.* Palo Alto, CA: Consulting Psychologists Press.

Neuhauser, P., Bender, R., & Stromberg, K. (2000). *Culture.com.* New York: John Wiley.

O'Hanlon, W. H., & Weiner-Davis, M. (1989). *In search of solutions: A new direction in psychotherapy.* New York: Norton.

Parker, G. M. (1992). *Team Development Survey.* Tuxedo, NY: Xicom.

Pasmore, W. A., & Mlot, S. (1994, July-August). Developing self-managing work teams: An approach to successful integration. *Compensation and Benefits Review, 26*(4), 15-23.

Quinn, R. E. (1996). *Deep change: Discovering the leader within.* San Francisco: Jossey-Bass.

Richardson, C. (1998). *Take time for your life.* New York: Broadway.

Rogers, C. (1951). *Client-centered therapy.* Boston: Houghton-Mifflin.

Rosenfeld, J. (2000, December). The man who loved chairs. *Fast Company,* pp. 232-247.

Sashkin, M. (1996). *The visionary leader: The leader behavior questionnaire* (Rev. ed.). Amherst, MA: HRD.

Schein, E. H. (1994, Winter). How can organizations learn faster? The challenge of entering the green room. *Sloan Management Review, 35,* 85-92.

Schein, E. H. (1996). Leadership and organizational culture. In F. Hesselbein, M. Goldsmith, & R. Beckhard (Eds.), *The leader of the future* (pp. 59-69). San Francisco: Jossey-Bass.

Schutz, W. (1996). *Fundamental Interpersonal Relations Orientation—Behavior (FIRO-B).* Palo Alto, CA: Consulting Psychologists Press.

Schwarz, R. (1994). *The skilled facilitator.* San Francisco: Jossey-Bass.

Senge, P. (1990). *The fifth discipline.* New York: Doubleday.

Senge, P. (1994). *The fifth discipline fieldbook.* New York: Doubleday.

Senge, P. (1999). *The dance of change.* New York: Doubleday.

Shaffer, J. (2000). *The leadership solution.* New York: McGraw Hill.

Shore, B., & Shore, W. H. (2001). *The cathedral within: Transforming your life by giving something back.* New York: Random House.

Spears, L. (1998). The power of servant-leadership. *Perspectives in Business and Global Change, 12*(4), 41-53.

Staub, R. (2000). *The heart of leadership.* Provo, UT: Executive Excellence.

Teal, T. (1996, November-December). The human side of management. *Harvard Business Review, 74,* 3-10.

Thayer, L. (2001). *On being the best: Lessons for leaders.* Unpublished manuscript.

Thomas, K., & Kilmann, R. (1974). *Thomas-Kilmann Conflict Mode Instrument.* Palo Alto, CA: Consulting Psychologists Press.

Tichy, N., & Charon, R. (1995, March-April). An interview with AlliedSignal's Lawrence A. Bossidy. *Harvard Business Review, 73,* 69-78.

Tuckman, B. W. (1965). Developmental sequences in small groups. *Psychological Bulletin, 54,* 229-249.

Wetlaufer, S. (1994, November-December). The team that wasn't. *Harvard Business Review, 72*(6), 22-27.

Wheatly, M. J. (1999). *Leadership and the new science.* San Francisco: Berrett-Koehler.

Whitmore, J. (1996). *Coaching for performance.* San Diego: Pfeiffer.

Whitworth, L., Kimsey-House, H., & Sandahl, P. (1998). *Co-active coaching.* Palo Alto, CA: Davies-Black.

Wiltens, J. (1995). *Goal express.* Sunnyvale, CA: Deer Crossing.

Witherspoon. R. (2000). Starting smart: Clarifying coaching goals and roles. In M. Goldsmith, L. Lyons, & A. Freas (Eds.), *Coaching for leadership* (pp. 165-185). San Francisco: Jossey-Bass/Pfeiffer.

About the Authors

Virginia E. Bianco-Mathis is a Partner with Strategic Performance Group and a Professor at Marymount University, School of Business. She has held leadership positions at AT&T, Lockheed Martin, and The Artery Organization. Her teaching and practice is concentrated in the areas of organizational development and change, strategic planning, performance management, and leadership development. Her previous publications and national presentations include *Organizational Change: Best Practices,* "Consulting Dilemmas: Lessons From the Trenches," *The Full-Time Faculty Handbook* (Sage, 1999), *The Adjunct Faculty Handbook* (Sage, 1996), "Cross-Functional Teams," and "A Multidisciplinary Approach to Implementing Total Quality Management." Her major clients include America Online, Goodwill Industries, the U.S. Department of State, and Teleglobe. At Marymount University, she teaches in the master's programs for organization development and human resource management. She received a master's degree from Johns Hopkins University and a doctorate from George Washington University.

Lisa K. Nabors is a Partner with Strategic Performance Group. She has served as an Adjunct Professor for Marymount University and for George Washington University, where she has taught graduate-level courses in strategic planning and organizational communication. She has over 18 years of experience in the field of human resource and organization development. She regularly works with business leaders in the private and public sectors who are interested in developing as coaching leaders. In addition to working individually with leaders, she frequently works with teams, clarifying long- and short-term goals and creating the systems necessary to support the teams in achieving and surpassing them. Her major clients include the U.S. Department of Education, America Online, and the American Association of Retired Persons. She received her master's degree in education from the University of Maryland, where she has also completed doctoral-level course work in social bases of behavior and human development.

Cynthia H. Roman is a Partner with Strategic Performance Group and founder of the Graduate Certificate Program in Leadership Coaching at George Washington University. She also teaches leadership courses at the University of Maryland. She has over 18 years of experience in coaching executives, training managers, facilitating teams, and helping leaders plan organizational change. She specializes in using the theory and skills of action science to facilitate new approaches to learning and change. She coauthored *Organizational Change: Best Practices* and has given numerous national and regional presentations on coaching, consulting, mentoring, training, and facilitating. Her major clients include the American Red Cross, the U.S. Department of Education, and Host Marriott. She received a master's degree from the University of Georgia and a doctorate from Virginia Polytechnic Institute and State University.